HOW *to* SAVE *the* WEST

Ancient Wisdom for 5 Modern Crises

Spencer Klavan

Regnery Publishing
WASHINGTON, D.C.

Regnery® is a registered trademark and its colophon is a trademark of Salem Communications Holding Corporation

Cataloging-in-Publication data on file with the Library of Congress

ISBN: 978-1-68451-345-1
eISBN: 978-1-68451-393-2

Published in the United States by
Regnery Publishing
A Division of Salem Media Group
Washington, D.C.
www.Regnery.com

Manufactured in the United States of America

10 9 8 7 6 5 4 3 2 1

Books are available in quantity for promotional or premium use. For information on discounts and terms, please visit our website: www.Regnery.com.

How to Save the West

How different is the one who devotes his soul, pondering the law of the most high. He will hunt out the wisdom of all the ancients, and pore tirelessly over the words of the prophets. . . .

I am like the moon: I have grown full. Listen to me, you holy children, and put forth your blossoms like a rose planted near a gushing stream.

—The Wisdom of Ben Sira, Chapter 39

For Joshua

ἀτεχνῶς, ὃ ἔφη Ὅμηρος, "μένος ἐμπνεῦσαι" ἐνίοις τῶν ἡρώων τὸν θεόν,
τοῦτο ὁ Ἔρως τοῖς ἐρῶσι παρέχει γιγνόμενον παρ᾽ αὑτοῦ.

*What Homer says is simply true, when he talks about a
god "breathing valor" into some champion or other. That
is exactly what love does, by its distinctive influence, to a
man in love.*

—Plato, *Symposium* 179a-b.

CONTENTS

A Note on Translations

When I cite works in languages other than English, I usually either write my own translations or combine various existing versions. For this reason the endnotes give references to the original works themselves, rather than to any one English translation. But I have also relied on a range of excellent modern translations to guide and check my own, and readers can find my recommended editions in the bibliography.

Introduction

The twenty-first century seems to threaten civilizational collapse at every turn. Every new event provokes apocalyptic speculation, and every news cycle provokes more certainty that the end is nigh. "The fall of Kabul may serve as a bookend for the era of U.S. global power," wrote Robin Wright in the *New Yorker.* "What we have seen is...the end of the West's triumph and its dominance," declared Juan Manuel Ospina in *El Espectador* as Russian forces made their way into Ukraine. "Was Jan. 6 the beginning of the end of America?" asks Brian Bethune in *Maclean's,* discussing Canadian essayist Stephen Marche's book *The Next Civil War.* "Coronavirus makes America seem like a civilization in decline," writes Noah Smith in *Bloomberg.* Log onto Twitter and, predictably, the panic gets worse. "Russia's invasion of Europe is life or death for Western civilization," declared one user to the tune of more than 6,000 likes. Whether the culprit is white nationalism, or cancel culture, or COVID-19, or the election of Joe Biden, the constant refrain seems to be that America and the West will soon be history.[1]

To be fair, the West is always on the verge of collapse. The world being what it is, war and self-sabotage have a way of deflating even the grandest civilizational ambitions. History is full of stories to remind us that even great nations can fall suddenly and far. The intoxicating rise of Athens in the fifth century BC came to an abrupt and gory end in the Peloponnesian War. No sooner had the ancient Israelites made their way to God's promised land than they strayed after foreign gods and suffered under foreign oppressors. The Western Roman empire crumbled into warring tribal territories; France's revolution devolved from utopian optimism into terror and bloodshed; Communist uprising in Russia led to socialist dictatorship and millions of deaths.

It is always possible to look back and see in retrospect how everything went wrong. In America, a favorite conservative game is to pinpoint exactly the time when the country was set on its current path toward dysfunction—was it the Cold War, or the Civil Rights era? Perhaps the Revolution itself? But because humanity is broken, even our noblest aspirations can go astray—which means that any era, no matter how prosperous, and any philosophy, no matter how sound, has the potential to veer toward dystopia down the road. Look closely, and you can see the beginnings of destruction even in the best of times.

Some of this may just boil down to a natural human tendency for nostalgia: we are always prejudiced against the present, inclined to think our best days are behind us. "By some venomous defect in humankind, the past is always held in high regard, while the present is an object of contempt," says the lawyer Marcus Aper in a short work by Tacitus, a Roman imperial historian whose own outlook on the state of civilization was itself rather bleak.[2] It is easy to be right when you predict disaster, because disaster is always looming.

On the other hand, disasters really do happen, and cultures really do weaken and die. It will not suffice to shrug off every warning of decline as so much more reactionary hysteria for the simple reason that sometimes decline actually *is* happening. Virtue and beauty are delicate things; they require constant maintenance, and humanity is rarely up for the job. "At all times sincere friends of freedom have been rare," wrote Lord Acton, the great nineteenth-century historian of liberty. Even when the friends of freedom triumph, they must do so in negotiation with a fallen world which will, in the end, bring everything man-made to ruin. No one and nothing lives forever—not even nations.[3]

In our day, signs of impeding collapse are everywhere: riots in America's streets and in her Capitol building, declining birth and fertility rates around the world, depressed further by a conviction among some would-be parents that looming catastrophe makes it irresponsible to foist life onto yet another unwitting soul, and a digital revolution in information technology as transformative as the invention of the printing press. It has all proved unsettling to say the least. The accompanying struggle for dominance of this new medium between governments and tech magnates—or governments working *with* tech magnates—is shaping up to be every bit as desperate and vigorous as the battle between the Roman Catholic Church and its detractors at the dawn of the age of print.

All of this leaves many people fearful that some crash or disaster is imminent. Perhaps it is already here. It feels as if old and established powers—and, in time, nations—may be dissolving into irrelevance and careening toward disaster. Political and cultural certainties that once seemed ironclad now appear flimsy and obsolete. One cannot help but wonder: Is the West about to fall?

No Man Knows the Hour

This book is not going to answer that question, because no one can. Prediction is a fool's game—and anyway, even if we could foretell with absolute certainty that America and Western civilization are thoroughly doomed, what would be the use? What could we do with that knowledge except curse God and die? The problem for normal people in times like ours is that we feel totally overwhelmed and helpless to affect the overall scheme of events. Despair is a sin, and grand prophecies of doom do nothing to alleviate it. The prophecies themselves are misguided anyway. Here is something we tend to forget in these sweeping debates about the fate of the world: the history of the

West is not the history of one nation, or even of a few extraordinary heroes. It is a story of disaster after disaster, and of people who took care to save what they could from the flames. In 410 AD, Saint Jerome looked with awe as the Visigothic king Alaric sacked and burned the city of Rome: "Who would believe that Rome would fall, she who had been built up by the conquest of the whole world? That the mother of nations should also become their tomb?"[4] But even when he wrote those words, Jerome himself had already completed a Latin translation of the Bible which would serve as a foundation stone of Christendom in western Europe. As Rome crumbled, the very language that it spread around the world was being used to usher in a new era.

Western history is full of stories like that—of men and women who thought the world was ending even as they were laying the groundwork for the next chapter. America's own founders, when they broke free of British rule, designed a republic using ideas recorded by statesmen like Cicero, who lived and worked in despair as his own republic was being overthrown. The plays, poetry, history, and philosophy that survive from the ancient world were often rescued from destruction and warfare, pulled from the wreckage of cities or civilizations that were falling to ruin. This is not to counsel quietism: our political future is not a matter of indifference. But neither should we mistake our daily battles for omens of the end times. The West does not die when nations do.

We have forgotten this, because we are being trained to forget virtually everything that happened before yesterday. Received conventional wisdom these days is that we ought to revile the past. "Western civilization" as a concept has come to be treated as another byword for racism and bigotry. This leaves us with no frame of reference, no depth of knowledge that might help put our present crises into context. To jettison the best thought of ages past is to leave ourselves fumbling through an eternal present.

Today we tend to imagine ourselves as enlightened moderns who have cast off a superstitious and unsophisticated past. I call this *chronological chauvinism*: the conviction that newer must always mean better, and that modern views are automatically more reasonable than ancient ones. It is an attitude that can only be maintained by people who have been conditioned never to read the classic books they so despise. Any sustained attention to the great works of Western culture will reveal that the eras which produced them were no more backwards or prejudiced than our own, and some were considerably less so. The narrative that old books are worthless is designed to keep you from discovering that they are not. For when it comes to the fundamental questions we are now facing, the answers that we find through the great traditions are saner and clearer than the options presented to us by our modern gurus.

Death Wish

The irony is that the classics of Western culture have become most maligned exactly when they are most needed. Many of the people who run our cultural institutions hardly seem to care whether or not the great pillars of our civilization crumble. It is an attitude that has been a long time in the making. Back in 1978, Edward Said wrote in his book *Orientalism* that westerners define themselves in opposition to invented stereotypes and caricatures of easterners: "The Orient as a representation in Europe is formed—or deformed—out of a more and more specific sensitivity towards a geographical region called 'the East.'"[5] It follows that the West itself is no more than a chauvinist fantasy, designed to unite "us" against "them." That idea found popular expression in 1987 when activist Jesse Jackson joined a mob of students chanting, "hey, hey, ho, ho, Western Civ has got to go!" The group was lobbying against an introductory humanities course at Stanford called "Western Culture," on the grounds that it unduly elevated European civilization. Stanford agreed to remove the course, replacing it with an array of options under the heading of "culture, ideas, and values," all of which would highlight "works by women, minorities and persons of color." Other colleges and universities quickly took similar measures.[6]

By 1993, in the midst of a culture war that would look tame to us today, journalist David Rieff wrote, "the reality is that no serious player in the business world has anything but the most vestigial or sentimental interest in Western civilization."[7] The same could now be said of many tenured professors, CEOs, and global politicians, who seem to view Western history and tradition as a source of embarrassment rather than strength. "Lest we get on our high horse," said President Barack Obama in 2015 at the National Prayer Breakfast, "remember that during the Crusades and the Inquisition, people committed terrible deeds in the name of Christ. In our home country, slavery and Jim Crow all too often was justified in the name of Christ."[8] Obama was chastising Americans for comparing themselves and their cultural heritage favorably with that of ISIS, which at that point was bathing great swaths of Syria and Iraq in blood.

Obama was ahead of his time. Today it is routine practice to flatten centuries of Western achievement and thought into a simple litany of horrors. The term "Western civilization" itself "has been used to justify racism since it was coined," wrote journalist David Perry and Professor Matthew Gabriele in 2019.[9] The West "became the story of an unbroken genealogy that stretched from Greece to Rome to the Germanic tribes to the Renaissance to the Reformation to the contemporary, white world." Similarly, in the *Guardian*, the celebrated philosopher Kwame Anthony Appiah argued that "there is no such thing as western civilization": most often the term is a "way of talking" which "notices the whole world, but lumps a whole lot of extremely different societies together, while delicately carving around Australians and New Zealanders and white South Africans, so that 'western' here can look simply like a euphemism for white."[10]

Educators in public and private institutions alike demand that white students feel guilt about, or even apologize for, Western civilization and its alleged oppressions, while working to dismantle the established canon of Western literature. "They are making my son feel like a racist because of the pigmentation of his skin," said a mother at the glamorous Los Angeles prep school Harvard-Westlake to reporter Bari Weiss in 2021.[11] In Massachusetts the previous year, a 9th-grade public school teacher named Heather Levine gloated, "Hahaha—Very proud to say we got the Odyssey removed from the curriculum...!"[12] She was contributing to a Twitter hashtag, #DisruptTexts, under whose banner teachers around the country are encouraged to "rebuild the literary canon using an antibias, antiracist critical literacy lens."[13] The premise is that Western literature, as traditionally taught, excludes minorities and teaches hatred.

What Is the West?

In light of all this criticism, perhaps I ought to say what I mean by the term "Western civilization." With a lowercase w, the word "west" simply means a place that sits "to the left" on a map. But when I capitalize the word, I do not mean by it any one geographic region. Broadly speaking, I use the term "Western" to encompass the vast and complex inheritance of "Athens" (the classical world) and "Jerusalem" (the Jewish and Christian monotheists of the near east). As we shall see, the history of interaction between those two great poles of Western civilization has itself been fraught with conflict and struggle. But that too is part of the story. The shared cultural products of those civilizations, and the grand adventures they have inspired, are sources of hard-won and transformative wisdom that we would be fools to deny.

I concede that it is a relatively recent practice to talk about all this history in terms of a grand narrative called "the West." And it is true that by talking this way we inevitably create edge cases and exceptions. For example, were the medieval Arab scholars who preserved Aristotelian texts "Westerners"? Perhaps not, but we can meaningfully say that they played a role in the history of the West. Every word has fuzziness around the edges. The word "tree" denotes a wide variety of plants, and some shrubs might or might not qualify for the description. That does not mean there is no such thing as a tree.

Historians and scholars who talk about "the West" are not inventing some "social construct" to shore up "systems of power," as neo-Marxists might put it. They are *observing*, in good faith, threads of continuity that stretch back through time and space. Cicero and Frederick Douglass, Aeschylus and Shakespeare, Saint Jerome and Julian of Norwich, Christine de Pizan and Hildegard von Bingen—all these writers and thinkers are bound by ties of history and tradition which we recognize and honor when we call them all men and women of the West.

In this capacity, Western civilization is not some ethnic or tribal marker designed to keep undesirables out. Just the opposite: it is a set of ideas and masterpieces shared among people from an enormous range of races and times. What are we otherwise to make of Cardinal Robert Sarah, a Guinean Catholic prelate and one of the greatest living Westerners today? Nor is Western thought a kind of dogma, a set of points to which all Westerners must ascribe. In this book we will discuss philosophers like Karl Marx and David Hume, who I believe represent wrong turns and dead ends in the Western journey. But they are Westerners, too, and I criticize them because I think our shared heritage points in another, better direction.

Already in antiquity, both Christians like Saint Paul and Saint Augustine, and pagan Stoics like Marcus Aurelius and Seneca, saw that certain truths and ideals could unite people from very different walks of life. "In Christ there is no Jew or Greek," wrote Paul (Gal. 3:28). And Seneca: "your slaves are men, companions, humble friends—indeed, they are your fellow slaves, if you consider how quickly fortunes can change."[14] In modernity, both Frederick Douglass and Abraham Lincoln—an escaped slave and the impoverished son of a carpenter—became titans of their age, in part by studying and embracing Western classics.

Years later, in a world of slaves made free by men like Douglass and Lincoln, the black sociologist W. E. B. DuBois wrote: "Across the color line I move arm in arm with Balzac and Dumas. I summon Aristotle and Aurelius and what soul I will, and they all come graciously with no scorn nor condescension."[15] He might as well have been communing also with the Florentine statesman Niccolò Machiavelli, who wrote from exile to his friend Francesco Vettori in 1513, "I enter the ancient courts of ancient men. Received by them warmly, I feed on the food which is mine alone and which I was born for. I am not ashamed to speak with them."[16] That is what it means to study the classics of the West.

The point is not to agree with or even like these many figures, or the movements they represent. It is to recognize that their centuries of striving have left behind for us a record and a tradition, and that we must turn to that tradition if we do not want to face our new and frightening age in blindness. "Is there a notion," wrote the political philosopher Leo Strauss in 1967, "a word that points to the highest that both the Bible and the greatest works of the Greeks claim to convey? There is such a word: wisdom."[17] Wisdom is what we gain from studying the legacy of the West and the suffering that has gone before us. Some small part of that wisdom is what I hope to offer in this book.

The Quarrel of Ancients and Moderns

Another thing people routinely say about the West is that at some point or other it suffered an irreparable "break" in continuity, so that ancient ideas and ways of life are fundamentally unrecoverable or unusable in the modern world. For some, the break between old and new ways of thinking comes with Machiavelli, the famously ruthless critic of Christian pseudo-piety and political naïveté. Enlightenment-era political philosophers like Thomas Hobbes and Jean-Jacques Rousseau are heralded as harbingers of a new age, in which self-interest establishes the foundation for all politics. In the nineteenth century, Swiss-Frenchman Benjamin Constant argued that modern people pursue a radical individualism and "security in private pleasures" that would have been incomprehensible to the citizens of an ancient city-state. Twentieth century philosophers like Martin Heidegger and Thomas Kuhn draw still more and sharper breaks in intellectual history.

My own understanding of the situation is different. My academic training is in ancient Greek literature, which might make me somewhat biased in favor of communion with the ancient world. And, of course, I don't deny that the past is another country. It takes some immersion to understand just how different the world might have looked to a medieval monk or an Athenian war veteran. But I don't think we ever cross over some unbridgeable divide. Instead, I think that different parts of the tradition become suddenly relevant at different times. You never quite know when a new development is going to dredge up some old volume that has been neglected.

Intellectual history, then, is less like a line broken up into segments than a vast ocean in which things sink to the bottom or come up to the surface, depending on the era. Take just one example: if you were a medieval scholar, seeking to uncover and elucidate God's plan for the universe, you would almost certainly have fixated on Plato's *Timaeus* as the masterwork of his career. Today's undergraduates, if they read any Plato at all, are far more likely to read his *Republic* than to have heard of *Timaeus*.

Different concerns make different projects important: in an age of world wars and the Cold War, the mystical cosmology of *Timaeus* can seem like so much speculative nonsense. More urgent is the *Republic*'s utopian vision of the perfect state—and its uncomfortable flirtations with authoritarianism.

Today, however, as theoretical physicists engage in vigorous debate over the order and structure of the heavens, *Timaeus* is suddenly relevant again. As digital technology comes into its own, it pays to rummage through the storehouse of Western treasures to see which old gems now shine with new luster. If the gems have been left to gather dust, the storehouse is nevertheless open and accessible to more people than ever before thanks to the internet. It's a strange new world, but that makes the old truths more important—not less.

Five Crises

This book is not a survey or a summary of Western history and thought. For that you would be well advised to read the magisterial *From*

Dawn to Decadence, by Jacques Barzun, and *The Western Canon*, by Harold Bloom.

What you'll get here is something a little different—an attempt to identify some enduring ideas that are particularly helpful today.

Our era has brought us up against some of the deepest challenges history has to offer. But the West has faced these challenges before. And there are records of those conflicts that offer us the wisdom of experience.

Underneath the daily headlines and tweets that cascade across our news feed, there are profound, central issues at stake. A crisis—*krisis*, in Greek—is a moment of conflict between two radically different and irreconcilable ways of looking at the world. I believe we face five essential crises today. I call them: the crisis of reality, the crisis of the body, the crisis of meaning, the crisis of religion, and the crisis of the regime. Each part of this book is dedicated to one of these five crises, and each part has two chapters. In the first chapter, I describe the crisis, show how it affects our daily lives and how it manifested itself in the past. In the second chapter, I describe how great thinkers of the West dealt with this issue and how we might deal with it now.

The crisis of reality is a choice between objective truth and relativism. Is the world simply what we make of it, or are some facts and moral truths eternal, no matter how many people deny them? Western philosophy begins with this question—and we must ask it again today, under the pressures of virtual reality technology and a culture of endlessly revisable and erasable online propaganda. The legacy of Socrates, Plato, and Aristotle teaches us how to hold fast to eternal truths in the face of chaos.

But the eternal truths of the soul can tempt us to hate or disregard the realities of the here and now. This is the crisis of the body—a choice whether to accept our physical forms or try to transcend them. Either our flesh and blood mean something, or the body is just meat for us to manipulate and rearrange at will. Today, transgender extremists and posthuman technologists say that our spirit can float out of its clay prison and into a world of purity and freedom. But that is an ancient and false promise, born out of disgust with the human animals that we are. Pagan, Jewish, and Christian wisdom alike can guide us into a healthier and fuller relationship with our own bodies.

Underneath both the crisis of reality and the crisis of the body lies the crisis of meaning. This crisis extends from art and the culture wars to science and pop philosophy. In evolutionary theory, we talk about the world as if it runs on reproduction. The age of memes and genes has revealed that everything, from DNA to the internet, is a game of imitation that the Greeks would have called *mimēsis*. But if we are copying and imitating things, then where is the original? Do our bodies and our works of art, our genes and our memes, refer to some meaning beyond ourselves? Or is it just imitation all the way down?

This leads us to the crisis of religion. A casual modern assumption is that science has displaced theology as the final and governing account of who we are and why we are here. But a survey of modern politics shows that man cannot live on material science alone. From ritual genuflection at Black Lives Matter rallies, to the increasingly fanciful multiverse theory that governs physics and Marvel movies alike, we are yearning to believe in something more than mere matter. Can we?

Once we have addressed these four philosophical crises, we will be better equipped to look at the last and most immediate problem before us: the crisis of the American regime. Lots of people, of every political persuasion, are worried that America, and the world order it upholds, is falling apart. Are they right? The last part of this book is about *anacyclosis*, the cycle of regimes. It is about how the West has learned to endure even its own destruction.

A Note on Tech

There is no way to talk meaningfully about these major challenges facing the West without also talking a fair bit about digital technology. Because our newest and most powerful tools are digital, the digital realm is where we make some of our most urgent decisions about what humans are and how we should live. Often, crises of theology and philosophy become most acute in fights over cryptocurrency, or the metaverse, or 5G. So though I am no tech expert, I will have occasion to briefly discuss how we should think through the problems and opportunities granted to us by the digital revolution.

These kinds of problems are made more fraught by the fact that a few corporations wield enormous power over these new technologies. My own comments will have more to do with how individuals can manage their own use of technology than with how governments can regulate the corporations themselves. But let me say a few words about how I think we should regard companies like Meta, Microsoft, Twitter, and Alphabet—the vast and growing conglomerates that together make up what we loosely refer to as "big tech."

To begin with, I take it for granted that these are no longer plucky garage startups: they are massive corporate entities buttressed by millions of dollars in government subsidies, tax carve-outs, and Congressional protection from lawsuits under Section 230 of the Communications Decency Act, which includes permission to kick people off of their platforms.[18] That is to say nothing of the direct investments the American government has made in big tech. During the Cold War, the Pentagon's research arm, DARPA, churned out dual-use technologies that laid the foundations not only of American superiority over Russia, but of the digital revolution itself. As new threats arose, new tech was called in to meet them. The Total Information Awareness program to monitor and track potential terrorists—designed in the wake of the September 11, 2001, terrorist attacks—was partially outsourced to Google to the tune of $2.07 million. Contracts with the National Security Agency proved no less lucrative. According to its former director, Michael Hayden, the Central Intelligence Agency "could be fairly charged with the militarization of the world wide web."[19] Today the federal government invests close to $100 billion dollars a year in information technology. There was no need for any sinister conspiracy—in each case, the goal was a reasonable one. The government has an interest in resisting Communist dictatorships and preventing terrorism. But the byproduct has been to make Americans more trackable and thus, potentially, more controllable.[20]

And so, as tech critic James Poulos points out in his book *Human, Forever*, "Technology has advanced to a point where it justifiably seems almost impossible that any truly private-sector person or group of people can innovate for reasons other than those of state."[21] The idea that companies like Facebook just naturally rose to the top of a neutral free market is a comforting myth that conservatives tell to avoid facing facts: big tech corporations are bloated monopolies empowered by the state to control its citizens, sometimes in ways the Constitution prohibits.

These were *choices* that our government made, not inevitabilities: they reflected certain values and priorities. The state helped make these companies—and it gave them power over us. But no matter how much big tech adds to America's gross domestic product, it becomes clearer every day that these companies' aims and goals are often *not* in the interests of the American people. They exert what analyst Rachel Bovard calls "state-like monopoly power over America's minds and markets."[22]

At the level of lawmaking, there is no reason why tech giants should have such an ironclad grip on technological resources and innovation. At the private and personal level, there's no reason why they should have control of your life, either. In policy, politics, and our personal lives, it should not be taken as "inevitable" that our data will be sold to the highest bidder, our children will be addicted to online porn, and our lives will be lived in the metaverse.

As a free people, we are entitled to exert *absolute* control over which kinds of digital products we consume, and in what quantities. Most especially, parents should control what tech products go to their kids. As the Daily Wire's Matt Walsh has pointed out, if you don't buy your kid a smartphone, he won't have one.[23] There is no need to put in his hand a device that enables him to indulge his every impulse without supervision;

nor is there any need to plug him into the metaverse, no matter how inevitable big tech wants you think this is.

So the guiding criterion for tech use and regulation should not be what we feel we must submit to, but what we believe to be good and right. For that reason the wisdom of the Western tradition is as indispensable in the digital age as it ever was—if not more so. The fundamental questions do not change when the tech does. To the contrary: when new machines radically alter what is possible for us, we desperately need guidance to help us chart a righteous path forward into the uncharted territory. The great works of the West can furnish us with that guidance.

The Last Line of Defense

Though this will not be an exhaustive survey of those great works, I hope to offer the most relevant historical, philosophical, and literary comparisons that I can. I routinely hear from followers of my podcast, *Young Heretics*, that they had no idea that Aristotle, or Aquinas, or Cicero, or Solzhenitsyn, could help them think through current issues that directly affect their daily lives. More dishearteningly still, they tell me they had been taught to think of great works and famous authors as impenetrable, guarded by some esoteric knowledge that only experts could obtain. One of the first things people often say to me is, "I'm not that smart"—by which they mean they lack initiation in the theories and complexities of academic discourse.

However, the people who tell me that they're "not that smart" are usually the most interesting people, the ones least constrained by abstruse ideological dogma or political piety. Writers like Aristotle and Heidegger take some time and care to interpret, it's true. But if these great works have any value at all, it is not because they furnish material for Ph.D. theses. It is because they have something to say to *you*—something about your mind and soul that will help you raise your kids, manage your household, and build your career.

The people who will preserve Western civilization, no matter how perilous its future, will be people like you, the reader of this book. I will not pander to you: some of the material covered here is complex. But it is also rich, and most of all it is not in any sense "above" you. It is *for* you. The whole inheritance of the West is for you. This book will help you take ownership of it.

At the end of Ray Bradbury's 1953 classic, *Fahrenheit 451*, the repentant book-burner Guy Montag meets a band of exiled intellectuals who have decided to preserve Western literature against destruction by committing it to memory. "We are all bits and pieces of history and literature," says the leader of the rebel band. "Byron, Tom Paine, Machiavelli or Christ. It's here. And the hour's late. And the war's begun."[24]

That's also where we are today: the hour is late, and the war's begun. The most important battleground in the culture war is the one most often forgotten. Within every human soul, within every family, within every day, there is a battle being fought over what principles, what beliefs, and what rituals will be accepted, taught, and passed on.

In that fight, you are the last line of defense. This book is designed to equip you to win.

PART I

Reality

We control matter because we control the mind. Reality is inside the skull.... You must get rid of those nineteenth-century ideas about the laws of Nature. We make the laws of Nature.

—George Orwell, *1984*

Is there really no life fuller and no love more marvelous than yours...?

—G. K. Chesterton, *Orthodoxy*

CHAPTER 1

The Reality Crisis

A World beyond Your World

Every year, the company formerly known as Facebook hosts a conference on virtual reality called "Connect." Since the COVID-19 pandemic began, Connect has not involved any in-person meetings. All the connecting happens online.

Somehow this manages to be both fitting and ironic at once, and Facebook's founder, Mark Zuckerberg, doesn't seem to mind. If you logged on at 10:00 a.m. Pacific Time on October 28, 2021, Zuckerberg greeted you with an enthused and thoroughly market-tested smile, seated in a carefully staged living room. He was there to deliver an offer: leave reality behind, and enjoy a world of wonders in return.

Whether you watched the video or not, this offer was meant for you. Zuckerberg will continue to make this offer, to more and more people, on a grander and grander scale. He won't be the only one, and you won't be able to ignore it or shrug it off. It would be good to consider now what your answer should be.

"We've gone from desktop to web to phones, from text to photos to video—but this isn't the end of the line," said Zuckerberg, announcing his company's transformation from Facebook into "Meta." "The next platform and medium will be even more immersive, an embodied internet where you're in the experience, not just looking at it, and we call this the metaverse."[1] "Metaverse" is a word that means "the universe beyond": it describes an immersive virtual world brought into being through digital technology. Put on a pair of goggles and reality is "augmented" or replaced with a new, and altogether better, kind of truth.

Near the beginning of his video, Zuckerberg demonstrates how the metaverse will facilitate "the most important experience of all: connecting with people." It turns out that "connecting with people" means projecting yourself into a digital "room" where other friends have "gathered." In physical reality (not pictured in the video), everyone presumably sits alone with a headset strapped to his or her face. In the metaverse, though, we see one another laughing and talking as "avatars," digital creatures shaped to look like anything the user chooses. Mark Zuckerberg decides to stay looking like Mark, but he's joined by a robot and a floating astronaut as they play poker with levitating cards.[2]

To some, this might seem like an outcome of dystopian fiction rather than a product launch. The word "metaverse" itself comes from Neal Stephenson's 1992 novel *Snow Crash*. But the best-known portrayal of what a metaverse could be is the Wachowski brothers' sci-fi classic, *The Matrix*, in which human beings suffer defeat at the hands of their own machines. Most people in the movie spend their whole lives trapped in pods that siphon energy out of their bodies for use by robots. These human batteries are kept docile and ignorant by the data streaming into their nervous systems, which compel them to exist in a hyper-realistic virtual world.

Now we are expected to enter the matrix voluntarily. We are supposed to like the idea of abolishing reality or blurring its boundaries, because of the pleasures and powers it will afford us. Not only at Facebook/Meta, but at Microsoft—which recently acquired the massive video game company Activision Blizzard in a deal valued at nearly $70 billion—industry leaders are betting that people will *want* to break free from reality as soon as possible.[3] That's why the idea has moved from science-fiction horror stories into the board rooms of Silicon Valley: gradually, some of the most powerful people in the world have come to think it would be a *good* thing to make human experience a largely virtual affair.

This is a striking philosophical attitude, and it is more than a matter of some new gadget. It's an entire way of looking at the world, a totalizing claim about what human beings are and how they can achieve their fullest potential. Does it horrify you to think about your body languishing away in what some people wryly call "meatspace"—the world of flesh and blood? Or in your heart of hearts, would you actually welcome a chance to leave your body and its limitations behind? When the metaverse beckons, will you be disgusted or relieved?

It would be rash to dismiss out of hand how appealing it might be to break the boundaries of real and unreal. Shakespeare's Hamlet, as he toyed with the idea of taking his own life, described "the thousand natural shocks / That flesh is heir to."[4] He was not the first or the last to wonder if it is worth living in a world that inflicts as much pain as ours does. But why take your own life when you could live a virtual one, free from the imperfections and malfunctions that torment us as we are in the here and now? Hamlet exclaims to his friends Rosencrantz and Guildenstern: "O God! I could be bounded in a nutshell, and count myself a king of infinite space, were it not that I have bad dreams." Hamlet here is limited by his debilitating mental state, but what if the dreams we dream in our personal nutshell could be good ones?[5] Who would dare lecture a quadriplegic about resisting the temptation to walk in the metaverse, or blame a burn victim for wanting an avatar's face? Real pain makes it hard indeed not to dream of sweet release.

The software engineer Beau Cronin goes so far as to accuse those who prefer non-virtual life of indulging in "reality privilege." It's easy to get misty-eyed about the virtues of the real world if you're well off—but most people aren't. "Reality has had 5,000 years to get good and is clearly still woefully lacking for most people," said the tech mogul Marc Andreessen in an interview. "We should build—and we are building—online worlds that make life and work and love wonderful for everyone, no matter what level of reality deprivation they find themselves in."[6]

Why *shouldn't* the world be whatever we make of it? What's so special about "reality"—if there even is such a thing? If we could simply dispatch with the distinction between real and unreal, there would be no more limits to what we could do. The promise of the metaverse is the promise that new technology will set us free from true and false once and for all. To some, it seems as if this is the final frontier of all man's struggles over nature, the promise on which our technology will at last deliver: the power to shape reality itself. "Beyond our world, there's another world," says the narrator of an advertisement for "Horizon," Meta's virtual social media engine. "Horizon isn't about 'rules' or 'limits'...so come. Join us. A never-ending, ever-changing world-beyond-your-world is waiting."[7]

Alternative Facts

It makes a certain degree of sense that this invitation to transcend reality comes at a time when true and false have become politically inconvenient concepts. In the wake of the 2016 election, it became popular to speak about "post-truth politics," as if wrestling for dominance over the public narrative had only just become a feature of democratic life. Much was made of a TV interview in which Kellyanne Conway, then a top advisor to President Donald Trump, defended Trump's press secretary Sean Spicer for saying that attendance at Trump's inauguration was the biggest in history (it wasn't). Conway referred to this as giving "alternative facts."[8]

This gaffe was portrayed as an unprecedented horror. But the problem of "alternative facts" is much bigger than comments from one or two Trumpian "spin doctors." In 2004, CBS *Evening News* anchor Dan Rather was shown to have repeatedly put forward false allegations that George W. Bush had been charged with insubordination when he was in the Texas Air National Guard. When the "Killian memos," on which Rather had based his allegations, were proven fictitious, the *New York Times* published the following headline: "Memos on Bush Are Fake, but Accurate, Typist Says."[9]

"Fake, but accurate" is an increasingly forgotten shibboleth for an old scandal, but it describes an attitude that has come to predominate in our era of contested truth. "The narrative was right but the facts were wrong," said *Newsweek* editor Evan Thomas in 2006: he was referring to the case of a black stripper, Crystal Magnum, whose false rape accusation against three players on the Duke lacrosse team were paraded in the press as evidence of white racism. Maybe Magnum had lied, Thomas argued, but her lie was in service of a higher, predetermined truth—the truth of rampant white evil.[10]

In much the same way, Congresswoman Alexandria Ocasio-Cortez complained on a *60 Minutes* interview that "there's a lot of people more concerned about being precisely, factually, and semantically correct than about being morally right." Ocasio-Cortez was offended that her demonstrably false claims about economic policy were overshadowing the obvious truth of her moral rectitude.[11] In 1998, the world scoffed at Bill Clinton's efforts to wriggle out of admitting to his affair with Monica Lewinsky by sputtering that "it depends on what the meaning of the word 'is' is."[12] In the twenty-first century, though, Clinton's gaffe has practically become the philosophical motto of American politics.

George Orwell described this sort of linguistic breakdown decades before. His classic novel *1984* was based, in part, on the example of Stalinist Russia, but also on the "groupthink" liberalism of the BBC, which was already showing signs of what we would call "political correctness." In 1946, Orwell pointed out that even in liberal democracies, widespread political dishonesty had corrupted language so that the "word *Fascism* has now no meaning except in so far as it signifies 'something not desirable'. The words *democracy, socialism, freedom, patriotic, realistic, justice,* have each of them several different meanings which cannot be reconciled with one another.... Other words used in variable meanings, in most cases more or less dishonestly, are: *class, totalitarian, science, progressive, reactionary, bourgeois, equality*."[13] We can now add words like "misinformation" and indeed "Orwellian" to Orwell's list.

Today, words are routinely used as political weapons rather than as good-faith attempts to describe reality. Physical and moral truth can be inconvenient for certain factions trying to shape political and media narratives. At the end of the Second World War, economist Friedrich Hayek wrote, "Once science has to serve, not truth, but the interests of a class, a community, or a state, the word truth ceases to have its old meaning;…it becomes something to be laid down by authority."[14]

This is the reality crisis: a moment at which it seems unappealing, inconvenient, or even naïve to believe that some things are more real than others. The reality crisis presents us with an age-old question: is truth independent of authority, including the authority of "experts" and of majority opinion?

The Death of God

Our version of this crisis was well described by Friedrich Nietzsche. Already in 1882, Nietzsche saw clearly that as Christianity had ossified. Europe was lapsing into what he called nihilism, a chaos of competing worldviews in which any sense of meaning is impossible to achieve, or else not even sought. Only the *Übermensch*—the strong man who jettisons old assumptions and imposes his personal will as a new, individual system of values—can thrive.

Nietzsche famously described this catastrophe as the "death of God," a total collapse of all that was once considered immutable and ultimate. "God is dead! God *remains* dead, and we have killed him," raves the visionary madman in Nietzsche's *Gay Science*. "Is the greatness of this deed not too great for us? Must we not become gods ourselves, just to seem worthy of it?"[15] Martin Heidegger, another German philosopher, later wrote that for Nietzsche, "God is the name for the realm of ideas and ideals."[16] Those higher realities—realities like virtue, goodness, and beauty—were once thought to be the standard against which all other truth was measured. But now they no longer carried conviction.

Horrified at the death of God and frustrated with the complacency of those who refused to acknowledge it or recognize its consequences, Nietzsche cast about desperately for any way to survive in a post-truth world. As he grew older, he grew more frantic and eventually suffered a nervous breakdown in 1889. But before he went mad, Nietzsche launched a powerful attack against objective justice. In his *Genealogy of Morals*, he argued that "it is meaningless to speak of just or unjust in itself; in itself, of course, no injury, assault, exploitation, or destruction can be 'unjust,' since life in its essence, in its basic functions, *operates* through injury, assault, exploitation, destruction...."[17]

Sick at heart with the softness of comfortable modern ethics, Nietzsche saw values like charity and humility as dirty tricks dreamed up by the weak in self-defense, to keep powerful men submissive and harmless. To make matters worse, modern relativists wanted to have their cake and eat it too: they wanted to live in the delicate and comfortable world of polite society, without believing in the absolute authority that made morality work. "The source of your feeling that something is right may be that you never thought much about it yourself and blindly accepted what has been presented to you as right since childhood," he wrote.[18] It couldn't last. Eventually, without the backing of absolute truth, morality as Europe had understood it would rot away.

Nietzsche more or less predicted the entire bloody path of the twentieth century. Throughout Europe, strong men like Adolf Hitler, Benito Mussolini, and Joseph Stalin did away with the old moral order, as best they could, and imposed their own. Here was good and evil stripped away and replaced by what Nietzsche called the "will to power": no pity, no softness, only one man's strength—or one party's strength—imposed upon everyone in sight.

But Nietzsche's observations were not only borne out by the rise of Nazism, Fascism, and Stalinism. The death of God—the crisis of reality—is also apparent today in the politics of the liberal West. In the twenty-first century, political demands often boil down to the assertion that the speaker's *point of view* or *identity* should be taken as an absolute authority. The various slogans we chant show this: "Believe women." "That's my truth." "Elevate black voices." Those who recite these mantras are demanding that their own personal outlook be accepted as the baseline reality against which all other claims should be judged.

Heidegger (who eventually joined the Nazi party himself), called this "the unconditional dominion of subjectivity."[19] Without God—without some shared, stable, objective basis for understanding what is true, moral, and real—we are left only with competing demands for power and competing attempts to control the facts.

Reality Integrity Policy

Digital technology has allowed for an enormous proliferation of information—but has also given unprecedented power over that information to a handful of people with their own political interests. One favored method for taking control of reality is to shut down debate about it altogether. Many in digital technology are sympathetic to this tactic, setting standards of censorship on political speech, restrictions on "misinformation," and even banning prominent figures—including the president of the United States—from social media platforms.

In the leadup to the 2020 presidential election, the *New York Post* broke a story about candidate Joe Biden's son, Hunter. His laptop contained emails and photos linking him to a Ukrainian energy company and potentially implicating the future president himself in a lucrative deal with CEFC China Energy, a state-controlled conglomerate. The *Post* was consequently shut out of its Twitter account, and Facebook reduced the reach of the story. "While I will intentionally not link to the New York Post," wrote Facebook's communications officer Andy Stone, "I want to be clear that this story is eligible to be fact checked by Facebook's third-party fact checking partners. In the meantime, we are reducing its distribution on our platform."[20] Before Twitter reversed its stance, people were blocked from sharing the article even over direct message. After the election, when President Donald Trump began making accusations of electoral fraud and claiming he had won, he was removed from Twitter, Facebook, and Instagram entirely. Over a year later, in March 2022, reporters at the *New York Times* dropped a casual acknowledgement that the laptop was in fact genuine.[21] This total revision of accepted truth came without apology or acknowledgement of how the establishment press and social media had previously smothered the story.

Twitter's corporate statement on Civic Integrity articulates a rationale for this kind of behavior: "Our service shows the world what's happening and democratizes access to information. And at its best, it also provides insights into diverse perspectives on critical issues—all in real time." But "the fight against malicious activity and abuse goes beyond any single election or event"—and so Twitter's overseers must determine what should and should not be said, "developing better tools and resources for finding and stopping abuse, and taking extensive action against activity that violates the Twitter Rules."[22]

In this context, as social media corporations labor to position themselves as arbiters of truth, Facebook's transformation into Meta starts to look less like a triumph of the human spirit and more like a consummation of the reality crisis. Making a bid to create the metaverse means making a bid to construct the contours of the world. It is an attempt to gain control, not just over what can be said, but over what reality itself looks like. And it is presented as a gesture of liberation, as if we are being broken free from a restrictive and outmoded reality. We are promised untold power and pleasure if we just abjure our responsibility to determine true from false—if we hand over the power to determine what is true.

The technology involved in this promise is new. But the promise itself is an old one. This is not the first time that pop philosophers and salesmen have suggested scrapping the basic distinction between real and unreal. In fact, the story of Western philosophy itself begins with just such a crisis of reality—and with one man who tried in vain to avert it. The man's name was Socrates.

Power Politics

Socrates came of age in Athens, at a time when the city was newly ablaze with daring political and philosophical speculation. According to the Bible's Book of Acts, when the Christian Saint Paul of Tarsus visited Athens many centuries after Socrates's death, "all the citizens and resident aliens passed their time doing nothing except hearing and talking about the latest ideas" (Acts 17:21). That had been the city's reputation ever since the beginning of the fifth century BC. Flush with a decisive and unlikely victory over the invading Persian Empire, Athens rose to preeminence as the intellectual center of the known world, her stages and marketplaces thrumming with debate. Socrates's student, Plato, captured the electrifying atmosphere of that moment in his dialogues, the subtle philosophical dramas that he composed with meticulous care. At the center of the dialogues is a character study of Socrates, that inscrutable sage who wandered barefoot through the streets, starting conversations that would one day cost him his life.

Socrates was competing for the attention of the city's best and brightest. The ambitious scions of Athens's great families were eager for knowledge and power alike. And since the city had embarked on a world-historical experiment in direct democracy, knowledge and power came to seem like one and the same thing. If a young man could become skilled in the arts of argument and persuasion, he could win the votes of his fellow citizens to take control of almost anything—the law, the military, and the economy. The techniques for seizing this new kind of power were hotly in demand, and sophisticated teachers came from all around the Mediterranean to supply instruction.

"If you give them money, these men will teach you how to win any argument—whether what you say is right or wrong." So says a scheming father to his son in Aristophanes's play *Clouds*, a knowing satire of

Athenian pedagogy from 423 BC.[23] "Making the weaker argument appear stronger" was a hallmark of instruction for aspiring democratic leaders.[24] A man who wanted to make his way in the world had to make his propositions seem attractive to the people. Teaching young men how to persuade was thus a lucrative business.

The men we now call "sophists" were selling intellectual agility. They offered exercises and techniques for defending any point at will, no matter how apparently implausible on its face. Teachers like Protagoras, a celebrity from the northern coast of the Aegean, made their names training promising young men to debate effectively on practically every topic imaginable. This is not in itself an ignoble thing: good debate teachers still train their pupils to understand and defend both sides of an argument. In *Clouds*, Socrates himself is depicted teaching this coveted skill—and even Plato portrayed his mentor as having the mental acumen to talk almost anyone into anything.

But there's a fine line between rhetorical aptitude and political cynicism. Gradually, the citizens of Athens came to feel they were being had, led astray by glib demagogues who were more interested in empowering themselves and enriching their coterie of friends than in getting at the truth. As the heady fifth century BC drew to a close, public opinion started to turn against the sophists, and with good reason.

Corrupting the Youth

The latter half of the fifth century BC brought Athens into the Peloponnesian Wars, decades of brutal struggle with Sparta over dominance of the Aegean. Athens eventually fared badly—so badly that Sparta was briefly able to install a puppet government that became known as the Thirty Tyrants. The tyrants enacted a punishing regime of state executions to chasten Sparta's defeated enemies, and some of Socrates's students were among those who led this reign of terror. After the democrats regained control, some accused Socrates of corrupting the young people of Athens, teaching them to disdain the city's gods, undermining ancestral wisdom to advance his own power, and colluding with the overthrown tyrants. Socrates found himself on trial for his life.

When he came before the court, the Athenians were jaded and suspicious of sophistry. It wasn't long before the name itself became a dirty word: *sophistēs* in Greek simply means "wise teacher," but after Plato, a "sophist" was nothing more than a glib hack. Plato's own student, Aristotle, would later write that the Athenians came to find the teaching of a sophist like Protagoras "obnoxious—and rightly so, for it is a lie which only seems like truth."[25] Athenians now understood that slippery rhetoricians could lead well-meaning citizens to self-destruction.

The Peloponnesian Wars had taught hard lessons about the unholy marriage between glib orators and angry mobs. The great historian of the period, Thucydides, wrote that self-interested charlatans led the people into disastrous military overreach by "wrestling for supremacy over one another, handing over even matters of state to the whims of the common man."[26] The problem was that democracy itself, as a system, contained no inherent limits on what could be decided. The *only* measure of worth was persuasion and narrative: anything that could be argued for could be voted for, and anything that could be voted for could be done. But, as the Athenians discovered, there could be terrible consequences when an irresponsible demagogue used the power of rhetoric cynically to get his way.

Beneath this was a deeper and older philosophical fight over the nature of truth. At the turn of the fifth century BC, a sophist named Heraclitus from Ephesus in Asia Minor (now Turkey) had made the observation that everything visible changes: people grow old and die, beauty fades, even the mountains erode and crumble over time. That much might seem obvious, but its possible implications about the nature of reality were not. For even basic sense data like colors and sounds can seem different to different people depending on their framing and presuppositions—spoken words of Greek sound like gibberish to one man, and like poetry to another. Nothing stays the same or, as Heraclitus put it in words that made him a sensation, "all things are in flux."

And so Heraclitus would have smiled to see the internet going ber-serk in 2015 over a photograph of a dress that looked blue to some people and yellow to others, or a sound in 2018 that some people heard as "Yanny" and others heard as "Laurel."[27] If all we have is the experience of our senses, and if our senses present to us a world in constant turmoil, then all permanence is an illusion. Heraclitus's sayings were like Koans, the riddles that Zen masters use to unsettle their students and drive them beyond their comfortable assumptions: for all the confident bravado of a culture hungry to know the eternal truths of the world, Heraclitus asked, *how can you know anything at all?*

To the young men whom Socrates encountered in Athens, this kind of sophistry seemed the height of sophistication. The pithy aphorisms of Heraclitus and the subtle arguments of Protagoras blended into a fashionable worldview for Athenian high society. In Plato's *Theaetetus*, Socrates interrogates the title character, a bright young thing who is at first very taken with philosophical relativism. As Socrates puts it: "according to Heraclitus everything is always moving, like a river cur-rent. According to the estimable Protagoras, wisest of sophists, man is the measure of all things. And according to Theaetetus, knowledge is nothing other than the experience of the senses."[28] Reality is what you make of it: all we can know is what we see, touch, smell, hear, and taste. Our senses show us a world that is constantly changing, and that looks different to different people. So, we must conclude that truth is in the eye of the beholder. And if truth is subjective, and if rhetoric is just the art of making people see things your way, then why not manipulate people to your own ends? There is, after all, no absolute moral or even physical reality to restrain you. In the *Republic*, Plato would put something like this argument into the mouth of another sophist, Thrasymachus: "justice is nothing other than what is good for the powerful" or, still more omi-nously, "what the powerful *think* is good for them is what the weak must do, and that is just."[29]

"There is nothing either good or bad but thinking makes it so," says Hamlet in his madness: that, in essence, was how the demagogues of

Athens justified their worst ambitions.[30] Thucydides records how an Athenian delegation argued that "The strong do what they can, while the weak suffer what they must" to excuse massacring the men of Melos for trying to remain neutral in the Peloponnesian Wars.[31]

It is no surprise then, that as the battle between Sparta and Athens dragged on, and as civil wars broke out in cities across the Aegean, language became a matter of politics. "They even changed the agreed-upon meanings of words to the opposite of the right ones," wrote Thucydides about the revolutionary chaos of a city called Corcyra. "Rash impudence was called 'courageous loyalty'; careful deliberation, 'specious cowardice'.... The cause of all this was hunger for power motivated by greed and ambition."[32]

Let truth go and you will not be set free: you will be cast into a brutal war of all against all. If truth is relative, then all that matters is power. This was the original reality crisis. And Socrates stood accused of causing it.

Vindicating Socrates

Addressing the tribunal that would decide his fate, Socrates insisted that, far from hawking cheap sophistication to conniving elites, he was intent on exposing the pretentions of the sophists—and not only them, but the sly politicians and pompous artists who peddled sham "wisdom" as well. The purpose of his pointed questions, Socrates said, was to show that the city's grand authorities were little more than conjurers, dazzling the public with their specialized rhetorical skills, but lacking real knowledge of the true and the good.

Even worse, he argued, the authorities believed their own hype. They considered themselves wise because they were clever, while Socrates confessed, "I know that I know nothing. Since I don't know, I don't think I do." This infuriated the impostors who ran the city: "many came to hate and resent me, with such fury and intensity that they started plotting against me." Political and cultural authorities, he asserted, do not like to have their ignorance exposed. And that was why he found himself standing trial.[33] Athens's crisis of reality was everywhere, just like ours: to a man, practically everyone in power had abandoned real wisdom for the sake of personal gain. For exposing this, Socrates stood condemned.

His self-defense was unsuccessful, and he went to his death. Plato devoted his own career to proving that the Athenians had been wrong, that they had condemned the one man who might have shown them the error of their ways. And so Plato's great question was: what did Socrates see that others did not? Or, to put it another way, what were the objective truths, what was the reality, that Socrates acknowledged but that others denied? Plato's was the question that inaugurated Western philosophy. We must make it our question too.

CHAPTER 2

Outside the Cave

These Things Remain

Plato began his defense of reality by conceding to the sophists that change, decay, and death are proof of a certain impermanence. But still, we know intuitively that though everything we can see and touch and smell may pass away, some things remain. Good and evil aren't matters of mere preference, and no one can really live as if absolutely nothing is permanent or true—in the end, that just means abandoning life altogether.[1] The world, as it is, as we sense it, might not satisfy us. But perhaps that is because there is more to the world than that. This is where Socrates and Plato began their departure from the sophists.

Socrates understood that there is no such thing as halfway relativism. (Sophisticated sophists acknowledged this point as well, though some of the shallower young men they taught failed to grasp it.) Either something, somewhere is true *no matter who disagrees*, or else *all things* really are in motion and in flux. For instance, try buying a block of wood and convincing yourself it's food. No matter how strongly you make the argument that it can feed your hunger, your digestive tract is likely to be unconvinced. Is your gut wrong, or your philosophy? Is there something true about the nature of wood that makes it different, always and everywhere, from a cut of meat?

The answer must be yes. Some things are simply true. And it goes far beyond the distinction between wood and meat. We can't look at the slaughter of the Melians or the death of Socrates—or for that matter at the Holocaust or the Soviet Gulag—and remain indifferent. Not only would that be callous, it would also feel profoundly *unnatural.* It is part of human nature to seek and apply an objective standard of the true and good. If we cut that part of our nature out, or deny it, we may gain godlike freedom (in the way Nietzsche understood it)—but it comes at the price of inhuman savagery.

Gradually, over the course of his career, Plato developed a theory about this unchanging part of existence. In the *Phaedo,* a doomed Socrates sits in prison with his closest disciples and wonders what will endure after he is put to death. His answer comes from the teaching of an old mystic named Parmenides: there is another world of being, or of "essence." The essence of things, the core of *what they are,* is something more than just matter. The essence of truth or of beauty is "always in the same state in the same way."[2] These things hold permanent even as everything around us changes. And the part of us that experiences beauty and contemplates truth is called the soul—or in Greek, the *psychē.* Your psyche is not just the "spiritual" part of you, the part that sings hymns or dreams up prophetic visions. It is your mind, too, and your capacity for reason. The soul, for Plato, is what makes you able to see and think about more than matter.

If your left hand holds two oranges and your right hand holds two apples, it is your soul that knows they add up to four. If your eyes see sunlight scattered through the atmosphere at dawn, it is your soul that perceives the beauty of the sunrise. The apples and the oranges themselves belong to the *sensible* realm, the realm of things we can perceive with our senses. But there is another realm, too: the intelligible realm, the realm of things like numbers and goodness. Things we can only perceive with the soul.

In his *Symposium*, Plato depicts Socrates stopping in his tracks at unexpected moments, gazing with his mind at a pure world of truth and beauty beyond what our eyes can see. "He has a habit of doing that," says Socrates's friend Aristodemus: "he just veers off and stops, wherever he is."[3] He was trying to refine that higher sense of things in their essence, the pure nature of things like goodness and beauty that cast their dim shadows through the material world. "What would you think," Socrates asks, remembering the words of a wise woman named Diotima, "if you could come to behold the beautiful itself—pure, simple, and unmixed? Not tangled up with flesh and men and things and all the rest of that mortal junk, but the beautiful itself—simple and divine?"[4] This is the world of the *eidē* (singular eidos)—literally, the "things which are seen" by the soul. The "shape" or "outline" of things beyond matter which we perceive with our minds. These are the pure "ideas" or, to use the technical term, the Forms.

Plato spent much of his career articulating the relationship between the world of the Forms and our world. How exactly is it that we see something eternal called beauty in the impermanence of a sunset, a human face, or a work of architecture? How can our ever-changing world of things "participate" or "share in" the unchanging Forms? Of all the allegories he used to answer that question, none is more famous than the allegory of the cave.

The Original Metaverse

In the seventh book of Plato's *Republic*, Socrates is trying to describe "the nature of humanity when it comes to education and the lack thereof."[5] His listeners, two brothers of Plato named Glaucon and Adeimantus, have yet to grasp the dire condition of the human soul. And so, says Socrates:

> Picture human beings as if they were in a rocky underground
> dwelling, like a cave, with an opening stretched out toward
> the light along the whole width of the cave. They are there

from childhood, their legs and their necks chained so that they stay in the same place and can only look forward. ... Light comes to them from a fire burning far above and behind them, and in between the fire and the chains there is a road leading up. Along that road, picture a wall....

And behind the wall, picture men carrying all kinds of artifacts—little statues of people and animals made of stone and wood and every kind of material. And we may imagine that some of the men carrying the sculptures are making noises, and some are silent.

What a strange image, says Glaucon, and what strange kinds of people. But no, says Socrates: "they're like us."

Dimly, at a distance, we glimpse the shadows on the wall and call them reality. Most people are born into almost total ignorance, watching a puppet show lit by an artificial light. A dark cabal of half-enlightened men—maybe the sophists, or the glamorous actors we see onstage, or the charming political leaders who overawe crowds with their eloquence—take advantage of the people's confusion to stage little simulations of the truth. It requires enormous effort—even divine intervention—to realize that behind the shadow play lies a light not made by man.

Plato's cave is the original metaverse, and we are already living in it. The Forms as they really are come into focus only by long study and careful reasoning. We can only climb out of the cave if our soul, and our reason, see beyond the things that change to the things that stay the same: truth, justice, and beauty.

Do you believe such things exist? It is in some sense the first question of philosophy and of life. There are different ways to talk about objective reality, and philosophers have argued—are still arguing—over whether there is a "world of Forms" "out there" existing in some perfectly spiritual realm, or whether absolute truth is more grounded in the things we see and do in the here and now. At a foundational level, though, the question is not *how* absolute truth exists but *whether* it exists at all. Does reality have a bedrock?

Life, Online

I suspect that if pressed, many of our most skillful tech entrepreneurs might answer this central question in the negative. When Mark Zuckerberg posted about making augmented-reality glasses that would overlay digital projections onto our vision, one commenter responded, "But when I wear glasses I want to see the world." Zuckerberg answered: "You'll be able to see the world. AR glasses will give you superpowers to see things you couldn't see otherwise."[6] So far as his public comments go, Zuckerberg seems unconcerned about putting digital creations on the same ontological level as physical objects.

"For decades, 'gamers' have been making 'fake' avatars and spending their free time in digital worlds," observes Matthew Ball, a tech entrepreneur and a widely read theorist of the metaverse. As the scare quotes imply, Ball is skeptical that our distinction between "real" and "fake" represents anything other than an old-fashioned cultural prejudice.[7] Zuckerberg himself, in a post on Facebook, described virtual reality glasses as "the key to bringing our physical and digital worlds together."[8] Once wearable tech is sophisticated enough, we can finally abolish the distinction between real and imaginary.

Ball claims, writing in 2021, that "The most obvious behavioral change of the past year has been the increasing amount of time we spent online and in virtual worlds. But more important is the destigmatization of that time." Shut in their homes during COVID lockdowns, people had to rely on digital technology for things they would normally do in person. Worried parents shopped for food online rather than risk a trip to the market. Wedding ceremonies were shrunk to a few "essential" attendees and the rest could attend on Zoom. In November 2021, the *New Yorker*'s cover art depicted a young woman gazing into a laptop on a "virtual" date with someone who sees only the video feed she sends him. Her elegantly dressed upper body stands out on the screen against her slovenly apartment and her unshaven legs. As far as her date is concerned, none of that physical squalor matters: only the digital image exists.

COVID lockdowns, Ball argues, normalized a level of dependence on high-tech interactions that would previously have been considered unthinkable, especially for older people and tech skeptics. That is true to an extent. But more astonishing, and perhaps more important, is the fact that so many people in power considered digital interaction an acceptable long-term substitute for life in person. As President Donald Trump extended his "fifteen days to slow the spread" to a month and a half, and as other countries like Australia enforced punishingly strict quarantine measures, it became clear that embodied life, in-person life, was simply not a big enough loss to matter in the eyes of COVID hawks. Zoom was enough.

Was it, though? Despite protestations to the contrary, evidence suggests that kids, especially, are suffering terribly from what's been done to them. In 2021, UNICEF and Gallup surveyed children in 21 countries and found that on average one in five people between the ages of 15 and 24 "often feel depressed or have little interest in doing things."[9] For more than a decade, an escalating number of teenagers have been suffering from depression, anxiety, and loneliness, but the pandemic lockdowns made things dramatically worse. Comparing early 2021 to early 2019, the U.S. Surgeon General reported that "emergency department visits in the United States for suspected suicide attempts" leapt by 51 percent for adolescent girls and 4 percent for adolescent boys.[10] A team of researchers at Brown University found "that children born during the pandemic have significantly reduced verbal, motor, and overall cognitive performance compared to children born pre-pandemic."[11]

History is full of anecdotes about callous kings who shut kids away without human contact just to see what would happen. The Greek historian Herodotus claimed that the seventh-century BC monarch Psammetichus (Psamtik) I of Egypt isolated a group of babies to find out what language they would speak, if any.[12] According to the monk

Salimbene di Adam, the thirteenth-century holy roman emperor Frederick II did much the same thing—with fatal results for the children involved.[13] The scholar Roger Shattuck called this kind of gruesome research "the forbidden experiment." But what we have done during the COVID pandemic looks eerily similar to a mass implementation of this supposedly forbidden experiment around the world, isolating young children at key stages of their development and depriving them of normal human interaction.

There are plenty of reasons why this cruelty and neglect might make kids despondent, but surely one of them is the constriction of their lives into cyberspace. Uploading our lives to the cloud has left children depressed and underdeveloped. Cutting ourselves off from the physical world has not, so far, produced encouraging results.

The Outside View

If deferring more and more of our lives to the digital realm is making us more and more miserable, why should we assume that making our lives *entirely* virtual will make us happy? If the internet makes us depressed and anxious, why would the metaverse make us happy and free? The promise of technological freedom from objective reality, like so many other utopian promises before it, goes something like this: "right now, we have only walked a couple steps down the path away from reality. It is causing us untold suffering and regret. But follow me *all* the way down that path, and life will be perfect. The pain of the present moment, the evidence of your current emotional state, is nothing compared with the treasures awaiting ahead if you will only silence that inner voice and press on. Paradise is just over the horizon of sorrow."

This never turns out to be a good deal.

For Matthew Ball, our quaint attachment to real life will pass in time. Ball cites a series of viral videos that have circulated since the early 2010s, in which toddlers raised with iPads make frustrated efforts to "scroll through" magazine pages by swiping up and down on them.[14]

What these kids have gained in facility with smart tech, they seem to have lost in comprehension of print: they simply can't grasp what a magazine *is*. "While we could easily understand what was happening" in these videos, writes Ball, "we couldn't truly appreciate how these frames of reference differed from our own."

Research by the networking firm Handshake supports Ball's observation: many members of Generation Z (those born between 1997 and 2012) "report feeling more 'seen' and psychologically safe online versus in person, which can counteract implicit bias or other behaviors that favor more outgoing and socially confident individuals in 'real life.'"[15] These kids—who are now well into their teenage years—are "natives" to the digital world. They see things differently than we do, and in time their comfort with virtual reality will erase the distinction between "real" and "fake."

Perhaps. One of the more discomfiting aspects of Plato's cave is that it's a matter of training. Plato has Socrates tell the story to describe "the nature of humanity when it comes to education and the lack thereof"—in other words, he is suggesting that we need rigorous work to strengthen our understanding and to develop our sense of what is real. Left alone, our capacity to discern truth from falsehood is weak enough already, and it atrophies further after long years of underuse.

But the power of the image is that it shows us what we really are *even if* we feel perfectly happy with our state of weakness and ignorance. The people chained to the cave do not think of themselves as pitiable. They probably think of themselves as comfortable, productive citizens. But we see how they look from an objective vantage point: shackled and bound to a dark wall, deprived of sunlight. The premise of the cave is that even if we do get used to swapping dreams for reality—even if we grow up that way—there will always be a basic level on which we are made weak and small by the exchange.

Pull back the camera, and it is still possible to get that bird's-eye view that Plato gives us in the cave. The images that do not usually feature in promotional videos are the images of what it looks like from *outside* the metaverse. But there are a few press pictures that do show Zuckerberg striding confidently down an aisle in a crowd of patrons, all but him strapped happily into virtual reality headsets. On the inside, they are experiencing wonders untold. From the outside, they look like the people in the cave: slack, immobile, and captive.

Some conservatives online have a saying: "I will not live in the pod. I will not eat the bugs." The slogan expresses an instinctive aversion to becoming the kind of person who would give up on objective reality and let politicians shrink life into a series of Zoom calls—the very kind of person who lies slumped at the bottom of Plato's cave.

At its root, the question is whether there is anything outside yourself. For the people sitting rapt in that lecture hall, staring into virtual reality goggles while Zuckerberg walks godlike amongst them, the world seems to have expanded into something new and wonderful. Soon, the technology may be advanced enough that those who enter the metaverse will have no way of experiencing the outside world if they would rather not. Zuckerberg's digital creations will look and feel real to them, and the way things are "out there" will not be able to get in and disturb them.

But if I stay outside, looking at the people of the metaverse from my own perspective, they will still just look like something out of the Pixar movie *Wall-E*: lethargic and placated, sitting motionless and staring at a screen. The minute you introduce someone *else* into the picture, someone who can look at you from outside, your view ceases to become absolute. Maybe in your perfect, hermetically sealed metaverse you look like a superhero flying through the stars. But to me you look like a brain-dead captive strapped to a nightmare machine. Does that matter?

The Hardest Realization

It must matter enormously, or else nothing can matter at all. One of Plato's many disciples in modern times was a woman named Iris Murdoch, a Dubliner who studied classics at Oxford before serving briefly in an Austrian refugee camp at the end of World War II. Murdoch was a fierce critic of the notion that good and evil were nothing more than functions of the individual will. In her book *The Sovereignty of Good*, she argued against the trendy worldview that "regards sincerity as the fundamental and perhaps the only virtue."[16]

This was an idea that worked in seminar rooms and lecture halls, but not in reality: Murdoch had seen too much real evil to believe that morality was simply a matter of personal choice. The gruesome horrors of the Nazi death camps, and the grieving families who fled across Europe to escape Hitler's war machine were definitive proof that wrong was wrong, regardless of what a moral relativist might contend. In other words, basic moral decency means recognizing that something immutably *exists* outside of yourself. "Love is the extremely difficult realisation that something other than oneself is real," wrote Murdoch in her essay "The Sublime and the Good." "Love, and so art and morals, is the discovery of reality."[17]

The dark secret of relativism is that it sounds sophisticated in theory and ends up gruesome in practice. Aleksandr Solzhenitsyn, who lived through hellish imprisonment in 1940s Russia, recalled that Stalin relied on a theory of criminal justice written by his chief prosecutor, Andrei Yanuaryevich Vyshinsky. Vyshinsky argued "that it is never possible for mortal men to establish absolute truth, but relative truth only.... Therefore, when we sign a sentence ordering someone to be shot we can never be *absolutely* certain.... The proofs of guilt were *relative*, approximate, and the interrogator could find them, even when there was no evidence and no witness, without leaving his office."[18] In Stalin's Gulag the link between erudite moral equivocation and violent physical brutality became absolutely, punishingly clear. Armed with the ideas in Vyshinsky's treatise, Stalin's police subjected prisoners to everything from sleep deprivation to rape and genital mutilation—all without anything that could be plausibly called evidence of guilt.

However well-intentioned they may be, those who blur the distinction between real and imaginary lay the groundwork for every kind of horror. That is why literary scholar René Girard made this biting assessment of how Nietzsche's ideas had fared after his death:

> To bury the modern concern for victims under millions and millions of corpses—there you have the National Socialist way of being Nietzschean. But some will say, "this interpretation would have horrified poor Nietzsche." Probably, yes. Nietzsche shared with many intellectuals of his time and our own a passion for irresponsible rhetoric in the attempt to get one up on opponents. But philosophers, for their misfortune, are not the only people in the world. Genuinely mad and frantic people are all around them and do them the worst turn of all: they take them at their word.[19]

From sophistical justifications of Athens's panicked violence as she groped for dominance in the Peloponnesian War, to the pseudo-intellectual defenses of the gas chambers of Hitler's Germany and the gulags of Stalin's Russia, what begins as trendy abstraction about morality ends in terror and bloodshed. It would be comforting, in a grim sort of way, if we could imagine this as some dark conspiracy on the part of philosophers to undermine civilization. But it is more tragic than that. Relativists sincerely believe that they are breaking old chains of oppression and ushering in a bright new future of unlimited freedom.

Either there is something outside of us, or there is not. I suspect that Mark Zuckerberg, like many of our modern "thought leaders," imagines that you can collapse the distinction between "real" and "virtual" without collapsing the distinction between good and evil. I also suspect he is fatally, terribly wrong. Morality *is* another version of stepping outside the metaverse, another version of realizing that there is some stable reality outside your own subjective preferences. If I cannot say with confidence that there is some truth beyond what I see in my virtual reality glasses, then I cannot say with confidence that there is some ethical standard beyond my subjective choices. The whole world, as I imagine it, becomes a matter of my personal will. There is nothing either good or bad, but thinking makes it so. We already know what that looks like.

The rise of social media brought an old advertising slogan from the 1970s back in vogue: if you're not paying, you're the product. In other words, "free" services online, like Google, make money by acquiring and selling your personal information. *The Matrix* dramatizes an even more disturbing truth: if you're *in* the metaverse, then someone else is *outside*, controlling it. Who? And to what end? Outside the virtual reality simulation, someone, somewhere, has appointed himself lord over a world of men in chains.

What Can Be Done

Does it have to be this way? Maybe. Facebook alone has tremendous market power, and its transformation into Meta was broadcast over the internet by what must surely be one of the most powerful PR departments in history. The video of Zuckerberg gazing into the universe of his prospective creation went so viral that it felt as if the metaverse was *already* everywhere. The walls were being built around us as we watched, and escape from this digital prison seemed impossible.

At the same time, other vast corporations have been laying the foundations of their own metaverse technology, more quietly but with no less determination: days after Zuckerberg's announcement, Microsoft released a video showing how Teams, its video conferencing platform, will soon allow users to replace images of themselves with CGI avatars.[20] Microsoft was already at work on Project Baraboo, a research and development venture that will generate a set of "mixed-reality" glasses called the HoloLens. Major brands, most notably Nike, quickly signaled their interest in adapting their retail strategies for a future dominated by metaverse technology.

These corporate signals combine to create a sense of inevitability, a gut feeling that this is the only future there can be. Sums of money that most people cannot imagine have been spent on technology that most people cannot understand. The pace is dizzying with no end in sight. There is an ambient sense of technological determinism: "once the toothpaste is out of the tube, there's no putting it back in." Once you split the atom, or build the printing press, that's that. New technology is developed, and it changes the world forever.

Those who resist this kind of change risk looking foolish to posterity. Efforts to suppress progress end up looking pitiable and small-minded in retrospect. Companies like Meta and Microsoft want us to think that resistance is futile: they want us to feel that when we criticize how they operate that we will end up on the wrong side of history.

There may be some truth to this. We are not going to stop virtual reality from existing or from becoming ever more realistic. You can already walk into a Best Buy and pick up the Oculus, a video game headset that transforms famous titles like *Resident Evil* into full-immersion experiences. There is obvious potential for devices like this to guide the hands and eyes of a brain surgeon in microscopic procedures, or to facilitate immersive new forms of art. We could, and probably will, find uses for virtual reality that will generate wealth, health, and no small amount of joy. None of that is to be sniffed at.

Technological transformations can be turbulent, unsettling, and, at a certain level, out of our control. But inventing a new technology is not the same thing as submitting to it, or demanding submission from others. As Harvard's Shoshana Zuboff writes in *The Age of Surveillance Capitalism*, companies that use technology are not *the* technology itself. Big tech corporations profit from uses of technology that "appear to be inevitable when they are actually meticulously calculated and lavishly funded means to self-dealing commercial ends."[21]

Products like Meta always come with a sales pitch attached. It is not only "we have this new tool" but rather "we should use this new tool to do *this*." For almost a century we have had the capacity to wipe out cities with nuclear bombs and generate enormous amounts of energy with nuclear power plants. We have done the former only twice, at Hiroshima and Nagasaki, in the extreme and desperate conditions of a protracted war with Japan. We do the latter far less than we should because politicians and lobbyists portray nuclear power as dangerous. Both of those facts are the result not just of the technologies themselves but of *intention*, not just having tools, but having ideas about how best to use them.

So the problem is not virtual reality itself, but the belief that we should let our real world melt indistinguishably into the digital one. This was Plato's great objection to artists and playwrights who passed off their fantasy creations as truth: they alienate us ever further from our sense of what is real. The more we let art, technology, and rhetoric blur the distinction between true and false, the more we condition ourselves to accept counterfeit virtue and sham beauty in lieu of the real things. As Plato warns, demagogues and poets become "imitators of phantoms of virtue and the other subjects of their creations": they give us reality at a double remove.[22] Put in these terms, the value proposition behind a totally immersive and ubiquitous metaverse becomes starkly obvious and seems somewhat absurd: "put on this headset and let a man become your god." Whatever else may be inevitable, there is nothing written in the stars that says we must acquiesce to *that*.

The Red Pill

The willpower to exert our authority over machines requires conviction. It is our lack of this conviction that makes technological determinism seem inevitable. Our gut tells us we *should* hold fast to reality, but we don't know *why*.

We are very easily convinced to ignore our gut instincts these days, in part because they are represented to us as unscientific, and therefore untrustworthy. This is a mistake. There are more ways to know something than by conducting a peer-reviewed study or performing a statistical regression analysis. Our instincts may need correction and refinement, but if we jettison them entirely we have blinded ourselves to a key source of moral and spiritual information. When we look with horror on product launches for the metaverse or insist that we will not live in the pod, that is not mere prejudice: it is our connection to a primal instinct that warns us that there is something deeply *wrong* about erasing the distinction between reality and fantasy.

That same primal instinct is expressed in all the myths and stories about virtual reality we tell, from Plato's cave to *Snow Crash, Ready Player One, Wall-E,* and *The Matrix.* These stories have the effect they do because they pull back the camera and show us an outside view, the perspective of someone who is free of the metaverse. That perspective reminds us that there *is* an outside, and it is *real.* There is a good reason why "take the red pill" has become such a powerful online rallying cry. The red pill, which frees skeptics from the matrix, has become a metaphor for seeing past cynicism and disingenuity in all its forms. People of various ideological affiliations—not all of them traditionally conservative—use the red pill to convey their sense that some truths are worth fighting for.

That is because stories like *The Matrix* portray our instinctive horror at being unmoored from reality—whether by the false erudition of moral relativism or the hollow promises of a high-tech future. We only become content to immerse ourselves in fantasy when the real world has either deteriorated to a point of collapse, as in *Snow Crash,* or when we are deceived by hostile puppet masters acting for reasons of their own, as in *The Matrix* and the allegory of the cave. The great artistic depictions of the metaverse are universally horrifying precisely because they express a true and primal horror. They record our instinct that no matter how painful the truth may be, it remains the truth despite our best efforts.

This is not "reality privilege"—it's not based on things going well or being pleasant. We should favor the truth even if it is painful, because the truth is meaningful in ways that fantasy is not. Precisely because things can go well or badly in the real world, precisely because the universe has rules that we cannot simply rewrite, our triumphs and failures carry a weight that they would not in a completely immersive metaverse. The ease of virtual reality is also what will make it a pathway to nihilism and dysfunction if we let it absorb us utterly.

Plato's story of the cave does not have a happy ending. The liberated philosopher, having escaped into the sunlight, does not return to receive accolades from his newly enlightened cave-dwelling companions. Instead, Socrates tells us, the true philosopher will face hostility and derision. He will stand accused of having his eyes corrupted by the sun. He will be held up as proof that escape is futile and, if he persists, his old companions will more than likely crucify him. Plato must have written that prediction in sorrow, knowing the Athenians had proved it true in their prosecution of Socrates.[23] Millennia later, as he looked out at a Europe that had already seen one world war and would soon descend into another, the poet T. S. Eliot wrote that "human kind / Cannot bear very much reality."[24] Plato would have agreed.

Before the end of my lifetime, we may have occasion to experience once more humanity's addiction to fantasy and emptiness. The nihilism that fueled the Gulag has engulfed civilizations before, and may do so again. I cannot promise that won't happen—no one can. But I can promise that none of our worst fears are *destined* to come true. And besides: there is a curious thing about the West. The truth that fails in the short term often turns out to be the one that lives for all time. We revere the name of Socrates, and not his executioners; we celebrate Solzhenitsyn and not Stalin.

"Unless a grain of wheat falls on the ground and dies, it remains but a single grain, with no life." So said Jesus to his followers not long before he was crucified. To the Athenians, Socrates said: "You are wrong if you believe that by killing people you will prevent anyone from reproaching you for not living in the right way."[25] We cannot live our lives forever calculating our chances of immediate success. Though prophets and visionaries arise to promise revolution, though every reality crisis presents itself as an unprecedented liberation from everything that came before, eternal truths seem, inevitably, to reassert themselves. It is our duty to defend these eternal truths—no matter how often they are denied, no matter how unpopular they become, and, as with Socrates, no matter the cost.

PART II

The Body

We do not want the world any longer furred over with organic life, like what you call the blue mould—all sprouting and budding and breeding and decaying. We must get rid of it.

—C. S. Lewis, **That Hideous Strength**

The devil, who had bragged and exalted himself above flesh and blood, had now been beaten by a man made of flesh. For the Lord was helping his servant, the Lord who took on flesh for our sake and gave the body victory over the devil.

—Athanasius, **Life of Anthony**

CHAPTER 3

The Body Crisis

Body and Soul

Flesh decays: about that much, Plato and Heraclitus agreed. The world of matter is a world of endless turmoil; only truth and beauty remain constant. But where does that leave *us*? Though we may seek and contemplate the eternal truths, we do so in the here and now. No matter how enlightened we become, we do not just float away into some cerebral heaven. We are not just souls; we have bodies too, and one day they will break down and die. How are we supposed to feel about this flesh of ours?

No one seems to have a good answer to this question. Pop culture in the digital age ricochets dizzyingly between extravagant depictions of physical beauty and aggressive endorsements of physical ugliness. "This is healthy!" screamed a January 2021 issue of *Cosmopolitan* magazine, as an obviously overweight woman grinned on the cover. In February 2022, Adidas advertised a new line of sports bras by plastering a grid of naked breasts all over Twitter, each pair selected to defy conventional expectations of beauty and proportion.[1] "One hesitates...to say anything that could be interpreted as praise of underwear

37

ads," writes the political and cultural commentator Mike Anton, "but, within living memory, the sirens of Times Square billboards were lithe and lovely; today they are, quite deliberately, obese and angry."[2] And yet on Instagram and TikTok, young women constantly lacquer over their real faces with digital filters in imitation of fitness influencers and supermodels, tossing their heads from side to side as the camera adjusts their proportions in real time. Our visual culture furnishes a bizarre mix of perfect airbrushing and defiant ugliness.

Some amount of this confusion over our physical selves may be unavoidable. Being human always comes with a certain itch of physical discomfort. We are spirits "in clay jars": our souls long to transcend the boundaries of space and time, but our bodies refuse to comply. This anguish persists despite the modern insistence that the eternal part of us—call it the soul, the spirit, or the mind—is an illusion. The fact that we continue to feel discomfort in our own skin suggests otherwise. Something about us is not happy with our flesh.

And yet today's sophists will tell you that there is nothing about us *except* our flesh, that the mind is just an outdated superstition. Science, they explain, has replaced the soul with an intricate web of electric circuity called the brain. The brain is quite different from the mind. The mind is where you experience thoughts or appreciate qualities like color or the timbre of a human voice. The brain, on the other hand, is the material object inside your skull where electrical circuitry lights up during cognitive operations. Some scientists, being materialists, argue that when we talk of being "scared" or "yearning" for someone's presence, it is merely the byproduct of electric sparks in our brains causing hormonal and other chemical reactions.

But though we may nod along in superficial agreement, this cheap modern wisdom does not satisfy the heart. You could map the entire limbic system, record every firing of every neuron in the amygdala, and measure serotonin in the blood down to the last milligram, without getting one inch closer to explaining human consciousness. Philosophers use the Latin word *qualia*, meaning something like "how things are," to describe experiences that cannot be reduced to mere physical events in the body. These experiences—memory, love, desire, and the innumerable things beyond description that we feel—are quite distinct from the biological events that accompany them.

This is sometimes called the "hard problem of consciousness." We know for certain we *are* conscious, and we find it impossible to deny that our consciousness involves a dazzling array of experiences: pleasures and pains, sights and sounds, emotions and memories, aspirations and desires. But what have any of those things got to do with electric circuitry or blood chemistry? The connection between them is totally opaque. "When billions of neurons send billions of electric signals back and forth, subjective experiences emerge," writes the popular historian of science Yuval Harari in *Homo Deus*. "Yet this explanation explains nothing. It merely affirms that the problem is very complicated. It does not offer any insight into how one kind of phenomenon (billions of electric signals moving from here to there) creates a very different kind of phenomenon (subjective experiences of anger or love)." Harari is an utter skeptic about the spirit, but he is smart enough to admit that the existence of consciousness remains a mystery.[3]

There are those who would say, just give it time: scientists will find a physical explanation for consciousness too.[4] But that is a category error, based on the assumption that when we look for consciousness, we are looking for the *kind* of thing that a scientific experiment could discover. We are not. All our most advanced models and scans of the human organism have furnished nothing that looks even remotely like consciousness, because consciousness does not "look like" anything at all. It has no physical contours or location in the body. If anything, it happens *to* or *through* the body, but even that language fails to capture the mysterious connection between the two. The secretion of adrenaline and cortisol (for instance) occurs at the same time as the experience of fear. But the relationship between them remains elusive.

Harari concludes from this that what we once mistook for a soul is simply a "frenzied collection of experiences [called] the stream of consciousness."[5] We are subject to one experience after another, from hatred to pride to anger to love, and though this is a surprising fact it says nothing about what we are—except that, in addition to our neural circuitry, we also have this curious thing called consciousness. "Unlike the everlasting soul," writes Harari, "the mind has many parts, it constantly changes, and there is no reason to think it is eternal." He also finds himself perplexed that such a thing should exist when there is no evolutionary reason for it: "The better we understand the brain, the more redundant the mind seems. If the entire system works by electric signals passing from here to there, why the hell do we also need to *feel* fear?"

You would think that this question would also give Harari pause about his certainty that the soul is a fantasy constructed from a "frenzied collection of experiences." There is something quite obviously missing from that account of things. We do not just have one experience after another in unbroken and unrelated succession. We also know *that* we are having those experiences: we are self-conscious, or self-aware. "Suppose that three sensations follow one another—first A, then B, then C," writes the Christian apologist C. S. Lewis in *The Problem of Pain* (1940):

> When this happens to you, you have the experience of passing through the process ABC. But note what this implies. It implies that there is something in you which stands sufficiently outside A to notice A passing away, and sufficiently outside B to notice B now beginning and coming to fill the place which A has vacated; and something which recognises itself as the same through the transition from A to B and B to C, so that it can say "I have had the experience ABC." Now this something is what I call Consciousness or Soul.[6]

This is quite a bit more sensible than Harari, and quite a bit older than Lewis. Aristotle, in his analysis of the soul, reflected on the fact that though we see with our eyes, we also *perceive* that we are seeing. And "even if some other sense perceives sight itself, then either that goes on into infinity, or else somewhere there is a sense which is aware of itself."[7] Either we see color with one sense, and perceive that we see with another sense, and perceive that we see that we see with another sense—and so on and so on forever—or else there is one unifying consciousness which is aware of all our senses, and of our self.

Saint Jerome, the priest who translated the Bible into Latin toward the end of the Roman empire, called this self-aware part of us the *scintilla conscientiae*—the divine spark of self-knowledge.[8] "It is distinct from the other parts of the soul and can correct them when they go wrong." This is what makes us more than just a "frenzied collection of experiences." We can see that we exist, and we can even judge between our different impulses and experiences. Our moral evaluation of ourselves—our feeling of guilt over lashing out at a friend, say, or telling a lie—suggests that we are something more than just a disconnected succession of impulses and appetites. It suggests that we have a soul.

This enduring self is the premise and ground of all rational thought: "without our being conscious that what we are thinking now is the same as what we thought a moment ago," observed the philosopher Immanuel Kant in 1781, "concepts, and with them knowledge of objects, are perfectly impossible."[9]

The soul is a logical and philosophical necessity, not an article of faith. And so the real question is not why we should have a mind (or a soul or consciousness) when it serves no evolutionary purpose. The real question is: given that we have feelings and experiences which transcend the physical world—like love, thoughts, and reason—why do we also need to have a body? The real question, in other words, is not whether the soul is redundant, but whether the body is. We can call this the body crisis. It is an ancient and perennial human discomfort: a suffocating feeling that the flesh is a trap, a longing to float up out of this skin and be free.

Prison Walls

"You must strive to return the Divine in yourself to the Divine in the All." Those were the dying words of Plotinus, a celebrated lecturer and interpreter of Plato.[10] Plato died in 347 BC, leaving behind a school—the Academy—that passed from hand to hand until it was destroyed by the Roman general Sulla in 86 BC. But Plato's work was bigger than any one school, and the fight over what his teaching meant was only beginning as Rome's empire billowed outward across the Mediterranean.

The days of Athens's blithe self-confidence were long gone after her defeat at Sparta's hands. The confederations of the Greek world fractured and fought amongst themselves until the conquering might of Alexander the Great swept through Greece in the fourth century BC. After Alexander's death, his kingdom too splintered into fragments. During what we now call the Hellenistic period, regional princes struggled for power with one another and with an increasingly expansionist Roman state until 31 BC, when a young Roman named Octavian brought order through force and became Augustus Caesar, the father of a world empire.

While kings fought over land, philosophers in Athens struggled to claim authority in the wake of Plato's and Socrates's deaths. Competing schools of philosophy—most notably Cynicism, Stoicism, Skepticism, and Epicureanism—vied for the attention and allegiance of truth-seekers everywhere. No Caesar arose to assert order or control over them.

This was the situation in 245 AD, when the wandering philosopher Plotinus arrived in Rome. He had a driving passion to see, as Socrates saw, what was eternal and unchanging in existence. Porphyry, a favored student of Plotinus, wrote that Plotinus "worked hard to free himself and rise above the bitter waves of this blood-drenched life . . . by the ways of meditation and by the methods Plato teaches in the *Symposium*, he was always raising himself up to the first and all-transcendent God."[11]

Plotinus pored over one of Plato's most mystical works, the *Timaeus*—a kind of literary sequel to the *Republic* in which the characters turn from plotting out the perfect politics to speculating about the foundations of the universe and its creation. Timaeus, the title character, bears wisdom from the ancient priests of Egypt who have passed down stories about how the world was made. The gods, said Timaeus, were all created by one God, the "demiurge" or craftsman. That one creator God made the universe as body and soul, a single great consciousness pervading all the heavens and setting the planets in motion. And "imitating the craftsman-god who had made them," the lesser gods "borrowed from the world, on temporary loan, portions of fire, earth, water, and air. These they molded together." Taking hunks of matter that they found in creation, they "bound the revolutions of the immortal soul into the body with its ebbs and flows."[12]

We will go wrong if we take this story literally, as an actual physical description of what happened at some point in time. Plato understood that the mysteries of creation and the soul were beyond literal description: "To tell what the soul really is would be a matter for a long discussion, and one totally beyond human power," Socrates says in the *Phaedrus*. "But a human being can describe it briefly, in an image."[13] These cryptic stories intimate something which can never quite be understood head-on, because it is the context and premise of all our understanding. The soul is the thing in us which perceives our own existence as more than physical beings. So how could it be perceived in physical terms? Only through metaphor and story can we turn the eye of the soul back on itself.

That was Plato's project in the *Timaeus*, and it was the project that Plotinus carried forward. "Imagine a stately and elaborate mansion . . . it has never been abandoned by its Architect—but still, the Architect is not confined to it."[14] That is the universe, the *kosmos*, according to Plotinus: a physical shell maintained by the governing spirit of reason. And the individual human being is like a universe in miniature: from one source in the Divine Mind there springs forth a cosmic soul, and from there the human soul springs forth and inhabits the human body.

There is more to this story than its mythical—not to say, kooky—exterior might imply. For one thing, it captures and expresses a strange phenomenon: the fact that the logic in our mind describes the logic of the world. When we calculate the trajectory of planets, we look up to find that the heavenly bodies are right where we predicted they would be, when we predicted it. When we look at two apples and two oranges, we come up with this strange idea called "two"—an idea not tied to any particular physical item but that lives in the mind, or the soul, abstracted from the sensible world.

Yet when we apply these abstract numbers to things like rocket ships and neuroscience, we find they behave in the outside world as they do in our mental calculations: the things "out there" conform to patterns we find inscribed within us. The myth of the *Timaeus* is in large part a depiction of this extraordinary fact: the one great mind that made the universe "endowed us with sight, so we can observe the rational revolutions of the heavens, and let them affect the revolutions of thought within ourselves (which bear a natural resemblance to those in the heavens)."[15] Plotinus found in this depiction an account of how our souls, though they descend into physical bodies, nevertheless reproduce in miniature the patterns of reason which pervade all creation.

But oh, what centuries of anguish are contained in that one word: "descend." *Katabainō*: the Greek word for plunging downward into the underworld, for the coming of death, for the soul's ruin. It is the first word of Plato's *Republic*, and the reason for all the trouble of our hearts. If the soul must move from its seat in the heavens into the body, it is hard not to think of that motion as a loss, as a fall. Plotinus was always yearning to reverse that fall and reunite his soul with the All, which is why he welcomed death. His discomfort with having his soul shunted into a physical body is expressed in the very first line of Porphyry's biography: "Plotinus the philosopher, our contemporary, seemed ashamed of being in a body." If the human soul is simply an emanation of the great All-Soul which hovers "out there" in the intelligible world, then the body into which the soul descends can hardly be more than an imposition, a dead weight. This is the painful caveat that Timaeus adds to his alignment of the heavens with our own minds: "our motions are turbulent, while theirs are calm." That is putting it mildly. While the planets wheel overhead in intricate mathematical harmony, our own desires and inadequacies drive us to madness. Our bodies want lovers we cannot have; they crave more food than we know we should eat; and above all, sooner or later, they die.

Plotinus felt the indignity of this situation keenly. He tried to ignore the fact of his flesh as often and in as many ways as possible. He refused to talk about where he was born and to whom, as if it disgusted him to have once been sheathed in the fluids of his mother's womb. Even the public baths, where he would have been surrounded by naked bodies, were too much for him. In his old age he suffered from intestinal discomfort, but couldn't bear to accept the prescribed treatment, which was delivered by enema. The disease festered and became diphtheria, of which he died: "his sight faded, and ulcers formed on his hands and feet," Porphyry reports. Day in and day out, Plotinus's soul pounded against the prison walls of his body. It was a life marked by the painful contortions of the body crisis.

Soul Dysphoria

The body crisis is making itself felt again. Plato's division between sensible and intelligible reality was famously reinforced in the modern era by René Descartes, a French mathematician who in the seventeenth century tried to prove his very existence by the fact that he could think: whatever else may be mistaken, we can be sure that we are having thoughts. *I think, therefore I am.* Less quotable, but no less important, is what Descartes says near the end of his *Meditations*: "Nothing else belongs to my nature or essence except that I am a thing which thinks.... It is certain that I am something other than my body."[16]

Descartes has been challenged at great length in the years since he wrote, but his stark division between body and soul has stuck firmly in the popular imagination. This is likely how most people now think of the soul, if they think of it at all: as some totally "other" essence which sits, perhaps, in the cockpit of our skull and guides our thoughts and emotions, while our physical brain guides the mechanical movements of our arms and legs.

"I see the body almost as a toy or a pet that I can play with," said Pippa Gardner, a transgender performance artist in a 2021 interview. "I am an inside and an outside. I see them as one inside the other.... I'm at a point where the exterior part is not behaving as well as it should, and the interior part is aggravated by that, saying, 'come on!'"[17] This is Cartesian "dualism" at its finest—but it would be wrong to lay the blame for it entirely at the feet of Descartes. Online technology has played a big role in dredging up our ancient discomfort with having bodies. The internet is, famously, a place where we can project an edited and perfected version of how we feel we *ought* to look. The intensity with which some people pursue this project was exemplified in 2021 when someone leaked an unretouched photo of Khloé Kardashian, whose celebrity depends in part on meticulously photoshopped images of herself. The Kardashian team issued severe legal threats to get the unretouched picture taken down, because in their view Khloé's natural human form is simply not enough.[18]

This helps explain where the "body positivity" movement comes from—it is a reaction against idealized, photoshopped images of presumed physical perfection. "Please be positive about your body, please use our movement to empower yourself. That's the point," said the obese pop star Lizzo on TikTok. She was defending "Big women, big Brown and Black women, queer women" who feel ashamed of themselves for being overweight or unattractive. To the body positivity movement, any physique, no matter how imperfect, undesirable, or unwholesome, is "beautiful."[19]

This kind of dishonesty is an unhealthy response to the equally dishonest practice of holding up photoshopped images as an ideal. But these two extremes have something in common: they are both about recalibrating and redefining the world to solve the problem of the body. Either pick a filter to smooth away your physical blemishes, or pick a crusade to reprogram people's expectations of beauty: either way, you're trying to reshape reality to cure your own dissatisfaction with your body. The unspoken promise is that somewhere you can find the right hair color, skin tone, plastic surgeon, body ideal, minority identity, or even animal or robot avatar that lets you finally be *you* without discomfort.

It is impossible to talk about this cultural moment without discussing the rapid rise in gender dysphoria among teenagers and young people. Previously referred to as "gender identity disorder," gender dysphoria is the name for a crippling and overwhelming sense that the sex of your body is misaligned with the reality of your soul or your inner self. In 2013, the *DSM-5*—an authoritative diagnostic manual for therapists and clinicians published by the American Psychiatric Association—defined gender dysphoria as "the distress that may accompany the incongruence between one's experienced or expressed gender and one's assigned gender," where "gender" refers not to one's biology but to "the public (and usually legally recognized) lived role as boy or girl, man or woman."[20]

The psychologist John Money popularized this way of speaking in the mid-twentieth century—it is the lasting legacy of his highly disreputable career. The word "gender" draws a stark—some might say Platonic—dividing line between "sex," meaning one's biological characteristics as male or female, and "gender," meaning the ways in which one behaves, feels, and is perceived. The runaway success of the philosopher Judith Butler's *Gender Trouble* in 1990 helped sunder these two ideas more starkly among the leftist intellectual class. Butler was wrestling with French poststructuralists like Michel de Foucault and post-Freudian feminists like Simone de Beauvoir, who had famously written that "one is not born, but rather becomes, a woman."[21] Pushing Beauvoir's idea further, Butler suggested that "sex does not cause gender, and gender cannot be understood to reflect or express sex."

But then, still more radically, Butler proposed that sex too is an invented idea applied to the body, so that even the most basic facts of our physical selves are subject to transformation and reinterpretation: "gender is not to culture as sex is to nature; gender is also the discursive/cultural means by which 'sexed nature' or a 'natural sex' is produced." Gender is a performance; binary sex is a social construct; our bodies are objects of hostile interpretations fabricated by the powerful. At the time these were explosive statements. Today, they are commonplace.[22]

When the word first became mainstream, most people thought that "gender" was just a more polite way of saying "sex." The public did not fully appreciate what this change meant until it was too late. In the twenty-first century we are increasingly learning to dislike basic facts about our bodies. It is no small wonder that ours is an age of skyrocketing gender dysphoria.

By all accounts, gender dysphoria is agony—a jagged mismatch between flesh and spirit. In 2016, BuzzFeed asked dysphoric people to depict how they felt. Women drew their breasts as balls and chains shackled to their legs; men imagined unzipping their own skin and emerging, newly female, from their old unwanted exoskeleton.[23] In children with gender dysphoria, puberty can be a time of acute distress when the maleness or femaleness of the body suddenly asserts itself in a dramatic way. The thoughts of gender dysphoric adolescents can turn to suicide, which is why many parents are willing to do anything—including irreversible surgery and hormonal intervention—to help alleviate the discomfort.

But it is telling to read in the *DSM-5* that gender dysphoria occurs in just 0.005 percent to 0.014 percent of natal males, and 0.002 percent to 0.003 percent of natal females. In 2013, when this edition of the manual was published, those numbers were current. They are already wildly out of date. Girls, especially, are developing gender dysphoria at an alarming pace: between 2006 and 2016, the number of referrals to London's Charing Cross "Gender Identity Clinic" nearly quadrupled. Between 2008 and 2015, another such clinic in Nottingham saw its referral numbers jump from 30 to 850.[24] A Gallup report in 2020 found that 1.8 percent of Gen-Z kids in the United States (born between 1997 and 2002) identified as transgender.[25] By 2021, it was up to 2.1 percent.[26] A shocking uptick in gender dysphoria, especially among girls, has blown the *DSM-5*'s figures out of the water. We are simply more uncomfortable in our bodies than we ever were before.

Perhaps some of this is because gender dysphoric people are more comfortable sharing their feelings as it becomes commonplace, not to say required, to accept and validate transgender people in American culture and society. But it is just as likely, if not more so, that causation goes the other way. Perhaps boys and girls feel more uncomfortable about their bodies as they are increasingly taught by adults and peers to view their physical sex as something detachable from their gender. Brown University health researcher Lisa Littman caused enormous controversy when she surveyed 250 families with dysphoric children and observed that 80 percent of the kids were female.[27] What Littman called "rapid-onset gender dysphoria" is a new phenomenon, a sudden self-identification as trans in girls who never showed signs of bodily discomfort before. Littman was attacked because her results suggested that our massive dysphoria epidemic might not be entirely spontaneous.[28]

More and more public schools have adopted the Human Rights Campaign Foundation's "gender snowperson," or other similar infographics, to teach that sex, sexuality, and gender are unmoored from one another.[29] But this kind of messaging goes beyond classrooms. One 2020 study in the *Journal of the American Medical Association* found evidence that in areas where kids are exposed to more media coverage of transgender-related issues, gender therapy clinics receive more referrals.[30] Studies have also shown that children increasingly shape their political beliefs and values (including their sense of gender identity) in conversation with one another in online forums like Tumblr. "Online engagement is not just isolated," said Tumblr's director of outreach Liba Rubenstein, "it really is attached to people's offline identities."[31]

Typically, this kind of peer-to-peer discussion is represented as a victory for liberation and inclusion. But online life is not just allowing kids to vent their discomfort with their bodies: it is also *creating* that discomfort where previously there was none. In this broader context the rise in transgender identification and gender dysphoria seems less like an authentic phenomenon in and of itself, and more like one symptom of the ancient body crisis, kicked into hyperdrive by the experience of internet life.

Abigail Shrier, a journalist who has spent much of her career documenting the rise of gender dysphoria in young girls, interviewed one teenager whose anorexia morphed into gender dysphoria as if the two sprang from the same source: "My goal went from diet pills to testosterone.... From fantasies about slicing off my thigh fat to slicing off my breasts. I bound them with duct tape. I couldn't breathe. It made me panic, but I felt brave." Buck Angel, a transsexual internet celebrity, speculated to Shrier about the association between widespread gender dysphoria and a disgust at the body more generally among teens, who are having less sex than previous generations and seem more comfortable in virtual than physical space. Shrier concludes that adolescent transgenderism "very often seems to be a sad cult of asexuality, like the hand-painted sign in an antique shop reading 'Please Do Not Touch.'"[32]

Persona Creata

Given the explosion of gender dysphoria among adolescent girls, this phase of the body crisis suggests a particular horror at the idea of womanhood. "Perhaps forever," writes Shrier, "but at least since Shakespeare's Viola arrived shipwrecked in Illyria and decided to pass herself off as a man, it has occurred to young women: it's so much easier to be a boy." The feminist injunction for women to "lean in"—to hunt out positions of power and dominance in traditionally male industries and pursuits—comes freighted with the implication that traditionally female pursuits are weak, contemptible, and dull. "I suppose I could have stayed home and baked cookies and had teas, but what I decided to do was fulfill my profession," sniffed Hillary Clinton, in a classic summation of this idea, during her husband Bill's first presidential campaign.[33]

Both implicitly and explicitly, our ruling classes express contempt for homemaking and motherhood. But this closes off the most primal path to resolving the body crisis. Women, by creating new life, bear witness to the possibility that body and soul can in fact be reconciled: in childbirth, human flesh becomes the medium of the divine. Poets have expressed this as the "eternal feminine," the strangely luminous power of women like Dante's Beatrice or Faust's Margarete to act as physical conduits for the life-giving power of God. "Woman, eternal, beckons us on," wrote Johann Wolfgang von Goethe in the closing lines of his *Faust*. This is the meaning of the Virgin Mary's consent to bring God into the world: her body will become the medium to deliver divine life in God made flesh.

This is not to say that pregnancy and labor are some sort of cakewalk that we should regard with misty-eyed sentiment. Ever since Adam and Eve were cast out of Eden, creating life has also meant facing pain. The delicate challenge of growing from girl to woman involves coming to terms with the blood and the sorrow of what it means to have a body in a fallen world. Now, though, that hard task is made harder by the constant social implication that to be a mother is to be brainwashed and oppressed. No wonder girls are fleeing womanhood, and small wonder this has intensified our sense that the human body is nothing more than dead weight. If our bodies are not at least potentially a source of divine blessing, then they are simply a burden. Shucking off that burden means turning women into mere body parts that can be removed, reconfigured, or appropriated at will. That means reducing the female body to its functions, recasting women themselves as "menstruaters," "chest feeders," and "birthing people."[34]

Thus adults who promote trans rights repeatedly indicate that bodily reality does not exist, or that the body has no inherent integrity and its meaning is entirely at the whim of its inhabitant. "Here's the thing about chest surgery," said Dr. Johanna Olson-Kennedy, a trans youth specialist and director of the Center for Transyouth Health and Development at the Children's Hospital in Los Angeles: "If you want breasts at a later point in your life you can go and get them." Reacting with alarm to Olson-Kennedy's statement, British journalist Douglas Murray asked: "Are people like blocks of Lego onto which new pieces can be stuck, taken off and replaced again at will?"[35]

Not yet, but perhaps that is the goal. Increasingly the objective is to abolish the boundaries of the body altogether, to liberate the human spirit and let it mold the flesh as it chooses. This is what critic Mary Harrington calls "biolibertarianism," the aspiration to remove bodily constraints and turn our physical forms into a set of customizable parts that can be interchanged or reshaped.[36] Harrington notes an anonymous 2018 paper, *Gender Acceleration*, which argues that surgical transition from male to female "breaks [a] lucky few free from the horrid curse of being human." A woman who calls herself "whorecress" expressed a very similar attitude in a video that went viral on TikTok: "I'm not body-positive," she declared, "I'm not body-neutral. I'm body-negative. I wanna be vapor. Or like, a plume of blue smoke. Or mist. Or a rumor—I'd be a rumor . . . 'cause like, gender? Humiliating. An ache, a pain? Needing to sit down? Spatial awareness? The vulgarity.... Every day I wake up and I'm subject to the burden of embodiment. How dare I be a shape? Disgusting."

Obviously this monologue was delivered with a certain irony. But like all successful humor, it articulated a real sentiment that the online audience connected with. Whorecress's *cri de coeur* against embodiment featured prominently on a Reddit discussion thread called r/voidpunk, which "is a subculture for those who often feel rejected or disconnected from humanity" and prefer to associate themselves with a more spectral or robotic form of life. r/voidpunk has just under 20,000 subscribers as of this writing, but the trend is much bigger than that: "transhumanism" is a growing movement among technologists, many of whom imagine a future where gene editing, virtual reality, and bionic enhancement render us free from the limitations of physical existence. Here is the modern culmination of our extreme body crisis.

The connection between transgenderism and transhumanism is made explicit by Martine Rothblatt, a transgender activist who has poured money and effort into transhumanist science. Rothblatt's book, *From Transgender to Transhuman: A Manifesto on the Freedom of Form*, argues expressly that gender transition is only the beginning:

I am convinced that laws classifying people as either male or female, and laws prohibiting people's freedom based on their genitals, will become as obsolete in the twenty-first century as the religious edicts of the Middle Ages seem absurd in America today.... Over the next few decades we will witness the uploading of human minds into software and computer systems, and the birth of brand new human minds as information technology. As we see our selves and our loved ones in these *transhuman* beings, and they make us laugh and cry, we will not hesitate long to recognize their humanity with citizenship and their common cause with us in a new common species, *Persona creatus* ([sic.] "the created person").[37]

The fullest available expression of the body crisis is not the hormone injection but the digital avatar: pick and choose how you will move through the imaginary space of the metaverse. The movement that began with "gender neutral" pronouns has now produced an enormous constellation of totally invented identities, going far beyond ze and zer to include neologisms like "pupself" and "demonself," for those who identify spiritually as animals or demons. What's going on here is bigger than gender: we are dreaming not simply of making men into women, and vice versa, but making ourselves into *anything*, at a whim.[38]

Desire and Happiness

"Gender? Humiliating." Whorecress was on to something. "How dare I be a shape? Disgusting." There is the body crisis in a nutshell.

And yet we can't escape the body except at a great and terrible cost. Much like virtual reality and online life, transhumanism holds out glittering promises on which it is singularly ill-equipped to deliver. It's not just that sex-change technology currently comes with mutilation, gruesome risks, and lifelong complications. Even if we imagine that rearranging or reconstructing body parts is painlessly easy (it is not), will it make us happy? What does "happy" even mean? Already Andrea Long Chu, a major transgender writer, has emphasized that happiness is not the point: "My new vagina won't make me happy," Chu wrote in the *New York Times*, "and it shouldn't have to." This is because "desire and happiness are independent agents."[39] Really? If our desires have no governing aim, such as happiness or virtue, then what is the use of them—or us—at all? Surely we follow our desires because they point us toward something *desirable*—if not, we are just aimless hunks of flesh pulled randomly in all directions by wants that have no connection to goodness or joy. This total dissolution of purpose would be one of the real wages of transhumanism, were it ever to become reality.

If we become fully free from the constraints of physical form, if we even develop the technology to "feel" whatever we want, then we really will become nothing more than a sort of computer-programmed robot, experiencing sensations that signify nothing; joy will be an electro-chemical occurrence, unrelated to falling in love or holding a newborn child. In our effort to liberate our spirits from our bodies, we will make our spirits and our very consciousness into the mere mechanical illusion that materialists already imagine it to be. Dissolve the boundaries of your body and you dissolve the boundaries of yourself. If you feel an instinctive disgust at this dystopian futuristic prospect, it is because you have a felt intuition of what we really are. Plotinus may have dreamed great dreams of ascending to be with the Divine All, but in real life he became a neurotic old man, crusted over with ulcers and boils. Our present efforts to transcend gender or even species, to become transhuman or to live as avatars in virtual reality, have left us looking ridiculous and feeling sick. As one wry observer noted of the cross-dressing celebrity Harry Styles, "'he's challenging gender norms' and he's losing."[40]

We can have compassion for gender dysphoric people without making them the central ideal of all our aspirations. Without a trace of malice toward them, we may observe that the measures they take to transform their bodies are not steps in a direction we find particularly attractive or healthy. It is no surprise that gender dysphoric people have high rates of depression. So do young people who spend their lives online. These are not ways that most of us should want to live. And yet we indulge in the fantasy that if these kinds of lives are pushed to the extreme—if the internet grows and swallows us up into the metaverse, or if the spirit gains total freedom from the body—then things will be great. If we continue down this path that is currently making us sick and miserable, we will eventually be happy and free. This, as always, is a dubious proposition.

CHAPTER 4

Spirit and Flesh

Not a Toy

The spectacular failures of our many efforts to disembody ourselves—and the horror of what might happen if we ever succeed—suggest that the body is *not* extraneous to us. It is not a toy, a pet, or an appendage. For all the problems it causes, this flesh of ours is an essential aspect of our very being. And so we hit once again on a philosophical issue much older than transgenderism or digital avatars. The union between body and soul was one of the major points of dispute between Plato and his greatest successor, Aristotle.

In *School of Athens*, a famous painting by the Italian Renaissance artist Raphael, the philosophers of the Greek tradition gather in a great hall to discuss and debate the questions of life. At the center of the composition stands grey-bearded Plato, pointing upward, and a virile young Aristotle, his hand outstretched over the ground. With Aristotle, Plato learned what it was like to have a brilliant and insatiable protégé, as Plato himself had been to Socrates.

Aristotle was born in 384 BC in Stagira, a coastal city in northeastern Greece. He travelled widely and, at the age of 17, made his first trip to Athens to study under Plato. In 343 BC he became a tutor in the court of Macedon's ambitious King Philip II. Writing after Aristotle's death, ancient biographers would claim that Philip summoned Aristotle to teach his son, the extraordinary young man who would one day be known as Alexander the Great—though what Alexander learned from Aristotle remains one of history's great unknowns.[1] He at last returned to Athens and founded the Lyceum, his own school; the small-town Stagirite had become a man of the world. Aristotle's surviving works are not dialogues but methodical treatises, exhaustive accounts of everything from the biology of insects to the origins and fate of the universe. His gesture in Raphael's painting, toward the ground, evokes his insistence on earthly reality. Plato, pointing at the sky, spoke allusively in his dialogues through myths and stories. But Aristotle did not want dreams: he wanted facts.

So it was that Aristotle grew frustrated with his teacher's talk of Forms, those unchanging and abstract ideas that we glimpse dimly beyond our physical world. What were the Forms, and where? "Plato says things exist by participation in the Forms," wrote Aristotle in his study of the supernatural world, the *Metaphysics*. "But what this 'participation' entails remains an open question."[2] "Participation," Aristotle suggested, was a fancy word that explained nothing,—a vague reference to some mystical union between the intelligible and sensible worlds.

It is not that Aristotle denied the existence of realities which are more than physical. Rather, he rejected the notion that such realities are in any sense "out there." He believed there was no special plane where the good, the true, and the beautiful floated in pure perfection. The world into which Socrates gazed was not some realm beyond, where Plotinus might hope to escape and leave his body behind. For Aristotle there is only this world, in which, though everything is made of matter, there are certain truths *about* matter that are not material.

Take, for instance, a circle: we may draw a circle in ink, or carve one out of bronze. It is a circle just the same—the shape exists independently of its material. But you have never seen, nor can you even imagine, an immaterial circle—a circle made of *nothing*. When you try to picture one, you may find yourself visualizing a plain black circle against a white background. But then all you have done is picture one version of a circle by drawing it in black ink on imaginary paper in your head. "Thoughts are not images, but they never take place without images," writes Aristotle in his study of the soul.[3] Things like circles are not bound by space and time, but neither are they *beyond* space and time. They are distinct from matter, but they exist within matter wherever we find or think of them.[4]

Take this idea further. Imagine a sculptor who carves two sculptures of the same man: one out of bronze, and another out of marble. The matter—in Greek the *hulē*, or "stuff"—is different. But the shape—the *morphē*—is the same. This is what forms were like for Aristotle: less "ideas" with independent existence in a far-off world than "shapes" into which stuff is carved.

From there Aristotle worked out a system of four "causes" (*aitiai*), or ways of explaining why things are what they are. The "stuff" itself is one cause: the *material* cause. Without a hunk of bronze or marble there could be no sculpture. But there could be no sculpture without a plan for its shape, either. This is the *formal* cause: the bronze is molded in a particular way, and no other way, because of the outline the sculptor has in his mind for it. That means the sculptor's art itself is another kind of cause—the *efficient* cause, the force that acts on the stuff to shape it into a form. But why does the sculptor choose to do so at all? That is the last cause, the "final" cause. The sculpture is being made for a reason—to decorate a temple or to celebrate the glory of man. This is its *telos*, its purpose or reason for being.[5]

Speaking very roughly, we are also like that sculpture. We are neither a lump of inert stuff, nor a magical ghost floating through space inside a meat sack. We are blood and bone and sinew, given shape by an organizing principle; we are matter arranged in just such a way that it is self-aware. That consciousness, what Jerome called the divine spark, is neither an accidental by-product of our physical existence nor a dreamlike self which deigns to operate a body of which it has no need. Instead, consciousness is the very thing that our bodies exist *to do*.

So the materialists are looking through the wrong end of the telescope. We do not have fears and desires and loves only because our bodies produce certain chemicals. It is just as true, and more essential, to say that our bodies produce those chemicals because their natural purpose is to live a conscious life. "If the eye were an animal, its soul would be sight," wrote Aristotle. "The eye is the matter of sight; if it loses its sight, then it is no longer an eye.... So too an animal is the soul and the body," and thus "the soul is not separable from the body."[6]

An eye is that which sees, just as the human body is that which lives and feels and acts in the world as humans do. That makes some sense of Aristotle's famous, if complicated, definition of the soul: it is the first actuality of a natural body that has life potentially.[7] Our bodies are the kind of stuff that can breathe and see and desire and think. The soul is the realization of that potential: it is the form of the body's matter, the fact that we are alive.

Here is a way of describing the soul that does not make it sound like a ghost in the machine. The technical term for Aristotle's mode of thinking about these things is *hylemorphism*—the belief that form (*morphē*) and matter (*hulē*) are always (or almost always) intertwined. But jargon does not do it justice: this is a union between body and soul that saves us from both pure materialism and pure dualism, a philosophy that conforms to our experience while also providing insight into how to live.

The Point of It All

Being a soul in a body means you are a certain *kind* of thing: you are matter so configured as to be self-aware. You are what you are both because of the stuff you're made of, and because of how that stuff is arranged to do certain things—you have a formal and a material cause. It follows that you also have a final cause, a goal. You can be a more or less perfect version of the thing you are, a more or less complete embodiment of the particular humanity that is you.

The state of perfection or completion—the *telos*—is the state toward which every natural being naturally wants to move. Virtue—excellence, or *aretē*—is being excellent at being the thing that you are. Humans, because of their capacity both to reason in the mind and to act in the body, have access to a unique kind of virtue called moral or ethical virtue. We are rational animals, meaning that we can bring the high principles of truth and beauty to bear on the messy and changing world of the here and now. The four principal ways of being excellent at being human are traditionally called the "cardinal" virtues: wisdom (*sophia*), self-restraint (*sōphrosunē*), courage (*andreia*), and justice (*dikē*).

Already before Aristotle, Plato had associated each of these ways of being excellent with what he called the three "parts," or aspects, of the soul: reason, daring, and desire. To be wise is to use your reason and logic, the *rational* part of you, to discern what is true and false, good and evil. Self-restraint means using that wisdom to guide and direct the many desires and appetites that you experience every day in the *appetitive* part of you, the part that wants. Courage means sticking to your guns and living out your wisdom against every threat or desire—this takes heart, which is what Plato calls the part of the soul that feels righteous indignation and passion for battle. The *thumos*, the heart or the chest, is the part that can follow through on the demands of wisdom. And justice is the art of putting everything in order inside and out, of letting your head guide your gut and not the other way around.[8]

Notably, these essential human virtues are quite worthless unless they are practiced in the real world. It is no good *knowing* that adultery is wrong if you're overpowered by your lust for another woman in the heat of the moment. It's no good thinking about what a generous person you are if you can't bear to part with five dollars to feed a hungry man. The wisdom of your mind and of the ages is useless unless you have the courage to stand fast by it, to speak up against the prevailing orthodoxy and suffer what slander may come if you do. In other words, human virtues are not just perfections of the soul: they are real actions of the body, things we *do*.

And so there is another virtue—practical wisdom, or *phronēsis*—which is the very art of making ideals real in the here and now. We strive for virtues with our soul, but we put them into practice—we make them real—with our bodies. And when we do this well, we sense it. We can *feel* virtue—not necessarily as physical pleasure, but as a kind of rich satisfaction that comes from excellence. This is human *eudaimōnia*, flourishing or fulfilment.

There is a reason why distorting and mutilating our bodies brings us pain and makes us ugly, even if we think it will make us free: what we long for is in a kind of feedback loop with what we do. Our bodies are the medium in which our soul lives, the language in which it expresses either its well-being or its decay. This is not to say that perfect health or a godlike physique is synonymous with moral excellence—just that there's no such thing as being so ethically pure in your soul that you make yourself and everyone around you miserable in the flesh. You are not going to make yourself better by floating free of your physical form.

The Divine Spark

"Virtue" in the sense of human excellence is a word you will not find used often by posthumanists or transhumanists, because they are not so interested in making us morally *better* as in making us smarter, faster, and longer-lived. In his essay, "Why I Want to Be a Posthuman When I Grow Up," Nick Bostrom of Oxford's Future of Humanity Institute defines being "posthuman" as having more than human capacity in at least one of three areas:

- Healthspan—the capacity to remain fully healthy, active, and productive, both mentally and physically.

- Cognition—general intellectual capacities, such as memory, deductive and analogical reasoning, and attention, as well as special faculties such as the capacity to understand and appreciate music, humor, eroticism, narration, spirituality, mathematics, etc.
- Emotion—the capacity to enjoy life and to respond with appropriate affect to life situations and other people.[9]

These are worthy goals so far as they go. It would be wonderful to live longer and healthier lives. But are mere strength and longevity the purpose of our being? Is excellence in emotion nothing more than "the capacity to enjoy life and respond with appropriate affect to life situations and other people"? What about the capacity to act with honor or love the good?

Bostrom goes so far as to exclude moral concerns from his discussion entirely: "any moral reasons [one] might have for declining the transition" from humanity to posthumanity "would only be relevant insofar as they would make the outcome worse" for the patient.[10] In other words, the question whether we should abandon our humanity is primarily a question of outcomes, not of morality. But how can we measure outcomes *except* by some moral standard? If moral excellence is irrelevant, what is the point of getting stronger or smarter to begin with—unless strength and intelligence are simply the highest goods?

By definition, the posthuman kind of excellence comes at the expense of our humanity—it rids us of the unique kinds of joy, sorrow, and triumph that come with being the rational animals that we are. But what other kinds of joy, sorrow, and triumph are there? What good will it do us to become super-efficient machines if "good" becomes simply a matter of power? This is that old fantasy yet again—the fantasy that by breaking free of our body's constraints, we will liberate the divine spark within us to have free reign over space and time.

And true enough, leaving the limits of the body behind was an appealing prospect even to Aristotle. Pure contemplation and mental perfection were, in his view, the highest form of *eudaimōnia* a human could attain. Bostrom has taken this to mean our reason is the best part of us, so we can safely develop our mental faculties and disregard every other human virtue. "If what is good for us is to develop and exercise our rational nature, this implies that it would be good for us to become posthumans with appropriately enhanced cognitive capacities (and preferably with extended healthspan too, so that we may have more time to develop and enjoy these rational faculties)."[11]

Aristotle himself seems to have been tempted to think this way: in a manner of speaking, he said, the intellect "is what each person really is, insofar as it is the dominant and better part." But he added that a man who achieved a life of only contemplation would not really be living a *human* life. "Such a life as this," he said, "would be higher than human: a man would reach it not in virtue of his humanity, but in virtue of something divine within him." To be fully human, on the other hand, is to be two things in one—both animal and rational, body and soul.[12]

It is not inherently evil to mend or even enhance the body with tools. Think of prosthetic limbs or cochlear implants; these are miraculous forms of technology that hardly threaten to make monsters out of us. No one who has watched a child see color for the first time using corrective glasses could feel anything but grateful reverence. But the difference consists precisely in the fact that healthy, life-enhancing technologies *restore* or *support* our humanity rather than attempting to transcend it. They help us to walk if we are crippled, see if our vision is impaired, breathe if we have asthma, and so on.

Transhumanism demands the exact opposite, threatening to dissolve the limits of our body, to redefine happiness and goodness as it redefines our humanity. The most likely outcome of this project is misery, ugliness, and neurosis. The human soul's goodness, honor, courage, and excellence must live in a human body—or not at all.

A Living Soul

Like a great deal of wisdom from classical antiquity, Aristotle's teachings on the union of body and soul have attracted many Christians, and repulsed many others. At the turn of the third century AD, Tertullian, a ferocious Christian polemicist from Carthage, asked: "What does Athens have to do with Jerusalem? What does the church have to do with the Academy, the Christian with the heretic?"[13] If the Bible contains all truth, then what need is there to supplement it with the teaching of unbelievers? It is a question that has often vexed the church, and in some cases still does.

But there is another strain of Christian thought, going all the way back to the New Testament. Saint Paul, writing to the infant church in Rome, said: "When Greeks, who do not have the law, do by nature things required by the law, they show that the requirements of the law are written on their hearts" (Romans 2:14–15). And so even though Scripture remains the final word, many Church fathers saw in Greek and Roman wisdom precursors or premonitions of Christian truth. There have always been Christians who seek to "reconcile all things to God through Christ," in the words of another Pauline epistle (Colossians 1:20).

But Aristotle, who seemed quite unsympathetic to such doctrinal necessities as human resurrection, was a problem for the church: plainly brilliant, but also plainly, historically pagan. Only a Christian philosopher of equal brilliance could square the circle. In the thirteenth century, the Catholic theologian Thomas Aquinas rose to the occasion, reconciling Aristotelian physics and metaphysics with Church doctrine. In his *Summa Theologica*, Aquinas attempted to give an exhaustive account of "whatsoever belongs to the Christian religion." As he proceeded with his deliberate, methodical account of questions high and low, Aquinas found in Aristotle a great philosophical ally. Like Aristotle's, Aquinas's hand was always outstretched toward solid ground—even as his eyes were turned up toward heaven.

Aquinas's view of body and soul is, in important aspects, distinctly Aristotelian. "The first thing by which the body lives is the soul," Aquinas wrote. "The soul is the primary principle of our nourishment, sensory experience, and spatial movement; and likewise of our understanding." Our consciousness is knit into our body: "it is distinct, yet it exists in matter."[14]

Aquinas was certain, where Aristotle was not, that the soul endures after death. But, like the rigorous Aristotelian that he was, Aquinas insisted that the soul must go *somewhere*: even after physical death, souls are not unmoored from corporeal space. Rather, in heaven or in hell, they await a moment when they will be resurrected bodily.[15] And so belief in resurrection is not belief in disembodiment. On the contrary, it is the belief that even after this earthly body has broken down, another kind of matter will be shaped in the form of that same soul. The sculpture will be made again, in gold instead of bronze.

It is worth noting that Aquinas was not simply appropriating Aristotle for the church. He was, if anything, noticing a deep and strange consonance between the most developed observations of Aristotelian logic, and the most basic assertions of Jewish wisdom. Long before Alexander the Great conquered Greece, or Christ set foot on earth, a prophet told the story of how God made man. "The LORD God formed a man from the dust of the ground and breathed into his nostrils the breath of life, and the man became a living soul" (Genesis 2:7).

Believers have read those words so often that it's hard to recognize this astonishing fact about them: they are perfectly hylemorphic. They describe an irreducible union of flesh and spirit. The "living soul" (*nefesh chayyim*) is not simply a molded lump of clay. Nor is it the disembodied "breath of life." Rather, the "living soul" is the total fusion of the clay and the breath together as one. Adam becomes alive in Genesis when God's life force joins together with a lump of "stuff" from the ground. From that point, Adam is—and we are—form in matter, clay given life, body and soul.

The Dwelling Place of God

Your body is not expendable, and your mind is not a mistake. Your body and your soul are inescapably connected, just as light is inescapably connected to the sun. You have never seen or shown love, patience, or generosity merely in the abstract: you have always embodied these virtues in action. You cannot simply help a man by feeling nice about him. You can only take bread in your hands, give it to him, and let him chew it and eat it. As it says in the New Testament: "Whoever says, 'I love God,' but hates his brother, is a liar. For if he does not love his brother, whom he has seen, how can he love God, whom he has not seen?" (1 John 4:20). Perfection of the soul comes through actions of the body.

Your flesh, for all its flaws and failings, has something to say about who you are. Your masculinity or your femininity is not something you perform; it is something you aspire to fulfil. Most men long to be manly because they carry in their bodies the potential to be fathers, protectors, and warriors. Women are, by and large, endowed with the grace to create, to make homes, to give life. These are things to be relished, not despised or discounted. Though the flesh has its discontents, they are nothing compared to what happens when we try to cast our bodies aside, discarding objective truths and judgements about our physical selves as arbitrary "gender assignments," "beauty standards," or "Western norms." Certain things *are* objective. Our biological sex is one such objective truth. Physical excellence is another. There is a reason why so many men find that their discontents are alleviated by the rigor of physical exercise, why "get jacked and tan" has become a rallying cry for young men who are fed up with the sickliness of hyper-online life. Men seek peace in strength: it is in their nature, and their nature is in their flesh. Likewise, it is not surprising that rates of female unhappiness have risen as increasing numbers of women forego marriage and childbirth. These are things most women feel drawn to at a profound physical and spiritual level, even if they also find fulfillment in work. Our bodies and the longings that come with them are not going to go away just because we mutilate and deny them.

This is not to say that every case of gender dysphoria can be cured with a vigorous weightlifting regime for young men or home economics classes for young women. But our current reigning orthodoxy prevents us from even considering relatively easy, time-tested remedies before leaping into surgery and hormone treatment. The danger of our present situation is that we have no north star. We sense that our bodies matter, but we have no idea how to live that fact out. We all know intuitively that wishing away our body or our soul, and willfully denying objective standards of excellence, will make us miserable. Why should chemicals and surgery have anything to offer us—what would the use of them even mean—without some final standard of beauty, excellence, virtue, and truth? The future will bring technological possibilities that we cannot imagine. We will have to decide how to use these technologies, whether for good or evil. But that will require knowing the difference—and living it out in our flesh.

Whatever good you will do, whatever excellence you may seek, will not exist in some imagined sphere of perfection. Your quiet actions of tomorrow morning—waking up early, working out, praying, making breakfast for your kids—will count for more than all the grand designs you dream up or the beautiful ideas you have about yourself. The dwelling place of God is with men, and the dwelling place of the soul is in the body. You are not on your way to some communion with the eternal or the infinite: the infinite is *already here*, expressed in the medium of your flesh and blood and the hard, solid world you can see and touch. The world of the spirit is our world, the world of humanity. Live in it: you might even like it.

PART III

Meaning

As the dance is the thing with which we are concerned and contains complete within itself its own arrangement and history and finale there is no necessity that the dancers contain these things within themselves as well.

—Cormac McCarthy, *Blood Meridian*

By the ancients, man has been called the world in miniature.

—Leonardo Da Vinci, Notebook
(Codex Leicester)

CHAPTER 5

The Crisis of Meaning

Life, the Universe, and Everything

At this point I expect plenty of intelligent readers will be objecting, in perfectly good faith, that Charles Darwin explained all this spiritual nonsense away long ago. The theory of evolution, some will say, accounts for how organisms come to be the way they are by means of natural selection. Genetic mutations which reproduce themselves better than others will always endure. Over time those species and characteristics survive which can do things like see, hear, and use logic to predict outcomes in the world around them.

On this view there is no need to resort to concepts like "virtue" or "the soul." The human brain is a marvel of complexity, to be sure, but its existence is only a stage of development in a history stretching back millions of years—from the ancient eel-like chordate *Pikaia gracilens*, to the gradual webbing of ganglia and dendrites across the body, on up to our highly advanced processing computer, the brain. What I have been calling the soul came gradually into being as a by-product, not a goal, of this delicate structural elaboration.

The story is a beautiful one, but only from our perspective as the self-appointed heroes of it. "The chimpanzee and the human share about 99.5 per cent of their evolutionary history, yet most human thinkers regard the chimp as a malformed, irrelevant oddity while seeing themselves as stepping-stones to the Almighty," wrote evolutionary biologist Richard Dawkins in a preface to *The Selfish Gene* (1976). But "to an evolutionist this cannot be so. There exists no objective basis on which to evaluate one species above another."[1] There is no inherent system of values or intentions in nature itself: there are only things that we, because of the kinds of beings we are, may find preferable. Ideas of a governing consciousness or law that we conform ourselves to are misplaced. Law, and consciousness, are in us and not some higher entity. In other words: there is no God.

Dawkins, neuroscientist Sam Harris, philosopher of cognitive science Daniel Dennett, and the late essayist Christopher Hitchens became known, in the early twenty-first century, as the "New Atheists." They denied not only the existence of God but the possibility of believing rationally in any religious system. Though these men came from different academic backgrounds, one thing they shared was a conviction that science can overrule virtually all competing disciplines or sources of truth. "We distrust anything that contradicts science," wrote Hitchens of himself and his fellow travelers in *God Is Not Great*.[2] Hitchens went on to cite with approval Dennett's famous argument that religion was a product of evolutionary happenstance rather than ancestral insight into any actual reality. For their fans, the New Atheists were authorities on religion precisely because they afforded to scientists the kind of authority once reserved for priests and clerics. In disputes about what can be known, they gave science the last word.

The ancients would have called a man like Dawkins a "natural philosopher"—he and his fellow scientists are professional seekers and lovers (*philo-*) of wisdom (*sophia*) regarding what happens according to nature (*physis*). *Physis* means, in Aristotle's language, "that which has its principle of change and being at rest within itself."[3] In plainer terms, "physics," or the study of nature, is the study of things that happen spontaneously—according to fixed laws that are inherent in the things themselves. It is inherent in a mass to be attracted by the force of gravity to other masses—in other words it is natural for a stone to fall to the earth when you drop it and for planets to orbit around the sun.[4]

These mechanical workings of the world have always been objects of academic and commercial interest, but knowledge about them has not always been thought of as a privileged or superior kind of knowledge. There are, after all, other branches of philosophy which study things that are not physical. One such branch is the philosophy called "metaphysics": the study of that which is beyond (*meta*) nature. Metaphysics describes not just the mere facts and rules of what happens in the physical world, but the principles of *why* such things happen and for what purposes.

There are still more branches: Ethics, the study of how we should behave, can be thought of as philosophy about how metaphysics comes "down to earth," or of how principles beyond nature can govern the natural world. If doing good means exerting something called free will—choosing one course of action over another—then morality must involve principles higher than mere physical law. If a starving parent gives up his dinner so his child can eat, he is resisting the natural inclination of a biological organism to eat when hungry. He does so under the influence of a virtue called charity or love. This is another reason why what I have been calling the soul, if it exists, cannot be physical: though it guides the actions of the body and inheres in its structure, it can make choices that are not predetermined in the physical mechanisms that the body is subject to.

In Latin, the equivalent of *meta* is *super*, and the equivalent of *physis* is *natura*: that which is metaphysical is *supernatural*. Strictly speaking, then, men like the New Atheists believe there is no such thing as metaphysics: everything, including the operations of our brain and the experience of consciousness that arises from it, behaves according to observable and predictable laws of nature. Nothing is supernatural, not even morals. Good and evil, for someone like Dawkins, have no basis in anything metaphysical or divine. Our conventional ethics can be explained in purely secular—indeed, in evolutionary—terms. This helps us understand why scientists have taken a place in our society akin to that of priests, and philosophers in others; if there is nothing beyond nature, then natural scientists become the authorities on all questions, including those once answered by metaphysics.

We call upon science now to explain not just how the physical world works, but how *everything* works, and why. Evolution is no longer simply a description of how organisms develop but a grand, unified field theory of all life: who we are, what our purpose is, and where we are going. In the first chapter of *The Selfish Gene*, Dawkins argues that "it was Darwin who first put together a coherent and tenable account of why we exist." Then he quotes with approval paleontologist G. G. Simpson: "All attempts to answer that question before 1859 are worthless and . . . we will be better off if we ignore them completely."[5]

If there is nothing but matter, then material science can explain everything—and indeed that is Dawkins's goal in *The Selfish Gene*. He takes the logic of evolution and expands it out beyond mere physical reproduction to explain life from the molecular to the civilizational level. Dawkins's aim is to account for everything with one rule: that which works, survives. Or, more precisely, things survive when they are good at replicating themselves. "All life evolves by the differential survival of replicating entities," writes Dawkins: things make copies of themselves, and if those copies vary just enough, then the resulting variety will produce various possibilities of which the ones that reproduce best will survive.

This rule explains not just why our bodies and brains have developed the way they have, but why human society and culture look the way they do. Dawkins's revolutionary insight was that not only do genes behave according to the law of replication, but cultural activities and practices repeat and mutate, too. Dawkins invented a word for patterns of behavior that replicate themselves in culture the way genes replicate themselves in biology: he called them memes.

Meme World

"Examples of memes," wrote Dawkins, "are tunes, ideas, catch-phrases, clothes fashions, ways of making pots or of building arches. Just as genes propagate themselves in the gene pool by leaping from body to body via sperms or eggs, so memes propagate themselves in the meme pool by leaping from brain to brain via a process which, in the broad sense, can be called imitation."[6]

"Meme" comes from a Greek word: *mimēma*. It means an "imitation" or a "replicated thing." Effective ideas and attitudes—the unrelenting curiosity of Socrates, the Christian rituals of mercy and absolution, perspective in painting and counterpoint in music—are carried forward into the future in the same way as physical strength and reproductive fertility. Whether encoded into DNA or patterned into the communal lives of successive generations, these things live on.

Our modern idea of the "meme"—an image or format that catches on and spreads around the internet—is just one example of this larger cultural trend. A "meme template" like the picture of "the Distracted Boyfriend" becomes popular because it expresses an experience—the experience of leaving behind one love or obsession for another—that takes different forms. As people label the same image with new text, the meme gains traction. So too behaviors and habits, like using charcoal in beauty products or acronyms in email, become so popular that they spread everywhere.

The idea of the meme was, of course, a sensation. By 2013 it had become viral enough to earn Dawkins an invitation to the glamorous "New Creators Showcase," a display of new artistic talent hosted at the Cannes film festival by the global advertising network Saatchi & Saatchi.[7] Dawkins cut an incongruous figure as he strode to his spotlight at the center of a dark stage and approached the lectern. He was dressed in a shirt with elbow-length floral patterned sleeves and looking to all the world like an absent-minded professor who had stumbled out of his offices and into a red-carpet fashion show. But his ideas had become glamorous enough to make him a celebrity in the art world too. As the applause died down, he explained to the eager crowd of artists and designers what art and design were all about. "Memes spread through human culture as genes spread through the gene pool," Dawkins said: great art, like any successful cultural act, means reproducing and imitating themes that stick in the memory.

Dawkins's own environment proved his point. The set design, such as it was, resembled not a glitzy Hollywood gala but a tech conference. Audience and stage alike were bathed in a seamless blackout. Only Dawkins and his spotlight could be seen: a bright island in a sea of darkness and possibility yet to be discovered. This is unmistakably the look made popular by Apple magnate Steve Jobs at the annual Worldwide Developers Conference, famous for hosting the announcements of new iPhone specs and operating systems. Jobs helped create the world in which a nerdy scientist could be treated like a superstar, could be featured onstage as a celebrity amid the heady atmosphere of Cannes. The elegant minimalist aesthetic, the fashionable enthusiasm for the hard sciences, the suggestion of an infinite dark universe awaiting illumination by man's searching intellect: these too are memes, spread by Jobs and his followers into every corner of our culture.

Like all viral memes, our new forms of behavior in the internet age have been so contagious as to become invisible: it is all just background noise, as if we had never known anything else. The internet memes which ripple across social media, mutating as they go, are made possible by radical shifts in behavior and commerce which are, themselves, memes.

Natural Reflection

Dawkins makes a show of discarding all the outdated, pre-scientific thought that went before Darwin. But he is actually touching upon truths that ancient philosophers grasped rather more fully than he does. Had he paid attention to those old philosophers rather than determining, with G. G. Simpson, to "ignore them completely," he might have found that he was not really the first to discover the phenomenon he would dub the meme. "Imitating things is natural to men from childhood," wrote Aristotle in his *Poetics*. "In this, man is different from all the other animals: he is the most imitative, and he learns his first lessons through imitation."[8]

Walk into any kindergarten and you'll find five-year-olds mimicking the teacher in the classroom, and each other in the playground. We memorize the alphabet and our multiplication tables by singing songs sung to us by parents and teachers. We learn how to behave in polite company by watching what our parents do. Even bullies mock other kids by acting like them, making exaggerated faces and parody versions of their victims. Imitation—in Greek, *mimēsis*—is an indispensable building block of our humanity.

This foundational truth about how we grow and form our culture began attracting new interest in the mid-1990s, when a group of scientists discovered parts of the brain called "mirror neurons" in the macaque monkey. In some primates—including humans—there are brain cells that activate both when we watch someone do something, and when we do it ourselves. If I watch you pick up an apple, my mirror neurons will behave in the way they would as if I really was picking up an apple. Monkey see, monkey do—or rather, monkey see, monkey feel like doing. This explains, for instance, why watching sports or a cooking show on television can be so involving. We look at people doing things and reproduce some part of their experience within ourselves.[9]

A materialist might say that mirror neurons therefore "cause" us to imitate one another. I would be more inclined to say that empathy is central to the human soul, and so the human body has a capacity to empathize. As often, the neuroscience, though interesting, only confirms what our ancestral wisdom could have told us: that we learn, grow, and connect by imitating one another. Perhaps it is fitting that in discussing this human tendency to pass on what came before us, I should cite my own father. In his book *The Truth and Beauty*, Andrew Klavan points out that the primal human instinct to imitate is reflected in the *Prelude*, an epic autobiography by the English Romantic poet, William

Wordsworth. "Blest the infant Babe," wrote Wordsworth, "(For with my best conjecture I would trace / Our Being's earthly progress,) blest the Babe, / . . . who with his soul / Drinks in the feelings of his Mother's eye!"[10] This was Wordsworth's "best conjecture" about the roots of our humanity: in the relationship between mother and child, a baby gains his first entry into the world of human thought and feeling. The mother smiles down at her baby—and eventually, the baby smiles back. The child sees his father walk, and after months of practice he takes his first step. "Imitating things is natural to men from childhood."[11]

As humanity evolves and becomes more refined, though, it does become capable of more elaborate kinds of imitation. This was Aristotle's central insight into what we might call art and what he would have called *poiētikē*—a word that literally means "making." Because unlike monkeys, humans not only mimic one another: they also create reproductions of what they see and experience in the world.

The monkey that sees a sunset might or might not feel something like wonder. But the man who sees a sunset can reproduce it using dye and canvas—that is, he can become inspired to paint an image of it. Or else he observes the grace of an athlete throwing a discus and hammers away at marble until it captures the lithe tension of the body at that crucial moment. This mirror impulse in us, the thing which makes us take within ourselves some part of what we see, also makes art moving: we do not simply look dispassionately on the sculpture of the discus-thrower. Study the sculpture long enough and you can *feel* the man's expectant focus, his sublime agony of effort and concentration. Our inborn habit of imitation, of *mimēsis*, finds expression in all the many elaborate patterns of interaction and ritual we call "culture." But nowhere is its emotional power more intense than in the thing we call art.

Word Painting

Perhaps the supplest medium of artistic imitation is words. This is not to say that literary arts are in some all-encompassing sense "better" than visual arts, any more than banking is better than agriculture because agriculture is older and more primal. But words are a strange and different kind of thing, unique in their powers of representation.

Each word is its own little symbol. I say "gold" and you conjure in your mind the idea of a colored metal—the same kind of thing I was thinking about. Only I couldn't have transmitted the idea straight from my mind to yours without the linguistic token of it, which we call a word. The ability of a word to convey an idea is called its "semantic" property, because each word is a *sēma*—in Greek, a "sign" or "symbol"—of some idea or set of ideas.

But by inventing that symbol we've called a totally new thing into being, a sound that can be made with the mouth or represented on paper as a series of written characters. Those characters and those sounds come with properties of their own that have nothing to do with the object they denote (the "referent"). For instance: "Gold" rhymes with "hold" and "told." It has one syllable. There's nothing about the word "gold" that obviously sounds or looks like the metal it describes: there's nothing particularly onomatopoetic about it. But the sound and sight of the word—its "aesthetic," or sensory properties—come with the word if I want to use language at all. The idea conveyed is its own thing. But the idea cannot travel from mind to mind without the sound and shape of the word.

When we put words next to each other in sentences to express relationships between them, we get not just combinations of ideas but also series of sounds. As the Viennese philosopher Ludwig Wittgenstein wrote, "the deployment of a word is not bound everywhere by rules."[12] Using our basic tools for meaning, we invent new ways of expressing the full array of our experiences, modes of expression that go beyond a cut-and-dry factual statement.

Here for example is the beginning of a sonnet by Wordsworth's younger contemporary, John Keats:

Much have I travell'd in the realms of gold,

And many goodly states and kingdoms seen;
Round many western islands have I been
Which bards in fealty to Apollo hold.[13]

Now "gold" isn't just a metal anymore: it's a sign of royalty and majesty, a rich adornment on the halls of kings. It lines the high archways of cavernous chambers, and—soaring at great distance across space and time, linked to the far-off word "hold"—it glimmers above the heads of poets who sing exotic songs "in fealty" to the god Apollo. These meanings and images come from the juxtaposition and combination of meanings (not just "gold" but "realms of gold"). But they also come from the linking and intertwining of sounds, the aesthetic properties of the word lending color and quality to the semantic meaning.

Here is another kind of hylemorphism, form mixed with matter: the aesthetic "body" of the word in mysterious and irrevocable union with its semantic "soul." This is in fact how the Stoics in the Hellenistic era described language: as a kind of sculpture, an arrangement of sounds and symbols to house ideas.[14] Joining the imagery and sounds of words to capture a feeling or conjure an image is another kind of *poiētikē*, the kind to which the word is most often and most directly applied. The kind of art we still call "poetic."

The term "poetry" does not just mean "rhyming or rhythmic words." It means words used in a certain way, used not just to denote facts but to reproduce and convey a certain human experience. As Aristotle observes in the *Poetics*, a medical textbook would not become poetry simply if it were rewritten in verses of twelve syllables each.[15] To really write a poem you have to be conveying something you could not convey in bare assertions of fact—capturing some experience or happening that goes beyond just physical events. Poetry, properly so called, is *mimēsis* that uses pitches, meanings, and rhythms as its media.

Sculptors take clay or marble from the earth and mold it into the forms of men and gods; painters take colored pigment and layer it onto canvas to reflect the world back at itself; poets shape their representations of reality out of tone, time, and thought. Words are like stones that catch different kinds of light when you turn them this way and that in your hand. Build a structure out of them and it can house human passion, can put the experience of another man or woman from centuries ago before your eyes or into your ears and, through your eyes and ears, into your very soul.

Consider, for instance, a sonnet by Sir Thomas Wyatt. Wyatt was a cunning diplomat in the dangerous court of King Henry VIII, a monarch who would become infamous for his power struggles with the Catholic Church. The point of contention was Henry's separation from Catherine of Aragon, his first wife who failed to produce a male heir, and his subsequent marriage to Catherine's lady-in-waiting, Anne Boleyn. Boleyn, if not classically beautiful, was nevertheless an arresting presence, made all the more alluring by her sheer consequence as an object of the king's desire. Here was the woman for whom an ancient nation would defy an ancient church, pitting the heir of Alfred the Great against the heir of Saint Peter. Wyatt had separated from his own wife on the grounds that she was unfaithful. Moving amid the court intrigues of the 1520s and 1530s, Wyatt watched Boleyn from afar.

The poetic structure in which Wyatt chose to convey that experience was a new one in England, the sonnet. Sonnets are gemlike little constructions of fourteen lines, a form perfected in Italy by the lovelorn Francesco Petrarca, known to us as Petrarch. Petrarch had refined sighs of unrequited passion for the enigmatic lady Laura into masterworks of literary art, and now Wyatt was doing the same for Boleyn. The speaker's desire for her in the sonnet is like the desire of a huntsman for a deer: it is as if he stands breathless and exhausted, dispirited from the hunt. But when at last the lady appears herself, at the end of the poem, we learn that even if her suitor caught her, he could never have her:

> And graven with diamonds in letters plain
> There is written, her fair neck round about:
> *Noli me tangere*, for Caesar's I am,

And wild for to hold, though I seem tame.[16]

The lines are in iambic pentameter: ten syllables in five groups of two, each group typically alternating between unstressed and stressed (da-DUM, da-DUM, da-DUM, da-DUM, da-DUM—like a heartbeat). But within these four regular lines, something extraordinary happens. The royal deer stops and turns. The huntsman meets his quarry at last, but in that moment the high cold majesty of her beauty forbids him to approach. For the royal seal of ownership is stamped on her, and the necklace around her neck is a prohibition. It is as if she had "graven with diamonds" on the pale skin of "her fair neck" the very words *noli me tangere*: don't touch me. The words of the resurrected Christ to his follower Mary Magdalene, before he ascended to God the Father.

Boleyn is impossibly high above her courtly lover though standing right in front of him; she belongs to a sphere of celestial majesty which only makes his desire for her more poignant and exquisitely painful. The sharp, clipped syllables themselves glitter and clink with the sound of jewels touching one another: "graven with diamonds . . . there is written . . ." until the Latin command comes from on high in ponderous long syllables: *noli me tangere*. Then the word "wild"—a single syllable that must be stretched out languorously into two beats, the sound of it somehow feral, as if struggling against the rigid constraints of the meter as Boleyn's own blood courses beneath the cold diamonds. "And wild for to hold, though I seem tame."

The full depth and complexity in that vision is preserved, five hundred years later, glittering under the translucent surface of the words. All the internal experience of the man, the catch in his chest he must have felt when he saw her, the ineffable inner realities that could never be reported outright, are there for us—who have never been politicians or poets in King Henry's court—to receive and experience. In the metaphors and the sounds some tiny portion of Wyatt's humanity, some little vial full of life's *qualia*, has been stoppered up and preserved throughout time. He could never have done it by simply telling us: Boleyn was there, and she was very lovely. He had to say it was *as if* a man were hunting a sleek and elegant hart. He had to make comparisons and paint pictures in the medium of syllables and images: he had to make a *mimēsis*.

Mimēsis All the Way Down

From the infant babe who smiles at his mother, to the poet telling tales of lovelorn awe, imitation is natural to men from childhood. We are mimetic animals. But the truly shocking and profound thing is that this natural human behavior reflects something fundamental about the nature of all life. The world itself runs on reproduction, at least according to the evolutionary biologists. Dawkins's idea about memes is so powerful because it links an ancient truth about human behavior with a fundamental law of the physical world: at a molecular as well as a cultural level, that which can replicate itself successfully can survive. "I think Darwinism is too big a theory to be confined to the narrow context of the gene," Dawkins wrote.[17] DNA, he was arguing, obeys the same universal law that humans do.

This is a curious thing: that the *mimēsis* which governs our most refined human activities also governs the cellular mechanics of all life on earth. DNA, like art, works by symbolism and representation. The four chemical bases which sit on a strand of RNA make up three-letter sequences, and those sequences literally *translate* into the amino acids that make up proteins: there is no resemblance between them, just as there is no resemblance between most words and their meanings. "Today it is clear that the genetic code is a *code*," writes the physician and psychiatrist Leonard Sax: the fundamental mechanism of life is not just reproduction but symbolism.[18] There is meaning at the heart of the world.

Dawkins may think he has cast aside all pre-Darwinian anthropology, but with his theory of memes he is actually touching on a truth that was observed long before the nineteenth century. He is advancing by half measures toward an account of the world very like the one Plato gave in the *Timaeus*. According to that dialogue, time and space are a copy, a *mimēsis*, of the infinite timelessness in which the one creator god dwells: "time imitates the infinite," Timaeus says.[19] And the whole of space was formed in such a way "as to be as much like the perfect, rational, living being as possible, in an imitation (*mimēsis*) of that being's eternal nature."[20] The interlocking revolutions of the heavenly bodies mimic the harmony and order of the craftsman-god himself, moving according to predictable patterns and emulating, in time and space, the eternal rationality of god—who made all things "with the desire that everything should be as similar to him as possible."[21]

This goes for us, as well, says Timaeus. God the craftsman created lesser gods, whom he commanded to imitate him in crafting human beings.[22] And so, "imitating their maker," in whose image they were made, they made man as a microcosm, a miniature model of the vast, mimetic world. When we reason well—when the image of the world in our mind aligns with the truth of the world as it is—we are "imitating the unchanging revolutions of God" within our own souls. These are the same revolutions that are inscribed into the heavens, a limited copy of the limitless God.

We are mimetic, in Timaeus's telling, because we are made to be. If the things around us shift and change, still they do so in ways that intimate a changeless truth beyond and behind the stars. Indeed, one of Socrates' main objections to art, in Plato's telling, is that it is a mere copy of a copy: artists see things around them in the physical world, which are themselves mere phantoms or emanations of the eternal Forms, and then they create imitations of those phantoms. And so though they may dazzle us with elegant creations, "they don't lay hold of the truth."[23]

I have been arguing here that art need not always be deceptive in this way—that artists can reproduce material things and events in the world *as a means* of getting at the experiences those things contain and produce.[24] But, in any case, the foundational observation in Plato is that we make reproductions because we are *ourselves* reproductions: our mirror impulse, our drive to emulate and recreate, is an indication that we, too, are products of reproduction. The creation of the universe was, in this sense, a work of art.

What Means?

Dawkins and Plato agree that replication—the endless copying and reproduction of things—is a fundamental mechanism of the universe that governs everything from cells to empathy to human culture. Plato thinks this copying has an origin and a goal: the objective reality of the true and the good is the prime model from which everything, the heavens no less than the atoms, is derived. Dawkins denies only this one point: that there is any "ground" or "final goal" of our reproductions. For him it is just copies of copies of copies, all the way down.

But if so, why should anything matter besides the mere act of copying? Life, like art, needs some origin or some model if it is to be judged as true or false, good or bad. Dawkins makes the argument that human beings' "conscious foresight" sets us free to resist the baser urges of our biological nature and transcend "the worst selfish excesses of the blind replicators" in our DNA, which tell us simply to survive at any cost.[25] But why should we do so at all? What can words like "baser" and "transcend" mean in such a context? Dawkins takes it for granted that things like altruism are not only possible but *good*, that we should desire them even in some cases over our immediate gain. Why?

Plato has an answer to that question; Dawkins does not. Just as we judge a work of art by how well or accurately it portrays the moral and emotional realities of the world, we judge human action by how perfectly it conforms to the harmony, logic, and virtue that the human person was designed to replicate. If there is no such ultimate harmony, logic, or virtue at the bedrock of reality, behind all the *mimēsis*, then why should one gene or meme be better or more desirable than any other?

If it is self-evident that love and charity are superior to hatred and rape, then that self-evidence must be grounded in something other than the physical world, which is simply a machine operating according to mechanical rules. A world of mere baseless imitation, without an ultimate object, produces not harmony but bitter competition of the kind that René Girard describes: "far from making ourselves independent and autonomous, we give ourselves up to endless rivalries," eternal loops of mimicry and one-upmanship with no goal or purpose except to exist.[26] The mere mechanics of reproduction have no morals in them unless they point to something beyond themselves.

"It will not do to take our ideal from the principle in nature; for the simple reason that (except for some human or divine theory), there is no principle in nature," wrote the Christian apologist and humorist G. K. Chesterton in *Orthodoxy* (1908).[27] Dawkins himself admits that something is not *good* simply because it has *evolved*: we should not want to endorse just whatever the primeval soup throws up at us. Likewise, physicist David Deutsch, in defending Dawkins's idea of memes, writes: "*biological* evolution does not have a 'better' or 'worse.'"[28] Like Dawkins, Deutsch wants to evaluate memes according to abstract ideals such as knowledge and tolerance. But on what basis do we consider knowledge worthy of pursuit, man worthy of preservation, or art worthy of appreciation? We must get these ideas from some final reality, or not at all.

All imitation has to be imitation *of* something. When a poem or a painting or a human face reflects some emotion or truth, we say there is *meaning* in it: some reality lies behind the symbols and reproductions that we create every day. If that is not true—if it's just memes all the way down—then what we have is a crisis of meaning. If everything is just matter, nothing can really *mean* anything. In Dawkins's world, all our reproductions and repetitions can't point to anything beyond us—for the simple reason that according to Dawkins, there *is* nothing beyond us.

The problem is not so much that evolution has "explained away" metaphysical and spiritual reality. It's that evolution *needs* metaphysics to make any humane kind of sense. Unless there is a final model which everything is designed to copy, we have no way of saying that this or that achievement or action is "better" or "worse" than anything else. This crisis of meaning—our futile attempts to hold onto our moral decency without letting go of our materialism—threatens to make both our art and our lives empty. If there truly is nothing beyond nature, both art and life are meaningless.

CHAPTER 6

Life Imitates Art

The Funnel to the Soul

The crisis of meaning and the power of *mimēsis* help to explain our ongoing political battles over popular art. For decades now, Americans have been lining up on one side or the other of the "culture wars." One of the major fights has been over what kinds of art and music should be celebrated and accepted. Underneath that fight is a deep disagreement about what art is even *for*, and what kind of moral responsibility artists have. In other words, people are disagreeing more and more about why we even do this thing called culture at all.

In 2018, when the rapper Kendrick Lamar won the Pulitzer Prize for his album, *DAMN.*, the committee called it "a virtuosic song collection unified by its vernacular authenticity and rhythmic dynamism."[1] The 11th track on *DAMN.*, called "XXX.," includes these lines: "I'll chip a nigga then throw the blower in his lap / Walk myself to the court like bitch I did that." Unsurprisingly, the announcement of the prize was met with mockery and outrage from conservatives who feel that both pop art and the institutions of supposedly "high" culture have become sources of degradation and moral subversion. Which raises the question: what is art *supposed* to do, anyway? Is it supposed to depict—or to help shape—some reality beyond itself?

That is an ancient question, and it is no surprise that we ask it most often about music, TV, and film. These are our most powerful kinds of *mimēsis*, our most popular and widespread ways of depicting the world and making art. The emotional force of *mimēsis* has always presented a certain kind of moral danger, especially when it acts on us in ways we do not fully understand. Music in particular has a power to stimulate our emotions whether we like it or not. In the *Timaeus* this is represented as a kind of consonance between musical harmony and the human soul, which in turn mirrors back the ordered motions of the heavens: "Harmony . . . has motions akin to the revolutions of the soul within us, and was given by the Muses . . . as an auxiliary to the inner revolution of the soul, when it has lost its harmony, to assist in restoring it to order and concord with itself."[2]

Aristotle, too, though less prone to mythological speculation, saw that musical melodies and rhythms are like pure emotion transmuted into sound. "In rhythm and melody we find a real resemblance to the true nature of anger and gentleness, courage and temperance, as well as the other qualities of character," he wrote. "This is clear from what music does to us: in listening to such melodies, we experience a change in our souls."[3] Other forms of *mimēsis* work through a medium of some kind: I remember or imagine feeling a certain way, I represent that feeling in imagery or recreate the experience that led to it in words, and the art fires off emotions within you akin to those that once prevailed in me. But music knows no middleman: it is unfiltered, weapons-grade emotion, anger and joy and desire themselves mimicked in the contours of melody and rhythm.

This raw emotional force makes music more than just a pastime. It is a mistake to think of melody as something that merely fills silence, something we have on in the background. It has far greater powers than that. Picture for example a man in white riding on horseback, coming into sight at the top of a hill. There is a story somewhere in that image, but the meaning of it is obscure. Now imagine that as the rider hits the summit, Howard Shore's majestic orchestration from *The Lord of the Rings* surges along with him. Instantly we become aware that this is a moment of triumph, long-awaited. We know this even if we have not yet realized it is Gandalf coming, the great white wizard with his cavalry to turn the tide at the Battle of Helm's Deep. Even if we don't know exactly what is happening, music tells us *how we should feel* about what is happening, in a way we find hard to resist.

Because of this, music—and to some extent all emotionally compelling art—has ethical power as well as mere entertainment value. "There is no greater path for instruction to reach mind than through the ear," wrote the Christian philosopher Boethius in the sixth century AD. "When rhythms and harmonies enter the mind by this path, they undeniably affect the mind and remold it into their own character."[4] Something in us—that mirror impulse—picks up cues from the art we consume. There is no staying neutral in the heat of song, even if we come back to our senses when the singing ends.

Plato described this experience as "pouring sweet and sad and melancholy airs into the soul through the funnel of the ears."[5] The Roman statesman Cicero, applying Plato's and Aristotle's observations to the sphere of rhetoric in his *Orator*, said that a well-constructed speech can *movēre*, *delectare*, and *docēre*: move, delight, and instruct. Everyone is perfectly comfortable with the first two. We know that good speeches, just like good songs and poems, move us emotionally and bring us intense pleasure. But it follows naturally that things which have emotional power over us leave us with a sense of how the world is and how it ought to be.

Obscenity and Art

Art has political power: this is perhaps Plato's most infamous idea. From the moment of birth children are being taught in more than conscious ways. They are hearing songs sung in the nursery and learning fairy tales from their elders. All of this artistic conditioning creates in them a sense of the world before they can reason for themselves. This is still a recognized fact about childhood psychology: "As a child listens to a fairytale," writes psychiatrist Bruno Bettelheim, "he gets ideas about how he may create order out of chaos for his inner life."[6] Before we know anything at all about romantic passion, we learn from the story of the little mermaid that it is something irresistible and dangerous, something that draws you out of a safe, familiar world of family into an adventure that will change you forever. Before we know about war or heroism we hear about King Arthur or Beowulf or Prince Charming: we see them charge into the heat of danger with the trumpets blaring, and some combination of recognition and longing makes us think: *I want to be like that.*

The point is not whether these particular "messages" are good or bad. The point is that they are *not* messages. These myths and stories are not arguments or propositions that can be considered or rejected. They are depictions, *mimēseis*, of who we are, and what the world is like. If such things could be put directly into words, there would be no need for art to begin with. We breathe in stories like oxygen, and they shape who we become. Especially in our impressionable years, when we are children, art teaches us what logic could not—things we will have a hard time unlearning even if we try.

For Plato this meant that any statesman worth his salt should keep a tight control on what stories children and even adults hear. And so the Socrates of the *Republic* decides that art is too emotionally powerful to be wielded by just anyone. In the perfect city, most poets will have to be carefully scrutinized or exiled altogether. Moreover, only the state and its leaders can tell fictional stories for the moral good of the masses. "It is appropriate for the rulers, if for anyone at all, to lie for the good of the city in situations involving enemies or citizens. No one else can undertake anything of the sort," says Socrates.[7]

Today, the idea of "censoring art" has become associated with small-minded prudery, but that wasn't always the case. Over the course of the past century, a revolution in sexual ethics and public morality has made it taboo even to think about dictating what artists can and can't say—at least when it comes to criticizing traditional moral norms. It is customary to lay this revolution at the feet of the Hippies and their Vietnam-era antics, and certainly the epoch of "free love" was a transformative one for American mores. But long before then, artists and intellectuals had already been locked in debate over how, if at all, to legislate morality. It was in 1933 that the U.S. District Court for the Southern District of New York decided the landmark case *United States v. One Book Called Ulysses*. James Joyce's novel, *Ulysses*, published 11 years earlier, had ravished the literary world and scandalized the general public.

Ulysses is a meticulous recreation of one man's experience on a late spring day in Dublin. As a work of art it succeeds because it turns human life inside out—rather than the realist depiction of external events and behavior which was popular in earlier novels, Joyce produced a "stream-of-consciousness" masterwork, an exacting image of what it is like inside a man's head. The man in question, Leopold Bloom, comes across with all his contradictions and complexities intact, his spontaneous impressions and half-thoughts unedited by any conscious filter. This is also what offended the public: Bloom's nobler aspirations are placed alongside his mundane reflections and his lewd desires. The space between his ears is a chaotic mix of the sacred and the profane. The book includes a second-by-second description of his trip to an outhouse, a dismissive parody of his half-understood Catholic faith, and, most infamously, a graphic concluding soliloquy from Bloom's promiscuous wife Molly as he comes home to bed with her.

The charge against the work was that it was obscene, which would have allowed the state to confiscate and destroy copies of it under the Tariff Act of 1930. Judge John Woolsey, when he at last dismissed the charges against *Ulysses*, wrote that he had spent many weeks contemplating "whether the intent with which it was written was what is called, according to the usual phrase, pornographic, that is, written for the purpose of exploiting obscenity." He found that "in *Ulysses*, despite its

unusual frankness, I do not detect anywhere the leer of the sensualist."
There followed a sincere attempt to describe and evaluate Joyce's literary
technique—his efforts "to show how the screen of consciousness with
its ever-shifting kaleidoscopic impressions carries, as it were on a plastic
palimpsest, not only what is in the focus of each man's observation of
the actual things about him, but also in a penumbral zone residua of past
impressions."[8]

Woolsey was not questioning the existence of pornography and
obscenity—he took it for granted that the First Amendment's protection
of free speech did not extend to work that existed merely to excite lust.
But he was arguing that the definition of obscenity should not include
serious artistic efforts to depict the world as it is. As Judge Augustus
Hand wrote in a decision upholding Woolsey's judgment on appeal, the
novel's obscene passages "are relevant to the purpose of depicting the
thoughts of the characters and are introduced to give meaning to the
whole, rather than to promote lust or portray filth for its own sake."[9]
This was already a line of reasoning that found favor among the literary
elite, and in the years since Woolsey's decision it has become a kind of
received wisdom that almost no one explicitly questions. Debates over
Vladimir Nabokov's depiction of pedophilia in his novel Lolita had much
the same outcome in the 1950s, as did the public discussion of D. H.
Lawrence's Lady Chatterley's Lover in the 1960s. Today, after a series
of Supreme Court cases throughout the 1970s and 1980s (especially
Miller v. California in 1973), material can be outlawed as obscene only
if 1. the "average person, applying contemporary community standards,"
would find that the work "taken as a whole" incites "prurient interest,"
2. the work depicts or describes sexual conduct defined by applicable
state law in a way that is patently offensive, and 3. the work lacks literary,
artistic, political, or scientific value.[10]

The "Miller test" is famously subjective: it depends expressly on
the atmosphere of public opinion. What counts as offensive in the view
of the average person, and what counts as literary or scientific value
according to a person who is "reasonable" by prevailing standards, is

a matter of taste. Taste is not arbitrary: it can be good or bad insofar as it accurately measures a work of art's success as a depiction of human realities. But neither is taste democratic in the way the Miller test requires it to be: the average person's sensibilities can be vulgar, or prudish, depending on the moral atmosphere in which he was raised—a moral atmosphere shaped at least in part by the very artistic depictions with which he grew up. "We have forgotten . . . that our minds and spirits, no less than our lungs, can be damaged when the air they breathe is fouled by pollutants," wrote the critic Norman Podhoretz in 1997, reconsidering his former role as a defender of pornography and explicit literature.[11] There is an inescapable feedback loop here; art is not only the object which receives our moral evaluations but also the teacher which informs them.

We live today in a society that talks as if it does not recognize this truth, but acts as if it very much does. In 1956, discussing the reaction to *Lolita*, Nabokov all but dismissed the very idea that art might have something to say about good and evil: "*Lolita* has no moral in tow. For me a work of fiction exists only insofar as it affords me what I shall bluntly call aesthetic bliss."[12] As this attitude was gaining popularity, and as the courts were finding it harder and harder to recognize anything as truly obscene, the internet seemed to render the question moot by making it impossible to keep even pornography out of the public square. "Today...no thoughts, images, or pornographic words are 'unimaginable' because all are realized on the Internet," wrote Louis Menand in a 2016 retrospective on the *Ulysses* case. It was work like *Ulysses* itself that had helped inure audiences to scandal: "that we are not outraged by words in a book today is largely because of [Joyce]," Menand wrote. "'Ulysses' is the reason we are no longer shocked by 'Ulysses.'"[13]

Morality Wars

It may seem natural to us now, but "art for art's sake" is a highly unusual manifesto in the scope of human history. Only if art has no meaning can we treat it as if it has no responsibility for the moral changes it effects in its audience. In fact, it is unsustainable to think this way, and it is not really how we think even now—though we may protest otherwise. We often think of the "culture wars" as a losing battle waged by conservatives against liberal iconoclasm or amorality: the Right demands tighter constraints on what can be shown, while the Left seeks—and achieves—ever greater license to publish smut. Last century, when it was Nabokov, Joyce, and Lawrence versus middle-class American traditionalists, that may have been an accurate description of the situation. But the "laissez-faire" liberalism of yesteryear has given way to something entirely different, and now the fight is more accurately described as a war over *whose* morals will distinguish acceptable from unacceptable art.

By and large it is true that conservatives deplore the casual ubiquity of sex, violence, and foul language in popular culture. In this they explicitly recognize that culture shapes moral attitudes, especially among children. When Netflix hosted a stateside release of the French film *Mignonnes*, or *Cuties*, the promotional material featured pre-pubescent girls in sultry poses and revealing outfits, teasing the movie as a story of female liberation through underage twerking. Hundreds of thousands of people signed online petitions to have the movie removed from the Netflix library. "Netflix, what you are doing is called grooming," wrote the Christian pundit Carmine Sabia. Pro-life activist Lila Rose wrote that the film "encourages pre-pubescent girls to explore their 'sexuality' and act in sexual ways."

Cuties was a particularly egregious misstep in an era when conservatives were already feeling embattled and outraged about perverse sexual content on school shelves and in classrooms. But milder controversies have simmered around other violent films and television shows like HBO's *Game of Thrones* and even the Daily Wire's *Run, Hide, Fight*. Perhaps because so many dominant cultural outlets are so openly hostile to their values, conservatives feel keenly that art has power to mold the soul for good or ill.

But those who defended *Cuties* also did so in terms that implicitly acknowledged the moral weight of art. "Okay, so what the fuck you're not going to do is petition to get a coming of age film about a little black girl by a black woman director, maimouna doucoure [*sic*], removed from netflix [*sic*]," tweeted Danielle Dash.[14] Dash's website features movie and television reviews about intersectional feminism and "misogynoir"—her work is plainly informed by a set of beliefs regarding race and gender that has come to predominate in the Left's cultural vanguard.[15] Chief among those beliefs is the conviction that what people watch, read, and listen to should reinforce in their minds a certain set of ideas about who should have power, what rules should be followed in private and public life, and how American life especially should be restructured.

"If you remove homophobia [from your storylines] you are not giving homophobes any arena to see themselves," said the Canadian actor and writer Dan Levy about his show *Schitt's Creek*. The sitcom won ten Emmys and garnered critical approval for depicting a world in which the main character David, a pansexual, was regarded with total love and acceptance. "It's completely normalized," said one fan in an interview with the BBC: David's eventual marriage to a man shows that "it can be a natural and normal relationship."[16]

The technical term for this is "representation": the imperative to portray people of minority races, genders, and sexualities as both normal and admirable. When Apple TV+ adapted Isaac Asimov's mid-twentieth-century sci-fi classic, *Foundation*, showrunner David S. Goyer said it was important to him that two of the main white male characters be recast as black women. "I was conscious of the fact that there are a lot of people underrepresented in a lot of these sort of seminal works," he said.[17] More recently, a private meeting of Disney executives leaked by journalist Christopher Rufo featured repeated injunctions to add more trans and gay characters to children's films.[18]

Falling afoul of these values can come with its own censure, no less passionate or moralistic than the conservative reaction to *Cuties*. Disney's own ideological project was inspired by a Florida law that prohibited instruction about alternative sexualities to kindergarteners and elementary school students through the third grade. The law prompted a furious outcry across the country from left-wing teachers and activists. When comedian Dave Chappelle made jokes about the intolerance of the transgender movement in a Netflix special, critics demanded that the work be de-platformed: "These words have real world consequences," tweeted former Netflix showrunner Jaclyn Moore, referring to the leftist concern that culturally insensitive material can embolden bigots to commit hate crimes and enforce feelings of inadequacy or shame among minorities.[19]

What this amounts to is not a fight between moralists and libertines, but a struggle between two firmly held and totally incompatible moral visions. Both sides of that struggle recognize the enormous ethical power of imitation, reproduction, and depiction—of *mimēsis*—to set the emotional limits of what the public finds acceptable and abhorrent, attractive and disgusting. The Right wants to retain traditional limits on sexual propriety and public decency. The Left wants us to feel comfortable seeing and talking about almost any kind of sex act or religious blasphemy, but to shy instinctively away from criticizing abnormal sexualities or acknowledging racial differences unless the comparison is favorable to black and brown people. At their extremes, both sides want, as the Socrates of the *Republic* did, to seize control of art to saturate the atmosphere with messaging that reinforces their preferred ideals.

"In the twenty-first century we are looking for meaning, not subverting it," writes the hard-bitten old-school liberal Camille Paglia in *Glittering Images*.[20] She shows more understanding than both the Right and the Left do about the culture wars. Neither side is fighting to free art of every moral constraint or consideration. Both sides are fighting, and intensely, over whose moral outlook should be expressed and reinforced by the art that is most widely displayed and afforded public honor. At a certain point it becomes impossible to fight for, or over, nothing. The question is not whether art should be moral, but whose moral vision is truer.

Nihilism Chic

Thus, the culture wars are beginning to reveal what Richard Dawkins seems to have ignored: all imitation is imitation *of* something. Art and life alike are *expressive*, which suggests that there is some model from which they are made. We cannot assess them sensibly unless we begin from the premise that they point beyond themselves—that they have meaning.

In art, we show the world of human experience not just as a set of value-neutral facts, but as a moral and emotional universe where things have real ethical properties—where actions are good and evil, generous and miserly, heroic and cowardly. Are we right about that? Do the moral realities we depict exist in the real world, or only in our heads? When we say that something is right or wrong, and depict it as such, are we referring to any independent truth? We must be, or there would be no point in having the argument at all.

If this is so, then conservatives might consider refining the demands they make of art and artists. Moralists have a way of talking as if they want the world scrubbed clean of everything bad. "I once called *Game of Thrones* 'torture porn' and refused to watch it," wrote the blogger Erick Erickson: "I had tried, several times, to watch it and I found that it was filled with blood, gore, nudity, and sex—not something a Christian should engage with."[21] But Erickson revised his opinion, and rightly so: because blood, gore, nudity, and sex are all real things. They are described and depicted, sometimes in great detail, in the Bible itself.

Art that does not acknowledge humanity's dark and dirty realities might be fit for children, as they are growing and learning to process the harsher truths. It is absolutely right to demand that companies like Disney, if they insist on warping kids' sense of what is sexually normal, should be censured and boycotted. But adults cannot simply label the bad stuff as "not fit for engagement" and leave it at that. As a personal choice it amounts to isolating yourself from one half of reality. At the level of a culture war, it amounts to a losing strategy, because adult society has not been and never will be able to survive without art that is honest. If conservatives are right that society is lapsing into barbarian debauchery, then they cannot afford to adopt a position that is at once childish and ineffective.

A smarter set of conservative demands would focus not on *what* is depicted but on *how*. Take for instance Cardi B's extravagantly graphic rap song, "WAP," which describes the singer's state of arousal and desire in lurid detail. The conservative radio host Ben Shapiro went viral by simply reading the lyrics of the song aloud, without music, to make the point that the words were empty and degrading when stripped of their rhythm and accompaniment. And true enough—but *why* are the song and its attendant music video so vile, even for adults? Not because they describe a woman in a state of sexual arousal: even strict traditionalists aren't against women having sex drives.

But the song, like all songs, doesn't just depict physical facts: it casts those facts in a certain moral light. "Certified freak / seven days a week . . . make it cream / make me scream / out in public / make a scene." Cardi depicts promiscuous sex, in public, as something fun and consequence free—something that is perhaps best leveraged for financial gain ("I don't cook / I don't clean / but let me tell you how I got this ring. . . . / ask for a car while you ride that dick"). In reality, this is a recipe to end up loveless, shallow, and possibly diseased. Normal people who treat sex as Cardi does in the song will most likely become embittered and ashamed, because the actions she is proposing have a real moral nature. Sex is an expression of passion as well as a physical act. Treating it lightly has a tendency to cheapen the soul and decay the body. Cardi doesn't depict those truths. She uses her enormous wealth and team of stylists to conceal the consequences of her actions, to show mercenary promiscuity as something carefree, alluring, and fun. In other words, she is not just *showing* sex: she is *lying* about it.

In this sense conservatives shouldn't be demanding *fewer* depictions of sex and violence: they should be demanding *better*, more *honest* depictions of it. Consider a play like Shakespeare's *Macbeth*. If we really took Shakespeare seriously, rather than regarding him as just another "old white man," we might have all the same moral concerns about him that Plato's Socrates had about Homer. Why don't we? *Macbeth* is an almost unremittingly bleak depiction of a man's descent into nihilism, goaded on by his conniving wife. It depicts murder and brutality in unsparing terms. Yet it is a great work of art precisely because it depicts the moral reality that a man who defies the moral law, even if he escapes detection, will be haunted by his own evil until the day he dies. Lady Macbeth is driven to madness and probably suicide, while her husband ends up nervy and dejected, famously muttering to himself about the emptiness of life:

> Tomorrow, and tomorrow, and tomorrow,
> Creeps in this petty pace from day to day,
> To the last syllable of recorded time;
> And all our yesterdays have lighted fools
> The way to dusty death. Out, out, brief candle!
> Life's but a walking shadow, a poor player,
> That struts and frets his hour upon the stage,
> And then is heard no more. It is a tale
> Told by an idiot, full of sound and fury,
> Signifying nothing.[22]

Even before facing justice, Macbeth is hollowed out by his own tormented efforts to escape his own culpability: "I am in blood / Stepp'd in so far that, should I wade no more / returning were as tedious as go o'er."[23] The horror of this descent, to a hellish eternity of nothingness that begins from the moment of Macbeth's regicide, and carries on without end or pause, is what the play is really about. This is not just gore for gore's sake but honesty about the moral reality of murder. It is not just prurience or voyeurism. It is art.

A winning strategy for conservatives would be to demand that public space be afforded, and public honor be given, to art that tells the moral truth about the world—including its bleaker aspects. Art is representation, and representation is representation *of* something—ours might as well depict the real world.

Through a Glass Darkly

So much for art. When human beings make poems and paintings and movies, we do it to convey something—to speak about some reality and reflect it back to one another. But if that's the case, then what does that say about the *mimēsis* that runs the world? If replication explains everything—if reflection and reproduction are built into the very fabric of the universe—then *what* is ultimately being reflected, imitated, and reproduced? Is there a meaning behind it all, or not?

"The world is divided into things that look designed, like birds and airliners," said Richard Dawkins on the Saatchi & Saatchi stage, "and things that don't—rocks and mountains. Things that look designed are divided into those that really are designed—submarines and tin openers—and those that are not designed, but look that way, because they result from Darwinian natural selection—sharks and hedgehogs." One may wonder what made him quite so sure of this. How confident can we be that things which look designed, are not designed? How sure are we that the language of the world means nothing?

Dawkins was identifying, with considerable insight, a universal pattern of replication and imitation. *Mimēsis* is built into everything, from the molecular fabric of organic life on up to the choices we make and the way we know things. Aristotle would hardly have been surprised to find us retweeting one another's Willy Wonka screenshots, or watching our memes surge across the surface of the internet like waves of sediment over the sea of public opinion. Nor would Timaeus, in Plato's dialogue, have been surprised to hear Dawkins compare human memes to genetic replication. Most ancient philosophers would have found it remarkable, though, that Dawkins imagines no final object of imitation, no original source of copying.

Why do things reproduce themselves? According to hardline materialists, the answer is: because they do. That is the world we live in, though we could live in any number of other possible worlds. Why did infinitely replicating genes create infinitely replicating creatures then? Why did evolution produce beings who produce art? Why should a world of genes lead to a world of memes, or a universe in which self-conscious life no less than animal biology functions by emulation and reproduction? Dawkins's answer is: just because.

Whatever else this answer may be, it is an article of faith no less dogmatic than any church doctrine. Human consciousness might have developed via Darwinian natural selection, but the very driving force of that selection process—the replication and mutation of genes—has produced a creature whose higher faculties are patterned according to this one basic logic of replication and transformation. At the very least, there is no evidence whatsoever to prove that this patterning itself does not have a mind behind it, an origin beyond the mere fact of its existence. Indeed, there is ample reason to believe that it does. Replication is replication *of* something; imitation means something is being imitated.

Some may accuse me here of sneaking religion in before I have really turned to the question of God properly. But that is just the point. In these sorts of questions religion confirms basic truths; it does not invent them. It is Plato and Aristotle, and even Dawkins, who raise the necessary question: if the world is one giant factory of replication, then *what*, ultimately, is being replicated?

All the Bible does on this score is pose an answer: God. "We are his craftsmanship," wrote Paul to the Ephesians (Eph. 2:10), and the Greek word of the original is *poiēma*. Humanity is a kind of poem God writes, a work of art he makes to depict himself. "Let us make mankind in our image": from that one statement comes an answer to the question of memes and of morals, of DNA and natural selection. When John writes in his Gospel that "in the beginning was the Word, and the Word was with God, and the Word was God," he means that creation is an act of self-expression. *Logos*, which means both "reason" and "utterance," is the heart of it all. The "word" at the core of things is the one great meaning, expressed every moment in a thousand ways—in the reason that governs the heavens, and in the mind of man which sees and reflects creation.

Our mirror neurons are no evolutionary accident but a key to what we are, the sign and substance of everything we were made to be. The source of truth and of beauty—even difficult truth, or terrible beauty—impels us to make true and beautiful depictions of a world that is itself a reflection of that source. We see God "as through a glass darkly," wrote Saint Paul, and so it is: the glass, the mirror, the reflector, is us. (1 Cor. 13:12)

No one can be forced to believe in God, and no one should be. But anyone who wants art and human life to have significance should *want* to believe in God—otherwise, we have no ground to stand on. It's popular to assume that belief in God is mere superstition, tribalism, or prejudice. And there is plenty of that around. But if we are going to make sense of anything, there's no escaping this question, the question to which all our crises are leading: can we believe?

PART IV

Religion

The only people who have been able to posit the existence of multiple universes are people for whom the cause of the world is chance, not governing wisdom—such as Democritus, who taught that this world and an infinity of others came into being from the clash of atoms.... The claim that many worlds are better than one demonstrates an obsession with the value of mere numbers.

—Thomas Aquinas, *Summa Theologica*
Part I, Question xlvii, Article 3

The stars are like the trees in the forest, alive and breathing. And they're watching me. What I've done up till now, what I'm going to do—they know it all.

—Haruki Murakami, *Kafka on the Shore*

CHAPTER 7

The Crisis of Religion

The First and Last Question

So far I have described three foundational crises that motivate our daily arguments over how we should live. I have argued that the problems and conflicts which make the news are outward signs of deeper, more awful crises churning under the surface. These crises raise ancient questions about who we are and what the universe is.

Each of these questions in turn has boiled down to one fundamental choice: meaning or meaninglessness, grounded reality or infinite change. At every turn we have been confronted with the problem of whether anything *stays the same*, whether behind all our works of art and theories of life there stands some truth, goodness, or beauty to which everything refers and against which the morality of actions can be judged. I have tried to stress that these are the only two options: either an immutable bedrock of something that just *is*—however dimly we perceive it, however haltingly we approach toward it—or else a howling wasteland of arbitrary power and aggression.

Strictly speaking, however, this does not prove anything. Maybe the howling wasteland is the truth of things; maybe our reason is a cruel illusion and our sense of truth a side-effect of our torturously complex brains. The fact that we need to *act* as if some baseline reality exists does not in itself prove that our precious baseline reality *actually* exists. If it does not, we are deeply in trouble. But that is no proof that it does.

I am not going to furnish such proof in this section. I would be foolish to try. As I have been hinting throughout, the question of an ultimate final reality is the question of God. I have adduced a few citations to indicate that Jewish wisdom and Christian theology are in harmony with the pagan ideas whose truth can help alleviate our current anxieties. But I have avoided relying too heavily on chapter and verse simply because my intention is not to evangelize you into a particular sect. I belong to one such sect myself, and I can say confidently that everyone in the world should convert to it. But we are nowhere near having that conversation: the questions we are grappling with as a society are far more basic than which sect to join. They are not, for instance, *"Does God have three persons?"* or *"Do Christians need a pope?"*, but *"Is there such a thing as truth at all?"* These are not questions I am going to answer by whacking you over the head repeatedly with the Nicene Creed. Nor am I going to produce from out of my hat some Definitive Proof that renders unbelief impossible.

But if our sanity and survival depend on the existence of some fundamental reality, and if that reality includes such things as beauty and goodness, then we had better examine the likelihood or unlikelihood of such a reality existing. It is time to face the question head-on.

One major obstacle to evaluating the likelihood of faith is the common notion that something called "science" has disproven something called "God." People who say that often mean that they have attempted to exclude from their thinking every kind of reality other than the ones that can be described in coldly mechanical terms. But this is impossible, since it erases from view the whole spectrum of truths that matter to human beings—truths like beauty, desire, love, aspiration, joy.

Every worthwhile account of human life and experience depends on reference to concepts that have no meaningful location on a brain scan.

You can narrate every hormonal change that occurs when a man looks at the Grand Canyon for the first time, without even touching what it means for him to have the quality of experience we call "awe." Even supposing you could stimulate the exact neurons which produce that experience in him while he sat at home in a chair, an outside observer would immediately see that this manufactured awe was different from the genuine article, because it did not refer to the actual experience in the world. The man who really visits the Grand Canyon experiences awe, and an essential part of that experience is the perception that his feelings refer to some real quality of the world outside him.

The man sitting at home receiving brain stimulation has the same feeling of seeing something wondrous, but he is mistaken: nothing wondrous is there. And if this distinction obtains for aesthetic experiences like awe, how much more so for moral qualities, like virtue? I might feel a rush of camaraderie when my character in *Call of Duty* saves yours from a grenade, but since the danger is not real the action is not one we would describe as "courage"—only the real thing, done truly in the heat of battle, can qualify for the name. But courage, like awe, is nowhere on a map of the physical world. Though these things can be observed in time and space—I can watch the soldier take a bullet for his friend or see the man's eyes widen as he looks out at the view of the Grand Canyon—they are not themselves physical. They are instead ways of looking at the physical world as if it had meaning, as if the truth of things were not exhausted by material facts.

Idols of the Mind

Science has never shown that supernatural truths do not exist: it has only proposed to explain events without invoking them. This is a strategy, and a good one, for finding out what can be known "empirically"—that is to say, by using only the evidence of our verifiable experience (or in Greek, our *empeiria*). If you can observe something happening and explain why, you are doing science. Since the supernatural often cannot be observed and can never be exhaustively explained, it may be true—but it is not science.

In sixteenth- and seventeenth-century Italy, the mathematician and astronomer Galileo Galilei found that he could unlock enormous new regions of knowledge by performing what he called *cimenti*, or "trials." These were tests designed to examine whether Galileo's theories could explain and predict the behavior of things in the world—in other words, experiments. Thanks in large part to Galileo's English contemporary, Sir Francis Bacon, empirical experiment eventually became a scientific touchstone against which the truth of all theories was to be measured. In 1620, while serving as Lord Chancellor to the Protestant King James, Bacon presented his *Novum Organum*, a new handbook on the ground rules of logic and philosophy.

For centuries, a collection of six foundational essays by Aristotle had served as the basic scaffolding of all knowledge and inquiry. Later Philosophers called these six essays the *Organon*, the tool for determining what can be known, and how. But Bacon thought the *Organon* took too much for granted. It asserted theories without checking them against observed reality. This might be appropriate if we could trust our intuitions and the principles handed down to us by our ancestors. But, said Bacon, the mind of man does not come pure into the world: it is a factory of idols. In the 1500s the Reformation theologian John Calvin had rattled the West by denouncing man's heart in these same scathing terms.[1] Now, less than a century later, Bacon wryly deployed the same idea to suggest that no mere gut instinct or conviction could be axiomatically trusted.

Bacon identified four idols in particular that cloud man's vision of the real world around him. These four idols are ancestral prejudices (idols of the tribe), personal character and educational background (idols of the cave), social and economic milieu (idols of the market), and prior philosophical commitments (idols of the theatre).[2] Our upbringing, our social surroundings, and our personal psychology produce in us feelings of certainty that have no basis in fact. Bacon gave as an example "the fiction that all celestial bodies move in perfect circles." The mind by its nature "easily assumes a greater order and equality in all things than it really finds," and so the real, observable orbits of the planets were obscured by mere conjecture for far longer than they should have been.[3] Knowing the truth with any certainty meant clearing away all those presuppositions which might impede one's real vision of things—religious dogma included.

Across the sea, as Bacon wrote, church authority suffered an altogether different kind of assault. From 1618 to 1648 there raged the Thirty Years' War, a brutal conflict over who would rule what is now Germany and parts of Eastern Europe. Since 1555, the states of the Holy Roman Empire had been governed by different faiths—some Lutheran, and some Catholic—as religious conflict had transformed the organization of the empire, and would eventually reshape the continent. But this delicate arrangement began to collapse as Protestantism gained traction among the people of Europe. When the Emperor Ferdinand II undertook to re-impose Catholic fealty, Protestant dissidents in a state called Bohemia (roughly the present-day Czech Republic) staged a short-lived but cataclysmic revolt. Huge portions of Europe, from France and Spain to Sweden and Norway, were eventually drawn into the vortex of the conflict. Millions died as kings fought for the authority to rule under the auspices of their chosen faith within a new balance of power.

The treaties collectively known as the Peace of Westphalia brought an end to the war and established a religious non-intervention pact: each king was to go his own way and govern his domain as either Protestant or Catholic. No one church would ever again set the limits of good and evil for the West. As princes contended with popes, and as empirical study unlocked the secrets of the natural world, the sure and certain truths of the faith looked ever more up for debate.

The new era that dawned shortly after Westphalia is known as the Enlightenment, in part because scientific and philosophical inquiry seemed to have broken free of religious constraints. As Europeans looked back on the conflicts of the seventeenth century, religion came to look less like the font of absolute truth and more like a source of superstition, dissension, and bloodshed. In France, especially, Enlightenment-era philosophers or *philosophes* like Diderot, Voltaire, and Julien Offray de la Mettrie scoffed at what they viewed as primitive fantasy stories told by clerics to keep the people compliant.

The French Revolution of 1787–99 set in motion a chain of political events that would eventually break the power of the Catholic Church and the landed aristocracy over French public life. But already before then, an atmosphere of consensus was emerging among the educated set that humanity had finished with its fanciful childhood dreams of God. Back in Britain, the Scottish philosopher David Hume labored to build an entire worldview on what he considered pure empiricism: "all our ideas or more feeble perceptions are copies of our impressions or more lively ones," he wrote in his groundbreaking *Enquiry Concerning Human Understanding*.[4] This made it impossible for Hume to believe in supernatural occurrences or miracles, because they violate the patterns of behavior which humanity has always observed in the world: "it is experience only, which gives authority to human testimony; and it is the same experience, which assures us of the laws of nature."[5]

The Ages of Man

By the nineteenth century, it seemed obvious to a man like Auguste Comte, founder of the philosophical school known as "positivism," that man's story was one of progress from religious barbarism to enlightened liberty and science. Mankind, wrote Comte in *The Course of Positive Philosophy*, "passes successively through three different theoretical stages: the Theological, or fictitious; the Metaphysical, or abstract; and the Scientific, or positive." Theology and divine narrative could be associated with a kind of childhood, a nursery-life in which fairytales and shadow puppets tell a vague story about who we are and where we came from. Eventually in adolescence we give up the myth of a personal God in favor of abstract reasoning, until finally we arrive at pure logic based only on the facts we can experience and confirm. "All sound thinkers have agreed, since Bacon's time, that there can be no real knowledge except that which is based on observed facts," Comte proclaimed.[6]

Gradually, Bacon's empiricism became not just a tool for scientific progress but the single source of truth to eclipse all others: either we can demonstrate a fact with experiment and observation, or we cannot know it at all. By now, in the twenty-first century, Comte's view of religion as a relic of humanity's infancy has become a casual assumption of the chattering classes, one which hardly seems to need defending. The godfather of psychoanalysis, Sigmund Freud, gave this view the imprimatur of his new science when he told the story of mankind's first religious impulses in *Totem and Taboo*. "Psychoanalytic investigation of the individual teaches with particular emphasis that god is in every case modelled after the father," wrote Freud, "and that our personal relation to god is dependent upon our relation to our physical father, fluctuating and changing with him, and that god at bottom is nothing but an exalted father."[7] The physical sciences continued turning out their astounding products, and the once-unassailable dominance of Christianity disintegrated. Irreligion came to seem like the obvious path for any thinking man.

This assumption—that no sophisticated person really believes in God anymore—has persisted in the popular imagination. Shortly after Darwin revealed what seemed like a new origin of human life, two books established firmly in the public mind the idea that science and religion are irreparably at odds: John William Draper's *History of the Conflict Between Religion and Science* (1874), and Andrew Dickson White's *A History of the Warfare of Science with Theology in Christendom* (1896). But the intriguing thing is that few people, if pressed, can say why or how science "disproved" God, what experiment conclusively refuted his existence, or what the battle lines are in the "war" between science and religion. That is because the war was never really fought. In reality, what happened is that philosophers of science wrote God out of the picture—sometimes because they viewed the church as a socially regressive force, and sometimes simply because they wanted to define a sphere of investigation that did not rely on received wisdom or pre-determined convictions.

It is one thing to disregard certain kinds of truth for the sake of studying the material world. Isaac Newton, himself a committed (if eccentric) Christian, argued that objects attract one another with a measurable and predictable force. He made no conjecture about *who* or *what* was exerting that force, because he considered it a question that his research did not answer. *Hypotheses non fingo*, he said: I will not make up hypotheses where none are necessary or demonstrable. Science, by definition, means developing testable hypotheses and then making empirical observations that can either falsify or affirm them. It also then means leaving out irrelevancies, ignoring unanswered questions that the research cannot answer and is not designed to raise.

But it is another thing entirely—and a remarkable act of question-begging—to pretend that by disregarding those questions you have definitively answered them in the negative. We have gone from asserting that scientists should not ask or answer whether there is a God, then to believing that the only truths are those which science discovers, and finally to concluding that God does not exist because scientists cannot prove he does.

Subjectivity for Me, but not for Thee

As historian of science Stephen C. Meyer shows in his book *Return of the God Hypothesis*, some leading figures in the scientific community are beginning to consider God a perfectly plausible answer to the ultimate questions that precede scientific inquiry. Materialism, however, remains fashionable in elite intellectual circles. Consider even the derisive way we use the word "subjective": when we say that someone's appreciation of a painting or taste for fine wine is "subjective" we mean simply that it is *arbitrary*—that one person's taste is as good as any other's. Subjective experiences are understood as mere feelings with no real basis in the outside world.

This notion stems, in part, from the philosophy of Immanuel Kant, an eighteenth-century German thinker who defined scientific study as a realm of *objective* inquiry: "If something is valid for anybody in possession of his reason, then its grounds are objective and sufficient," he wrote.[8] But we go far beyond Kant when we imply that our subjective experiences—our convictions, our hunches, our fears and joys—have no grounding in anything real. When we say, "well that's just your subjective opinion," what we mean is that the other person has no basis for believing his opinion might be true. There is no physical proof that a man really is in love, or sees God, so we assume that God and love are all in the man's head.

At the same time as we have lost all grounds for believing in objective truth, each of us has stopped believing in any subjective truth except our own. Philosopher Martin Heidegger's "unconditional dominion of subjectivity" extends only so far as is convenient for any given political moment. Our public discourse has largely become a game of positioning one's own views as "objective" and "scientific" while deriding other views as merely "subjective," which is to say, "arbitrary" or simply "false." A remarkable example of this was when Professor Annelies Wilder-Smith of the London School of Hygiene and Tropical Medicine stressed that "we need to educate a lot of doctors and medical students, and the scientific community because they are part of the conspiracy theories" regarding COVID-19. In other words, trained scientists who come up with a disfavored interpretation of the relevant evidence are no longer scientists but dangerous conspiracists. Apparently "trust the science" is a mantra that applies only to those scientists who agree with Annelies Wilder-Smith.[9]

Something strange is happening here. The more confident we become in the pure objectivity of science and its total claim to explain everything, the more mystical—indeed, the more *theological*—science becomes. Examples of this abounded during the COVID era, most notably when Dr. Anthony Fauci proclaimed that his critics are really criticizing, not him, but science itself because "I represent the science."[10] This is not an empirical statement based on verified experimental results. It is rather a claim to clerical authority and esoteric knowledge. Popular representations of Fauci in the garb of a Christian saint communicate much the same idea: science is a source of absolute truth not just about physical facts but about what our purpose is and how we should live. Only certain experts—that is to say, ordained priests—have the authority to communicate these higher truths.

Fauci often made it clear that he considered himself just such a priest, entitled to manipulate the public in ways he considered moral. Admitting that he had discouraged the use of face masks even though he thought they were effective, he said, "It was at a time when . . . the N95 masks and the surgical masks were in very short supply."[11] Later on he told the *New York Times* that "When polls said only about half of all Americans would take a vaccine, I was saying herd immunity would take 70 to 75 percent [vaccination]. Then, when newer surveys said 60 percent or more would take it, I thought, 'I can nudge this up a bit,' so I went to 80, 85."[12] Throughout the pandemic, he thought of himself as a man authorized not simply to determine facts accurately, but also to tell noble lies: to discern the limits of good and evil and to falsify the facts accordingly. That is a claim to moral or political knowledge—and without even evaluating its merits on those terms, we can see already that it is nothing like what Isaac Newton or Francis Bacon would have called science.

So it is that science has become for us the final wellspring of *all* truth, physical or otherwise. We now turn to scientists not just for empirical data, but for guidance and speculation that would have once been offered by priests. In one sense this is of a piece with American politics more generally, which has taken on a worshipful character as traditional forms of religion have declined. During the summer of 2020 we saw Black Lives Matter activists demanding and receiving ritual genuflection from white supporters in a plea for absolution. At the 2021 Conservative Political Action Conference, supporters of Donald Trump caused controversy by wheeling out a golden statue of their beloved leader. And when ex-gubernatorial candidate Stacey Abrams helped win Democrats a congressional race in Georgia, Michigan governor Gretchen Whitmer celebrated by lighting a prayer candle in her honor.

"America is a nation with the soul of a church," wrote G. K. Chesterton.[13] And, in the words of Georgetown professor Joshua Mitchell, identity politics "has turned politics into a religious venue for sacrificial offering."[14] Perhaps science worship is just one of many ways in which we fulfill our inescapable need to worship *something*. But that need is bigger than just America, and it speaks in turn to the impossibility of looking at the world from a purely empirical, merely material, point of view. What the current state of science really demonstrates is that man cannot live on material facts alone. Kick faith out the front door and it will come in the back; banish mythology and religion in favor of natural science, and natural science will become the domain of a new religious mythology.

This has already been happening for some time in the field of evolution, where the grand story of our development from "lower" life forms is recited as an inspiring parable of all we can achieve in the future. In this new origin myth, life calls itself forth from the chaos of primordial soup and blindly but inevitably staggers toward ever-greater triumphs of intelligence and strength. But the mere fact that we have become more intelligent over time is no argument that we *ought* to become any smarter, let alone any more virtuous, in the future. Evolution alone has no grand aspirations or moral ideals: we provide those for ourselves by talking *about* evolution as if it were a creation myth. Nietzsche saw this already in 1881, when he contemplated the implications of Darwinism:

> In the old days, people looked to feel the grandeur of man by pointing to his divine origin. This path is forbidden now, for at its entrance stands the ape, along with other dreadful beasts, grinning knowingly as if to say: no further in this direction! So now people look in the other direction: the way mankind is *going* shall serve as proof of his grandeur and kinship with God. But this too is useless![15]

To retain any kind of sanity and purpose, humanity needs not just facts but values, not just data but stories and meaning. We need answers to metaphysical questions. Materialists, having closed off such questions entirely, are now trying to answer them in scientific terms. This is the crisis of religion. We feel that we are more than flesh—we yearn for some way of expressing the truth of that feeling. But every outlet is closed to us except material science; no truth is valid unless it can be proven in cold mathematical terms. So math and science become a kind of religion, a way of telling stories about our divine destiny.

In his speech before the Athenian jury, Socrates described how his fruitless search for wisdom among men took him at last to the "craftsmen"—those who could make things with their hands. "I knew I would find that they had knowledge of many lovely things," said Socrates. "I was not wrong: they knew things I did not know, and to that extent they were wiser than I. But, gentlemen of the jury, the good craftsmen seemed to me to make the same mistake as the poets: each of them, because of his success at his craft, thought himself very wise in other most important pursuits."[16]

Our scientists are like the craftsmen of Athens: they are exceptionally skillful at their craft. Thirty years ago it would have seemed miraculous that a telephone the size of a human palm would become the portal to a vast library of thought and information. "We can do anything now that scientists have invented magic," says Marge Simpson in a futuristic episode of *The Simpsons*.[17] We may laugh, but Marge is us: dumbstruck before the power of our new machines, we have become like tribal worshippers of occult sorcery. We are so dazzled by technological skill that we have gone blind, bowing down before the iPhone and the rocket ship, singing hymns to power, speed, and size, and looking to scientists for spiritual guidance as if surgeons could tell us how to heal our souls.

Material capacity is not the same thing as wisdom. Mathematics was never made to be a god, and physical facts have no power to answer the questions of theology. We have not replaced religion with science: we

have only turned science into a kind of religion—and the most primitive
kind at that.

CHAPTER 8

The Real Story

Many Worlds

This crisis of religion is most obvious in the development and popularity of multiverse theory. The idea of the multiverse is relatively simple: our universe is only one among very many parallel or alternate universes. It was an idea that attracted the attention of Erwin Schrödinger, a forefather of quantum physics, who proposed a "many-worlds interpretation" to help resolve the famous paradox of his dead and living cat.

The thought experiment known as Schrödinger's Cat was designed to criticize the "Copenhagen Interpretation" of quantum physics, according to which a particle, until it is observed, can be thought of as occupying multiple places or states at once. To emphasize the counterintuitive nature of this idea, Schrödinger invited his audience to imagine a cat trapped in a box with a mechanism that might or might not kill it based on the indeterminate behavior of a single radioactive particle. Is the cat dead and alive at once until observed? In 1952, Schrödinger proposed his "many-worlds interpretation" as an alternative to this uncomfortable possibility: maybe the cat is not dead and alive at once in our universe, but dead in one universe and alive in another. If equations predict multiple possible outcomes for a given situation, maybe they all occur at once in parallel realities.[1]

Schrödinger never carried this suggestion further. But another variant of multiverse theory has become very much in vogue lately, as a way of interpreting Stephen Hawking's famous "String Theory." String theory describes the universe as made up of one-dimensional strings, which vibrate to produce what we experience as the fundamental laws of physics. The equations of string theory can be solved in many ways, only one of which describes our universe. Recently, scientists have suggested that perhaps *all* solutions are accurate, because the others describe different universes beyond our own.

This idea has become popular because it helps answer another question that troubles modern physicists, namely: why is anything alive at all? It turns out that life as we know it relies not only on the sophisticated representational language we call DNA, but also on certain mathematical constants and conditions that just happen to be exactly what they need to be for us to live. There is no obvious mathematical reason why the balance between mass and energy should have been exactly what it was when the universe began. Nor is there any inherent necessity for elementary particles to exert exactly as much electromagnetic force upon one another as they do. But if these numbers were even minutely different, nothing could live. We know of at least twelve such parameters, all of them precisely calibrated to make possible the world in which consciousness and life have come into being.[2]

How can that be unless some care was taken in the making of the universe—unless the fabric of reality was planned out by some mind? This "fine-tuning" argument started coming into focus with physicist Brandon Carter's observations about the strength of interaction between charged particles in 1974. Carter advanced what has been called the "weak anthropic principle," which states that any universe with intelligent life in it is bound to be one that can support intelligent life. But since that universe had to be minutely conditioned, some observers began making a version of the "design" argument put forward by William Paley in *Natural Theology* (1802): if a phenomenon in nature looks tailor-made for a purpose, then only design can explain it. So who or what designed the universe to support life?[3]

Writing in *Nature*, mathematician George Ellis and physicist Joe Silk explain how multiverse theory is supposed to answer that question:

> The multiverse is motivated by a puzzle: why fundamental constants of nature, such as the fine-structure constant that characterizes the strength of electromagnetic interactions between particles and the cosmological constant associated with the acceleration of the expansion of the Universe, have values that lie in the small range that allows life to exist. Multiverse theory claims that there are billions of unobservable sister universes out there in which all possible values of these constants can occur. So somewhere there will be a bio-friendly universe like ours, however improbable that is.[4]

One widely cited form of multiverse theory is thus the inflationary string landscape model, which combines string theory with "inflationary cosmology," the theory of how the universe expands. In outline, the inflationary string landscape model proposes that different configurations of strings delineate universes with different laws and constants. As a universe expands, the string configurations "decay" in some areas and produce new universes, which have their own unique arrangement of matter and energy that then proceeds to expand from a new starting point. The result is a potentially endless proliferation of "bubble universes," local domains where the initial conditions and laws of physics are different from our own. The point of all this is to imagine a kind of "universe generator," an automatic process that could accidentally make a universe that supports life. It is a means of explaining away the fact that our universe looks designed.

Trust the Science

Multiverse theory is unprovable by its very nature. As Stephen Meyer points out, "to explain the fine tuning of both the initial conditions and the laws and constants of physics, the combination of inflationary cosmology and string theory needs to affirm numerous purely hypothetical entities, abstract postulates, and unobservable processes."[5] We cannot observe other universes, and the phenomena in our universe only show evidence of multiverse theory if we already believe in multiverse theory. For example: scientists can fire photons, the elementary particles of light, at an object called a "silvered mirror." The photons will pass through the mirror 50 percent of the time, and bounce off of it the other 50 percent. Does that mean that until we observe them, they are all both bouncing off the mirror *and* passing through it? Or that each one is bouncing in half of all universes which exist, and passing through in the other half? How we interpret the evidence of our experiment depends on the theory we have already decided to believe. A parallel universe is by definition one of which we have no experience, and so there is no *empeiria*, no empirical observation, that could confirm or falsify its existence. "Parallel universes may or may not exist," writes George Ellis; "the case is unproved. We are going to have to live with that uncertainty. Nothing is wrong with scientifically based philosophical speculation, which is what multiverse proposals are. But we should name it for what it is."[6] In other words, the multiverse is philosophy *about* science—it is not, strictly speaking, science. Yet some are so devoted to multiverse theory that they are willing to expand the boundaries of their field to claim scientific authority for philosophical speculation. Philosopher of science Richard Dawid, for example, argues that "the construction of the scientific paradigm is not a matter of logical deduction but a matter of plausibility, coherence, and success"—in other words, experiments and observation are not the only way to know something.[7] Multiverse theory is a plausible, if untestable, story about why things are the way they are. But to accept it as science, we have to broaden the definition of the discipline outside of the empirical realm that Bacon claimed for it so long ago.

No experiment or observation can interpret itself, as the Viennese philosopher Karl Popper observed in the twentieth century. Every test and every measurement is already laden with assumptions about what those measurements might *mean*. But still, Popper insisted, an explanation of natural phenomena must be testable in order to count as science: "the scientifically significant *physical effect* may be defined as that which can be regularly reproduced by anyone who carries out the appropriate experiment in the way prescribed," he wrote.[8] Popper saw that scientific truth depended precisely on identifying which questions can be asked and answered by experiment, and which can only be framed by theory: "The theoretician puts certain definite questions to the experimenter, and the latter, by his experiments, tries to elicit a decisive answer to these questions, and to no others. All other questions he tries hard to exclude."[9] Questions of metaphysics and theology are not answered by science because they are *prior* to it.

Now, though, public-facing experts desire authority to pronounce on all questions—questions of morality and theology as well as of matter and physics—so they are proposing to loosen the bounds Popper put in place. "In our opinion," write George Ellis and Joe Silk, "this is moving the goal posts." True enough: so long as scientists are in Popper's and Bacon's realm of experiment and observation, they have irrefutable expertise and authority that someone like you or I simply cannot challenge. It is scientists who know how contagious a virus is, or what value the fine-structure constant has: they know because they look and find out the answer. They are trained to do this in ways I am not, and within the bounds of that expertise I have no authority to say they are wrong unless they make some obvious mathematical or logical mistake. But once they start venturing opinions about how much risk of infection we *ought* to incur, or *why* the universe is so constructed as to support life, they are in the realm of philosophical speculation. What some scientists seem to want is the last word on the purpose of the universe and man's place in it. They want scientific authority over unscientific questions—that is, questions beyond scientific testing and observation—because they redefine science to deny that there *are* unscientific questions. But in the construction of "plausible, coherent, and successful theories" about the purpose of life I am at least as competent to speculate as any chemist or astrophysicist. "Physics as physics can make no assertions about physics," wrote Heidegger: science is expressly not designed to answer questions about the meaning of its own endeavor.

And so, if scientists want to start answering questions that science was not designed to ask or answer, about things for which no experiment can furnish evidence, then they are going to have to argue not with other scientists but with priests and philosophers. And in that arena multiverse theory is far from the most plausible, coherent, or successful explanation of things. It is not even a particularly novel explanation. In fact, it is almost exactly the philosophical system that was developed by Epicurus in the Hellenistic period, when Alexander the Great's death left in its wake a splintered world.

Perhaps in those days of political turmoil and division, multiverse theory looked plausible, because it is a theory of chaos. Like the earlier philosophers Democritus and Leucippus before him, Epicurus proposed that "the whole of existence is made up of bodies and void." "There is an unlimited number of worlds, some of them like ours, others unlike," wrote Epicurus to one of his students around the end of the fourth century BC.[10] Explaining Epicurus's philosophy to the Roman upper crust several centuries later, the poet Lucretius argued that all reality is one infinite expanse of atoms moving through the void, so that eventually there must be other universes (*kosmoi* in Greek):

> Seeds [or atoms], numberless in number, driven on in constant motion, fly in all directions in the fathomless universe. And it must not be considered likely under any circumstances that this one earth and heaven alone has been formed, and that all those particles of matter outside it achieve nothing—especially since our world was made by nature: the atoms themselves collided together spontaneously and by chance, crashing

blindly, unsuccessfully, and ineffectually in all manner of combinations, until at last those atoms coalesced which always had the potential, if suddenly forced into contact, to form the foundations of mighty fabrics, of earth, sea, and sky and the family of living creatures.[11]

Lucretius's and Epicurus's outlook was much like that of our modern materialists: particles interact at random and behave when they meet according to the mechanical laws of nature. Given an infinite number of such interactions, life of various kinds will eventually come into being somewhere, however improbable it is. Only a few fundamental laws govern the colliding and reconfiguration of atoms, and these laws make it possible to imagine infinitely many worlds coming into being.

No divine intervention is needed in this system: "nature is free," wrote Lucretius. "She does everything on her own steam. Divinities play no part." Since everything we can see is bodies moving through space, we must infer that there is an infinite expanse of atoms colliding and interacting with one another, forever. The gods are far off and impersonal, unconcerned with the problems we encounter as the ironclad laws of nature run their course.

Small wonder that Hume put his most controversial arguments in the mouth of Epicurus. Hume's chapter "on providence and a future state" is presented as a speech that Epicurus might have given before the Athenians, defending his own serenity in the face of an endless and uncaring universe. "Why torture your brain to justify the course of nature upon suppositions, which, for aught you know, may be entirely imaginary, and of which there are to be found no traces in the course of nature?" asks Hume's Epicurus.[12] We can find no evidence in ourselves of anything that endures after death; no experiment produces anything like a soul or a miracle; so why believe in anything but infinite matter and infinitely varied worlds?

Already by the days of the American founding this attitude was gaining ground: "our modern philosophers are all the low groveling disciples of Epicurus," groused John Adams in 1801 (thinking, perhaps, of his contentious relationship with self-proclaimed Epicurean Thomas Jefferson).[13] But Adams could hardly have guessed how pervasive the neo-Epicurean outlook would become. Nowadays it is the stuff of casual assumption and pop philosophy: we live in an infinite void of particles, interacting in infiniteways, producing infinite universes and life at random.

What If?

Today, the multiverse is so in vogue that it governs some of our most popular storytelling. That is what moviegoers discovered as the various franchises of the Marvel Cinematic Universe (or MCU to the cognoscenti) assembled their many plotlines into the grand finale of *Avengers: Endgame*. Screenwriters and studio executives immediately revived the narrative by zooming out into innumerable timelines of which *Endgame* represented just one. Properties like *Loki* (2021), *Eternals* (2021), *What If?* (2022), and *Doctor Strange in the Multiverse of Madness* (2022) left the supervillain Thanos and his once world-threatening evil far behind in time and space. In *Eternals*, the cataclysmic battle for the fate of earth is only one among many such battles that have occurred on Earth, and Earth is only one among many such planets. In *What If?*, a mysterious figure called the "Watcher" looks down on a kind of Schrödinger's comic book, where familiar characters take unfamiliar paths into alternate endings. "Time. Space. Reality," says the Watcher in the opening sequence of each episode: "it's more than a linear path. It's a prism of endless possibility, where a single choice can branch out into infinite realities, creating alternate worlds from the ones you know."[14] The multiversal vision of reality, which had previously been a peripheral factor of the films and the comics they were based on, suddenly became the governing idea behind the Marvel Cinematic Universe's main narratives.

Multiverse theory and materialism are not the results of our experiments but the *premise* of them, the background context of assumptions in which we operate. As such they are more mythology than science: they express our cultural convictions and prejudices. The Marvel Cinematic Universe conveys in the language of legend what multiverse theory says in the language of philosophy: that the universe is random, and there is no God. But the shallowness of these ideas is evident in the failure of the stories to inspire. What makes the Marvel Cinematic Universe increasingly tiresome and artistically sterile is precisely the constant abandonment of one reality for another, the constant revision of questions that look settled. Characters die and come back to life or show up again in another universe; eventually, even the event of their deaths carries almost no emotional weight. Audiences were moved to see Tom Holland's Spider-Man dissolving into space dust at the conclusion of *Avengers: Infinity War*. But once he and others re-materialized in *Endgame*, it began to look like none of the events in the series had any lasting consequence.

That is because in real human experience, events occur irrevocably. This gives them their weight and meaning. In the multiverse, all events are at least possibly happening somewhere at all times simultaneously. I am sitting here and writing in this universe; is there some parallel reality in which I have already died? Certainly there must be many in which I never existed at all. But in such a context what does the word "I" even mean? Just one among an infinite number of random possibilities, here not for any reason but simply because spacetime has churned up every possible combination of events.

This explains why the Marvel Cinematic Universe, and other expanded universes like *Star Trek: Discovery*, have become narratively inert the more philosophically "multiversal" they have become. Since in the multiverse no event excludes the opposite event from happening simultaneously, stories are no longer dictated by the logic of human action but by the actors' contracts and the financial convenience of studio executives. Television viewers have always had to roll with a few plotlines that seem more invented to suit financial imperatives than earned organically by the development of the characters: an actress gets pregnant in real life and must become pregnant in the show, or an actor quits and his character must be killed off. But in multiverse stories, financial imperatives are the *only* real imperatives: the chain of events and consequences that usually drives good plots is totally broken, and all that remains is whatever new contrivance will drive ticket sales.

All storytelling takes place at the level of the human being. However epic the scale of time or space, the things we care about happen on the scale of human action. Every new Marvel movie effectively redefines that scale, rendering previous stories obsolete or irrelevant. This effect is achieved most subtly in *Spider-Man: No Way Home* (2021), which quietly rewrites the ending of every previous Spider-Man movie in order to tell a compelling story in its own timeline. This makes the film exciting, but renders every previous film in which audiences had once been invested into a dead-end and a hoax.

Similarly, *Eternals* fails as a narrative because it renders all that came before it moot: upon the arrival of nearly immortal beings wielding unthinkable cosmic power, every previous event and character becomes retrospectively insignificant, a mere blip in the lives of these new protagonists. The Eternals are now the ones that really count; their decisions come to matter, while other stories shrink to the level of background decoration. Nor, at the level of the blessed gods, do moral choices make much sense at all. Sersi, who emerges as the main character of *Eternals*, achieves a triumph which must eventually lead to the heat death of the universe. She feels at best ambivalent about this victory, and wonders if her course of action was the right one. And she is bound to wonder, since in an infinite and random universe of mere atomic flow, governed by no ultimate mind, words like "right" and "wrong" can hardly have much use at all.

"The objects of imitation are men in action," wrote Aristotle in the *Poetics*.[15] Fictional stories move us because we believe the events in them reflect the real kinds of sequences that unfold in our own lives. Even if the story is a fairytale and the world is one of outlandish creations—goblins and dragons, say, or light sabers and pod-racers—the fictional elements matter because they drive forward a narrative that is recognizably like human life. In real human experience, choices have consequences and some losses are irrevocable. If that is not the case, then what we're left with is a story devoid of meaning; it plays with our emotions for a moment, but can never be of lasting importance.

Audiences want grand adventures and noble triumphs; they want virtues and aspirations; they want intimations of a higher truth. But the multiverse renders that all illusory, and materialism makes it pointless. If matter is all there is, then it's hard to believe in anything other than material comfort. Epicurus was not a hedonist, as his bitterest detractors claimed. but his vision of the good life, of *eudaimōnia*, was defined by a comfortable state of sedation where "every choice and every aversion" was related "to the health of the body and the tranquility of the mind, since this is the goal of a happy life."[16]

Perhaps for Epicurus himself this was a recipe for gentlemanly good nature. But as a society-wide prescription it seems to be a recipe for listlessness and dejection. In July 2021, the *New York Times* published a lengthy profile of Justine Ang Fonte, a teacher of sex-ed and "porn literacy" who left her post at Dalton prep school amid controversy after parents became incensed about the content of her lessons.[17] Fonte often sums up her entire philosophy in three words: she hopes her students' sex lives will be "safe, fulfilling, and pleasurable."[18] It is practically an Epicurean mantra, and a rallying cry for our age. But who can build a good life, or even a good sex life, on safety, fulfillment, and pleasure? That is a life for farm animals, not people. What about nobility and sacrifice? Fruitfulness and joy? These are absent from our neo-Epicurean credos because they require reference to higher forms of excellence and virtue that cannot be found in an endless sea of atoms.

And God Said…

Multiverse materialism is not some necessary fact that science has discovered. It is an explanation that some scientists have invented to account for facts that do not otherwise tell the story that they are supposed to tell. We live, it seems, in a universe that is delicately calibrated to support life, intelligible to us in our immediate surroundings but far stranger and more complex than we initially assumed. A materialist can invoke the idea of a multiverse to account for those facts while preserving the possibility of materialism. But that account comes at the expense of coherence at the level of normal human life. And it does not even really answer the question it is supposed to: if our world of life and reason was just coughed up by some giant universe-producing machine, who built the machine? As the philosopher Roger Scruton wrote in response to the unbelieving physicist Stephen Hawking: if the laws of physics created the world, "what created the laws of physics?"[19]

So, since we are just telling stories, let me propose one of my own. Let me propose that existence itself is a kind of story, a kind of language. What this language expresses cannot be put into words of the normal sort; the story cannot be told in Hebrew or English or French. But all those human languages are good metaphors for this universal language, the language of everything that is.

All languages have form and matter: there is the sound of a word or a sentence, and then there is the meaning it conveys. Words stand in as symbols for a certain range of ideas, and in relationship with one another they come to express a whole range of complex and subtle thoughts—from "this necklace is made of gold" to "much have I travell'd in the realms of gold." The matter of these sentences, the stuff they are made out of, is letters and syllables. But the form which lives within them is what they convey—the images, memories, and associations they evoke.

The whole of the universe works like this: it is matter so arranged as to contain form. Like language, the universe is subjective but not arbitrary: when I see light bouncing off the chair in front of me, it hits my eyes in such a way that my mind experiences the color called "brown." There is no "brown" in the atoms of the chair or the photons moving through space—at least not in any sense that I mean when I use the word.

The real brown, the visual quality of the thing, is something conveyed to me *through* and *in* matter—it is not the matter itself.

The atoms of the chair are not in themselves brown any more than the letters "c-h-a-i-r" are brown, any more than the sound I make when I say the word is something solid that can be sat on. But the word conveys to my mind the image, and the matter conveys to my mind the thing—the thing as it is to me, not in some abstract or clinical sense of molecular composition, but as a real and tangible entity that I know and relate to, like the favorite chair by my bookshelf where the cat sits above my shoulder as I write.

Everything works this way. The chair, the cat, and the bookshelf are best described not as conglomerate heaps of matter but as the real and solid entities which their atoms and molecules make in the world—beings with qualities and characters, with relationships to one another. Like language, the material world is not an end in itself but a pattern, a system of order and rules that gives shape to otherwise formless masses—masses of letters, of sounds, of molecules, and of flesh.

Under a microscope my chair will show itself to be made of so much synthetic material, various expanses of different metals and threads. I may, if I so choose, imagine those metals and threads as more "essential" or "real" than the chair itself. But who ever said that the truest way of looking at a thing was by holding it up an inch from your face? Who ever said that the best way to get the meaning of a word was to look at each of the letters one by one in isolation? The real essence of things, what they truly are, is best understood at the level of normal human perception. If you want to know what something really is, you get familiar with it in its entirety, as a complete entity, in the same way you get to know your best friend or your pet rabbit. The tool for reading the language of the universe is not the microscope, but the soul.

And the soul, too, is a kind of language, a kind of form in matter, a whole and complete meaning which all the parts of the body express. Your body has consciousness the way a word has meaning. Both are just inert stuff, empty letters and dry bones, until they come together in the right combination and the lights switch on.

What I am suggesting is that in the beginning, was the word. I am suggesting that expression, the act of investing formless matter with quality and meaning, is the mechanism at the heart of all creation. I am suggesting that God spoke, and that speech was and is what it meant for him to create light and grass and sky. So it is that Saint Augustine said to God, "you do not create in any other way than by speaking."[20]

I am suggesting that life is a language, from the heavens which declare the glory of God to the strands of DNA which synthesize living creatures into being from primordial sludge. "You, therefore, Lord, made these things," says Augustine of the heavens and the creatures of the earth:

> You who are beautiful, and so they are beautiful; You who
> are good, and so they are good; You who are, and so they are.
> But they are neither beautiful, nor good, in the way that you
> are.

The being and character of each thing is a sign, a symbol of the ultimate Being who made them all.[21]

And I am suggesting that when God had made all these things he turned at last to make one final soul in his image, one last array of neurons and dust which would represent him on earth just insofar as it could *understand*, could see snow on the ground, feel a fire's warmth, watch mothers expose the strength in their breasts to the delicate mouths of infants and say, "it is good."

The Heavens Declare

We are language-makers because God makes language, and the thing we try to express in all our utterance—whether in words or images or actions—is love.

There is a danger in a word like "love," which has been so belittled as to look pathetic. If we conjure up images of frilly Hallmark cards we will get entirely the wrong idea. But the fierce love of the Christian saints and mystics, the jealous love of Abraham's God, is an all-encompassing passion. Love is what says with unbridled intensity, "this is good" and, by comparison, "this is evil." Love is what drives a saint to go willingly to the gas chambers in place of another, what keeps a mother sitting by her child's hospital bed; it is the thing within us that would rather die or suffer than lose the beloved.

And so our yearning for truth—even if truth is ugly, even if to tell it we have to tell stories of loss and pain—is in itself a kind of love. At our best we talk to one another, we make art, we build civilizations, because we are trying to acknowledge honestly what is good in the world. And either there *is* something good—either our language and our culture and our virtues refer to some ultimate good above all others—or it is all a farce, an endless game of imitation without purpose or meaning.

Now at last I am evangelizing you, though not perhaps in any usual sense of the term. I am not trying to prove the existence of God to you, as the great Medieval philosophers did, or even to threaten you with hellfire if you get the answer to this great question wrong as if on some eternal gameshow. I am instead trying to suggest to you that the ancient texts of Genesis and John's gospel describe the world, which our modern science has discovered, far more accurately and coherently than the pop Epicureanism that some materialists and scientists have settled upon. And furthermore I am suggesting that you already *act as if* you believe in the world described by Scripture, not the world described by the multiverse and the Marvel Cinematic Universe.

You behave as if there is somewhere a final truth, a goodness, a meaning, and a ground of existence which gives coherence to words like "good" and "love." You do not act as if you live on one strand of an infinite and confused dimensional tapestry, a tangle of universes writhing randomly without any governing logic. You may have said you think it's all just atoms bouncing through the void. But in your heart of hearts, that is not what you believe.

I am not trying to refute or disprove any claim that science makes. I am trying to invest science once again with the glory it has stolen from itself by answering questions it was never designed to ask. This is not to say that belief means resisting new scientific discoveries that seem to threaten old ideas. It is rather to say that those new discoveries can be valued not simply for what they tell us about the world, but for what they illustrate about God.

Matters of Perspective

In antiquity and throughout the Renaissance there developed a system of classical education that put the different ways of knowing the world in order: the *trivium*, or "three ways," was the study of rules for clear speech (grammar) persuasive argument (rhetoric) and sound reason (logic or dialectic). Using these tools the student could progress to the "four ways" of contemplating mathematical truths. This *quadrivium* consisted of studying quantities (arithmetic), masses (geometry), how masses move (astronomy), and how quantities relate to one another (music).

But over and above them all was the discipline of seeking wisdom and final truth—philosophy, or theology. That was the search for ultimate answers to ultimate questions, the governing system which explained why science matters at all. What I have been arguing is that natural science moved beyond the questions of the *quadrivium*—the questions of what things are and how they move—to those of theology. In doing so it began to eat its own tail: scientists began inventing physical theology and material philosophy, trying to make of mere atoms the meaning of a life worth living.

It is a fool's game. We study the natural world because we think it contains truths worth knowing, not simply for the sake of our survival but for the sake of living richly and fully. If all creation is a language then all discoveries about creation contain within them signs and symbols of their creator. "Since our intellect knows God from creatures," wrote Aquinas, "it knows him as far as creatures represent him."[22]

Traditionally the study of outer space, like the study of all natural phenomena, was thought to reveal signs and symbols of the hand that made it. Music is a part of the *quadrivium* because the beauty of harmony and the elegance of mathematics are two human ways of experiencing the same scientific truth—the truth that rational order inheres in the cosmos, and it is good that it should do so. The "music of the spheres," a mystical vision in which the planets emit melodic notes in cosmic harmony, was as real for the groundbreaking physicist Johannes Kepler as for the masterful composer Igor Stravinsky: "music is a force which gives reason to things," wrote Stravinsky, "a force which creates organization, which attunes things. Music probably attended the creation of the universe."[23] Or in Shakespeare's terms, as Lorenzo says to his lover Jessica in *The Merchant of Venice*: "Such harmony is in immortal souls."[24]

Kepler and Shakespeare and Stravinsky were not childlike believers in some primitive fairytale. Rather they saw creation as a coherent and complimentary story that could be expressed in astronomical, literary and musical terms, and that pointed to something beyond themselves that was worth investigating and exploring.

Typically, religious believers are accused of a simplistic belief in a caricature "sky daddy," as if we really think that angel-aliens were sitting on a cloud or an asteroid in space. But the old practice of picturing heaven as situated above us has long been understood as figurative in the best sense—as an attempt to use God's creation to picture what true communion with God must be like.

This is what the heavenly guide Beatrice explains to Dante in *Paradiso*, the final installment of the poet's imaginary journey through hell and up to heaven. Having encountered various saints and angels in various parts of outer space, Dante wonders whether all the planets are really populated by celestial residents. Beatrice responds:

> They showed themselves to you here not because

> this is their sphere, but as a sign for you . . .
> Such signs are suited to your mind, since from
> the senses only can it apprehend
> what then becomes fit for the intellect.
> And this is why the Bible condescends
> to human powers, assigning feet and hands
> to God, but meaning something else instead.[25]

Understood as literal scientific maps of space, says Beatrice, myths like the one in the *Timaeus* are lies. But if Timaeus's stories are allegories, then "perhaps his story reaches something true": perhaps the expanding orbits of the heavens draw a picture for the eye that the mind can interpret, a picture of ever-magnifying glory. "This principle, ill-understood, misled / almost all of the world once, so that Jove / and Mercury and Mars gave names to stars."[26] But rightly understood, from the standpoint of a robust theology, this mythical kind of interpretation can give fresh meaning to science and myth alike.

So it is that other Christian allegorists have gone on telling stories of the heavens without in the least intending for them to challenge what scientists discover about the physical world. C. S. Lewis's *Space Trilogy* is one attempt to replace "the mythology that follows in the wake of science" with a story of adventure and majesty.[27] So is John Milton's *Comus*, a seventeenth-century court poem that uses the height of the heavens as an analogue for the heights to which the soul climbs in the moral life. "Love virtue," writes Milton: "She alone is free; / She can teach ye how to climb / Higher than the spheary chime."[28] If, as Psalm 19 says, "the heavens declare the glory of God," then everything we discover about them will be usable not only for what it tells us about the mechanics of the world, but also as metaphor or allegory pointing to something higher than itself. This works because the language of creation is intelligible, and the author intends to be known.

If the Copenhagen Interpretation of quantum mechanics is right, and a particle may be superposed in many places or states until it is observed, then the world is not a multiverse but a relationship: reality exists outside of us, but it takes its final and definite form only when interacting with human perception. This fact, which vexed Schrödinger so deeply, need not trouble believers very much at all. The universe of the Copenhagen Interpretation looks very much like the work of a God who invites us to participate with him in making the world, the kind of God who would make the animals, but call upon Adam to consummate their creation by giving them names. Reality is outside of us and cannot be whatever we want it to be, but it is also designed, from the photons to the planets, as a book for us to read—and books are just letters on a page until they meet with the kind of mind for which they were written.[29]

What You Believe

All science takes place within the context of philosophy—within a universe of meaning and understanding. The mythology that physical science has generated for itself, on its own material steam, is shallow and incoherent. It finds its end grasping desperately at meaning and authority where there is none, worshipping Dr. Fauci or Elon Musk, virtue in evolution, telling stories about the multiverse to escape the sneaking feeling that our world shows symptoms of deliberate design.

I am not here to tell you which church you should join. But I *am* here to insist that if you want your behavior and your philosophy to make sense, you should want to believe. You need not give up a shred of your vitality, of your intelligence, of your openness to discovery or space travel. On the contrary, if you want your language to mean anything, your space travel to be worthwhile, and your virtue to be more than an empty performance, there must be some ultimate truth to which it is all referring and against which it can all be judged.

You already behave as if that were the case: you already tremble at the thought of murder and make resolutions to be more courageous or more just or more disciplined at the beginning of every year. Why? Surely not because you think your soul is an illusion and your body is just one more chunk of undifferentiated dust vibrating through space. In a thousand ways both large and small, you already behave as if your actions and experiences in the world have value beyond the bare material facts—as if they communicated enduring values like love and justice which really do exist in some immutably solid way. In your actions, if not in your words, you already believe in something rather than nothing.

You should want to think and say the things that are implied by what you do, and you should want to act in ways that make sense given what you really think. In an effort to maintain our unbelief in God, we often act and talk in ways that make no sense at all. But our unbelief is based on nothing at this point except a vague feeling, a comfortable association between sophistication and doubt.

Why not proceed in the other direction? Why not talk as if our natural intuitions, our nobler aspirations, our loves and losses, mean something? No one should pretend to believe out of shame or fear. But no one should be guilted out of affirming the plain implications of his actions just because those implications feel gauche. What we need is less a conversion than a surrender, less a change of heart than an act of confession and acceptance. We ought to believe what we believe.

PART V

Regimes

The LORD almighty has a day in store
For all the proud and the uplifted,
For everything exalted:
They will be humbled.

—Isaiah 2:12

Time and time and time again the people discover that
they have merely betrayed themselves into the hands of
yet another Pharaoh, who, since he was necessary to put
the broken country together, will not let them go.

—James Baldwin, *The Fire Next Time*

CHAPTER 9

Regime Crisis

Time's Up

When the ancient Israelites came into the promised land, God gave a warning to his chosen nation. It had taken 40 years of grief, doubt, and hardship in the desert to reach this new home. At long last, there would be somewhere to lay down foundations, somewhere to grow crops and know peace. But this very relief could be the people's spiritual undoing. God warned: "Beware, lest you forget the LORD your God." (Deut. 8:11) Content in ease and prosperity, "you may say in your heart, 'my power, and the strength of my own hand, made all this wealth for me'" (Deut. 8:13–17).

So it was. So it always is. Again and again the ancient Israelites—standing in for all of us as the archetype of man's relationship with God—grew satisfied with material wealth and forgot to honor the deity who bestowed it. Again and again, disaster and oppression followed upon apostasy—but each time the Israelites were chastened, they found new faith. Perhaps the lowest point of this cycle came at the turn of the sixth century BC, when Israel suffered defeat at the hands of the Babylonian empire. The prophets saw this as a catastrophic act of divine judgement, with the Holy Land itself lost to foreign invasion. The Israelite leaders had not recovered their faith in time to avert their own doom. This raises the question: Is it possible to find God too late?

This, too, must be our question. It is easy to feel as if all of our efforts are in vain because the time is simply past for repentance. Whatever we recover or preserve from the wreckage, we might wonder whether the West is past saving altogether. Is our fate already sealed? Have we strayed so far from our cultural foundations that we can no longer find our way back?

Whittaker Chambers feared it might be so. During the late 1930s, Chambers realized with dawning horror that he had pledged his life and fortune to a mass murderer. He was a spy for the Communist underground, reporting to Joseph Stalin's Russia on American activities. But in those years Stalin was growing ever-more paranoid and erratic, condemning members of his own party to suffer and die in the Gulag on the thinnest suspicion of disloyalty. History would call it the "Great Purge"—a feverish orgy of political imprisonment that showed Stalin for the tyrant he was. Wracked with fear and sorrow, but aflame with a newfound Christian faith, Chambers renounced the Soviet regime and became an informant against Communists in America.

The dramatic trial in which Chambers exposed a State Department official named Alger Hiss was a shocking revelation of Communist activity at the highest levels of American government. In retrospect, it is easy to tell Chambers's story as part of an inevitable triumph, the victory of the West over Communist evil. But Chambers himself was far less sanguine.

Unimpressed by the rosy optimism of the dawning American century, Chambers made a grim prophecy to the prominent conservative intellectual William F. Buckley Jr. Stalin's totalitarian madness, wrote Chambers to Buckley, was not some foreign affliction that the West had now fought off. It was a symptom of internal breakdown within the West itself:

> On one side are the voiceless masses with their own subdivisions and fractures. On the other side is the enlightened articulate elite which, to one degree or another, has rejected the

religious roots of the civilization—the roots without which it is no longer Western civilization, but a new order of beliefs, attitudes and mandates. In short, this is the order of which Communism is one logical expression, originating not in Russia, but in the culture capitals of the West.[1]

Maybe America is living on borrowed time. When Chambers wrote those words in 1954, it may have seemed unlikely that the great nation would fracture and crumble. The foundations seemed unassailably sturdy. Now one wonders if they are even there at all.

Decline and Fall All Over Again

When American forces pulled out of Afghanistan in 2021, the predictions about what would happen next were quite dire. "Does Afghanistan Mark the End of American Empire?" asked Zalan Khan of *Al-Jazeera*.[2] "The American Empire Is Ready to End," wrote Amotz Asa-El in *The Jerusalem Post*.[3] The historian Niall Ferguson, who had written a history of America's rise to world power in *Colossus*, wrote in *The Economist* that the end of American hegemony "won't be peaceful."[4] It seemed Afghanistan, the "graveyard of empires," might claim the life of another arrogant invading power.

It wasn't just Afghanistan. For years already there had been talk of decadence, of wasting away or falling to ruin. During the Trump administration, America saw not just daily predictions of neo-fascist revolution, but more profound and structural anxieties about *Why Liberalism Failed* (from the University of Notre Dame's Patrick Deneen) and descriptions of the United States as *The Decadent Society* (from *New York Times* columnist Ross Douthat). All throughout 2020, as COVID sent the civilized world into crisis mode and racial unrest made streets unsafe, everything that had once seemed secure looked ready to dissolve.

For some, the sign of collapse was the sight of American cities on fire in the 2020 Black Lives Matter riots. For some, it was Trump's election in 2016; for others, it was his failure to attain reelection in 2020 and the suspicions of widespread fraud it evoked. When those suspicions led to a demonstration at the Capitol on January 6, 2021, and a small group of rioters broke into the Capitol building, federal prosecutions and fresh prophecies of disaster followed.

Then came Vladimir Putin's invasion of Ukraine, which further shocked and terrified those who thought of global conflict or national collapse as a thing of the past. It turns out there are still power-hungry autocrats, just as there have always been. And, as always, when powerful countries like America display weakness, their enemies are emboldened. "I fail to see in current Western strategizing any real recognition of how badly this war could go for Ukraine in the coming weeks," wrote Niall Ferguson, lamenting the naïve hope among NATO allies that Chinese and Russian global ambitions would simply fail. But even if Russian defeat does come to pass, it will not solve the problems that emboldened Putin—and, for that matter, China's Xi Jinping—in the first place. Unless we recover our own strength and confidence, the West's enemies, their aggressive plans, and our decline in global power politics are problems that are not just going to go away.[5]

Plenty of people are worried about American decline, but there is little agreement on the cause or possible solutions. That in itself is a telling sign of national crackup. Either our democracy is threatened by right-wing extremists who must be prosecuted—if not persecuted—with the full powers of the federal government, or our society is melting down under the corrosive assaults of neo-Marxism, Critical Race Theory, and gender extremism. Perhaps the solution is secession or localism, or perhaps it requires a massive extension of federal power, and more governors ruling by emergency decree as they did during the COVID crisis. Perhaps nothing will work and we are doomed to another civil war.

History, it is said, never repeats itself—but it does rhyme. Maybe we are like Rome's empire in the fifth century AD, facing cultural dissension within and vigorous foreign enemies raring to beat down our gates as we sleep. Maybe we are like Britain in the 1930s, wearying of imperial responsibilities and complacent in the face of power-mad dictators. Maybe our weakness, and our fate, will be worse than that of our predecessors—maybe the internet has so dissolved our moral sinews that we will not even lift a finger to avert our own destruction.

"Hopelessly beyond merely refusing to fight for king and country," writes the novelist and veteran Mark Helprin, "we are materially obsessed, paralyzed by imagined privations and exaggerated grievances, and anaesthetized by snacks, drugs,...addictions and entertainment."[6] Whatever your prior political commitments, it is hard not to feel despair in the face of forces beyond any normal person's control, while the endless wheel of history seems ready to crush us under its relentless advance.

But this, in itself, is a feeling that the West has faced before. Western civilization has a history of dealing even with its own decline, and has resources for facing what looks like the end. In this sense, the West has prepared itself, and us, even for its own collapse. Nations fall: that too is a truth that the Western tradition is big enough to incorporate. If the American republic were to fall, as someday it must, that would be a catastrophe of the highest magnitude. But it would not be the end of the West, which is curiously used to rising from the ashes of its own ruin.

The Pride before the Fall

Ancient Greece's first historian was no stranger to imperial decline or reversals of fortune. "Many of the nations that were once great have become small, and those that were great in my time were small before," wrote Herodotus of Halicarnassus. He was reflecting on Greece's unlikely victory over the Persian Empire, which was the story he had chosen to "investigate"—in Greek, *historein*. Before rapt audiences in Athens he read aloud from his investigation, his *historia*—the very first Greek "history."

The shocking about-face of Persia's enormous army, and its failure to conquer the upstart Greek cities which had fixated its rulers for generations, led Herodotus to take seriously the prospect that any great world power could collapse quite precipitously. "I know that human prosperity never stays in the same place long," he wrote, and it was as much a warning to the Athenians as a celebration of their victory.[7]

Herodotus's history is elaborate and meandering, but he always remains keenly observant of the sudden downfall that can come to kings and nations in the flower of their might. "God promises fortune to many and then utterly ruins them," says the Greek sage Solon to the rich king Croesus of Lydia. Sure enough, Croesus soon finds himself bereaved of his heirs and ruined at the hands of Cyrus, conquering ruler of the growing Persian empire. For Greeks who had improbably beaten back Persia, it would have been sobering to reflect that Persia itself was once an energetic young kingdom—not the brittle administrative state it had become.[8]

This sense of chastening dread found expression on the stage as well. Every year in March the whole city of Athens would gather for a festival in honor of Dionysus, god of foreign mysteries and drunken madness. That was the festival where playwrights brought the best of Greek poetry and music together into the grand pageantry of Attic tragedy. Only three of the many tragedians wrote plays that survived in full into the modern day: Aeschylus, Sophocles, and Euripides. It is the oldest of them, Aeschylus, who saw most clearly what Herodotus saw.

Aeschylus was himself a veteran of the Persian Wars and dared to put the anguish of his enemies onstage for his fellow Greeks to contemplate. The *Persians* appeared in the festival of 472 BC, making it our oldest surviving tragedy. Its genius consists in the setting: the play takes place not in Athens, but in the Persian court of Xerxes, the defeated king. Xerxes has lost the naval battle of Salamis to an Athenian fleet under the leadership of the general Themistocles. At a crucial moment before the Persian king returns home in disgrace, Xerxes's mother Atossa summons forth the ghost of her husband, the revered monarch Darius I. Darius, too, had failed to conquer Athens. But he had ended a number of internal rebellions and presided over a massive expansion of Persia's wealth and territory in Egypt, Europe, and central Asia.

Looking with disappointment on the misadventures of his son, he considers whether his dynasty was always fated to collapse:

> Alas, how quickly the prophecies did their work: Zeus
> Brought the fulfillment of the oracles down like lightning
> On the head of my own son. And here I thought for sure the
>   gods
> Would take more time to bring the end to pass.
> But when a man is impatient, then a god helps speed him
>   along.
> Now it seems a flood of disaster is welling up for all those I
>   love:
> My ignorant boy in his naïve self-confidence made it all
>   happen.[9]

Fate and foolishness are intertwined: the gods had foreordained Persia's fall, but Xerxes's impetuous pride hastened it along.

There was a word of caution here for Athens—but in vain. Aeschylus had not been dead 30 years before the two city-states which had led the fight against Persia found themselves embroiled in their own struggle for power over the Mediterranean.

Thucydides wrote that no matter how many other causes were alleged for the outbreak of the Peloponnesian War, the "truest cause was the one most concealed in official statements: the growth of Athens's power, and the alarm it caused Sparta, made war inevitable."[10] Imperial overreach and jealousy inspired in these two great powers a mutual distrust that the political scientist Graham T. Allison has called "the Thucydides trap": once two national powers grow strong enough, they cannot coexist.

Whether or not war really was inevitable, in retrospect Athens's downfall was a predictable result of *hubris*: the pride and complacency that leads great nations into disastrous ventures. Because of *hubris* Xerxes could not abide the existence of an independent Greece; and because of that same *hubris*, Athens herself became too jealous of power to retain it.

If Governments Were Angels

Looking back on these events in the post-Peloponnesian world of Alexander and the Hellenistic kings, Aristotle took it upon himself to describe what makes nations rise and fall. He did so by combining some of Plato's observations with a debate Herodotus had imagined between Darius and his allies when they took control of Persia.[11] In that debate, three would-be leaders had proposed three possible systems of government: rule by the many, by the few, or by one. Democracy, aristocracy, and monarchy.

When at last Darius had his turn to speak, he won the day for monarchy. Each kind of government had its benefits and pitfalls, he argued, but "take the three forms of government under discussion and imagine that each is of its best kind. I propose that monarchy is preferable to the other two." One ruler, if he really were the best and most virtuous man available, would have the kind of clarity and control that real leaders need. He could, in the words of the poet Alfred, Lord Tennyson, "make mild / A rugged people, and thro' soft degrees / Subdue them to the useful and the good."[12] There could be no civil war or mob rule in a truly efficient state; to keep order and make sound decisions an ultimate authority in the person of one king was needed.

To an extent, Aristotle agreed. But in his *Politics*, he noted also that what is best by nature becomes worst when corrupted. Had he been a Christian he might have observed that the brightest angels are in danger of falling the farthest: Lucifer is the chief of all devils because before he rebelled, he was the closest to God. And governments, like angels, do fall. When they do, their rulers stop ruling for the common good and start to use their power for their own gain. "Tyranny is monarchy with the advantage of the monarch in mind," Aristotle wrote. "Oligarchy is rule for the advantage of the rich. And democracy is rule for the advantage of those who are poor. None of them is oriented toward the common gain."[13]

Monarchy, aristocracy, and shared rule: these three different ways of organizing a city-state, or *polis*, represent three fundamental ways of regulating all human life. That, in Aristotle's terms, is all *politics* is: the natural practice of organizing our life together in community. Hence Aristotle's famous claim that "man is a political animal": wherever there are humans, there are traditions and forms of rule.[14] And wherever there are humans, even in the best of times, there is the temptation of corruption. So, the three forms of government decay into three vicious shadows of themselves: monarchy becomes tyranny, aristocracy becomes oligarchy, and what we now call democracy becomes mob rule.

Few understood this fact better than Polybius, a Greek soldier born a little more than a century after Aristotle died. When Rome began conquering the Greek world, Polybius saw the cities and governments he had known swept under and replaced by a newly growing empire. He spent his early life in dutiful and distinguished service to the Achaean League, a confederation of city-states that banded together not long after the death of Alexander the Great. Polybius's father, Lycortas, was an honored general in the league. Polybius himself showed all the signs of a promising military career. But that was cut short when Rome, having fought and conquered Alexander's successors in Macedon, turned its attention to shoring up support in Greece. Lycortas and others had resisted efforts to rally behind Rome in the fight against Macedon—and, in retribution for this lukewarm attitude, 1,000 Achaean noblemen were deported to Rome in 167 BC. Polybius was among them.

"Many of the nations that were once great have become small," Herodotus had written. How true that must have seemed to Polybius, whose whole political universe had been wiped out of significance. Once he vied with his Achaean rivals for prominence and honors—now they were all being made clients and captives, added to the long list of Rome's subordinates. In the years that followed, as an expatriate in Rome's high society, he set his mind to understanding how the glory of Greece had been extinguished by this astonishing new power.

Polybius's account of Rome's ascent to dominance contains the most famous and thorough description of how governments rise and fall. In his account, it is a cycle—the cycle of regimes or, in Greek, *anacyclosis*. It is not just that the three forms of government are subject to corruption, but that each as it decays gives way to the other. Monarchy is natural: a strong leader takes control of his people. But in time the pride of kings makes them perverse, and so, wrote Polybius:

> Monarchy first changes into its corrupted shadow-self, tyranny. Next, the abolition of all forms of kingship produces aristocracy. Aristocracy by its very nature degenerates into oligarchy; and when the masses become angry enough to take vengeance on this government for its unjust rule, then comes democracy. Eventually, the licentiousness and lawlessness of this form of government produces mob rule to complete the series.[15]

Complacent kings are unseated by restless nobles, and aristocracy is born. But the best and the brightest soon become corrupt themselves, and responsible noblemen give way to self-dealing elites. When oligarchs push their subjects too far, the people rise up and take control. But democracy too easily gives way to covetousness and class rivalry, which turns into mob rule—the ruthless struggle for majority dominance. This creates just the kind of chaotic power vacuum that a strongman needs to step in and take control. And so the cycle begins again.

Polybius's words are not prophecy, and history never follows a perfect script. Unexpected wars or accidents can intervene to arrest the cycle of regimes. But as a general pattern it is remarkable how often Polybius's cycle repeats itself. Once you understand the contours of the cycle you can discern little fragments of it unfolding everywhere, like snatches from a familiar refrain.

The engine of it all is *hubris*: the predictable arrogance of power asserted—whether by a tyrant or oligarchs or a mob—just before it is about to fail. It is, as Polybius wrote, "a natural process." Thomas Cole's famous 1836 painting, *Destruction*, is often used to represent the fall of Rome. But it's actually part of a series, *The Course of Empire*, which depicts the life cycle of all great civilizations from their ascendancy to their downfall at the hand of pride. United States Marine Corps veteran G. Michael Hopf put Polybius's ancient insight in modern vernacular when he wrote, "hard times create strong men, strong men create good times, good times create weak men, and weak men create hard times."[16] There's no rule that says this must happen except the rule of human fallibility: maybe we are not *destined* to get complacent and weak. But we always do.

The Perpetual Motion Machine

Rome was supposed to have found a way out of this cycle: the republic. Hypothetically, a republic is a kind of perpetual motion machine, a hybrid of all three basic forms of government that plays their strengths and weaknesses off of one another. A leading executive—in Rome, the two consuls—carries the decisive authority that a king would have, especially in wartime. The consul's powers are offset by landed nobles who make laws: in Rome this aristocratic power was chiefly concentrated in the senate, a word which literally means "a bunch of old men" and which in practice referred to the elder statesmen of the patrician elite. But those elites in turn were accountable to the weaker and poorer citizens whom they ruled. Over time more and more men were given citizen status, meaning they could vote to choose leaders or even run for office themselves.

The specifics of this arrangement were enormously complex and variable over time. Rome's republic was not without its internal revolutions. But in its broad outlines it struck Polybius as an ingenious antidote to the instability that plagued simpler forms of government.

Republican politics, however comically deadlocked and bureaucratic, was in principle a nimble and elegant solution to the fundamental problems of governance. This delicate Roman system of checks and balances was said to have replaced an earlier monarchy in the sixth century BC, and from then until 133 BC the experiment was a huge success. Romans bickered and debated, but for those almost four centuries they never took up arms against one another. Even as their power began to grow beyond all expectation on the world stage, the republic held fast. It seemed to be working.

Rome did not invent this concept. The word "republic" itself is a Latin translation of a Greek word: the Greek *politeia* becomes Latin *res publica*, which means "the public affairs." It refers to the whole array of systems and arrangements that keeps a society functioning. Hence Plato's dialogue, *politeia*, is now known in English as the *Republic*. Originally, *politeia* referred to a state's "constitution" with a small c: not just the written laws of the land, but the culture and custom of the people. Plato, and those who read him carefully, came to realize that healthy nations survive by holding three fundamental forces in tension with one another, like the balance of masses and charges that holds protons, neutrons, and electrons together in an atom. Gradually the word "republic" came to mean not just any constitution but this tripartite "mixed regime" in which nobles, magistrates, and commoners worked together in fraught but enduring harmony. Other cities—most notably Sparta—had tried this arrangement before and made a decent showing of it. But it was Rome that demonstrated the genius of the republic beyond any shadow of a doubt.

Looking back, the historian Livy mulled over the lucky set of circumstances that had allowed Rome to escape the cycle of regimes, at least for a long while. The city had been a monarchy once. Rome's founder Romulus, and his immediate successors, ruled justly. But Rome's kings became increasingly venal and abusive, until finally a coalition of disaffected noblemen organized a coup. They replaced the king with a system which ensured that no one class of citizens would be ground beneath the heels of another. Livy wrote that the nobles acted with propitious timing, because the Roman people, bound to one another by a long history of fellowship and the slow training of good laws, had become ready to govern themselves.[17]

Class Conflict

Republics, however, were not immune to hubris. One political theorist who knew this very well—both firsthand and historically—was Niccolò Machiavelli, an ardent student of antiquity. Since the early twelfth century, his native city of Florence had been a republic itself, and boasted a proud tradition of elected leadership. But at the time of Machiavelli's writing, that tradition had been repeatedly punctured by the intervention of powerful noble families, most notably by the cunning and multitalented Medici. Machiavelli's career had been a casualty of Florentine politics: in 1513, after a distinguished diplomatic career, he was sent into exile by the Medici on suspicion of having conspired against them. It was in this exile that he composed his best and most enduring studies on the dynamics of political power—how to acquire it, and how to keep it.

"All states, all powers that rule or have ruled over men, are or have been either republics or principalities," he wrote at the beginning of *The Prince*, a handbook aimed squarely at the Medici in the hopes of advertising his skills as an adviser.[18] Machiavelli's treatise on *realpolitik* made his name synonymous with scheming amorality in obtaining and exercising power. But elsewhere, in his *Discourses on Livy*, Machiavelli revealed himself as enamored with the ideal of a republic.

Machiavelli argued that a voting public can be "more prudent, more stable, and sounder in its judgments than a prince. It is not without reason that the voice of the people has been compared to the voice of God."[19] What has in modern times been called "the wisdom of crowds" made a strong argument, in Machiavelli's view, for relying on the common sense of the people to discern between true leaders and mere demagogues.

But if republics have the benefit of protecting against all the usual forms of civic decay, they are also vulnerable to another evil that can bring them down from within: class conflict. It was, wrote Machiavelli, impossible for even a republic as sophisticated as Rome to avoid tension and resentment between the common man and the elites. Those with power, wealth, and education will always be tempted to lord it over those without, and those without will always be incensed when they feel their lack of status too keenly:

> The fear of losing wealth arouses the same emotions in men as the desire to gain it, since men do not feel secure in what they already have except by acquiring still more. Moreover, these new acquisitions are themselves means of strength and power for abuse; and, worse still, the arrogant behavior and contempt of the nobles and the rich arouses not only the desire for wealth and position among those who have none, but also the hunger to avenge themselves by stripping the wealthy of those riches and honors which they see them employ so badly.[20]

Earlier, Plato had seen that extreme inequality of wealth made a city vulnerable to manipulation from outside: in such cases "there are two cities really, warring with each other: one city of the poor, another of the rich."[21] And in the end, as Machiavelli well knew, class resentment had indeed become the ruin of Rome's republic.

As foreign conquests incorporated new territories and expanded Rome's borders, veterans chafed to see the spoils of their victory taken over by a wealthy few. It was not supposed to be that way: technically, according to the law, territorial acquisitions were supposed to be divided into small lots. This would limit the amount of land that could be bought up by any one family, encouraging the creation of small farms and building up what we would now call a middle class.

But self-dealing plutocrats had long since invented workarounds to thwart this system, buying out extra lots under false names. By the late second century BC, according to the later Greek essayist Plutarch, wealthy landowners had dropped the pretense altogether and held vast tracts in their own names. That was the situation on the ground when Tiberius Gracchus, a daring nobleman whose charisma had earned him support from the common people, began canvassing for a government buyback that would redistribute the land more fairly.

According to Plutarch, Tiberius gave a moving speech in support of the new proposal: "The wild beasts that roam over Italy," he said, "have every one of them a cave or lair to lurk in; but the men who fight and die for Italy enjoy the common air and light, and nothing else. Without a house, without a home, they wander about with their wives and children."[22] The people must have felt that at last they had a voice.

Gracchus's movement was popular but ill-starred. First Tiberius and then his brother Gaius held the office of Tribune of the Plebs, in which capacity they were charged with defending the interests of the common man against the upper classes. But they were too dogged in executing that task to escape unharmed: a powerful coalition of the wealthy banded against the new arrangement, and both Gracchi brothers were killed in Rome's first episode of civic violence since the expulsion of the kings.

"No Roman was ever killed by a Roman, until Tiberius Gracchus," wrote the imperial historian Appian. From then on "the Romans openly took sides against each other" and "there were now many cases in which one man would not let go of power.... If one side took possession of Rome first, the other made war—in theory against the rival faction, but in fact against their own country."[23] Tiberius's death inaugurated one hundred years of bloodshed and terror that augured the eventual end of the republic.

Class warfare quickly devolved into mob chaos, and mob chaos—as surely as if Polybius himself had foretold it—created an opportunity for strongmen. First came the military dictatorship of General Cornelius Sulla, and then eventually the epoch-making reign of Augustus Caesar. Rome submitted to rule by one man. The empire was born, and peace, for a time, was restored.

A New Republic in a New World

More than 1700 years later, King George III's colonial subjects in America protested against Parliament's excessive taxation and unjust interference in their internal affairs. And so a group of American leaders declared that they should "dissolve the political bands" that connected the American colonies to Great Britain.

The aristocrats of the eighteenth century who devised the American republic undertook to establish a tripartite system, modeled on the Roman Republic and the tradition of English law and parliamentary government with which they were familiar. The new government would comprise an executive branch, led by the president, a legislative branch in Congress, elected by the citizenry, and a judicial branch appointed by the executive to adjudicate national court cases.

Unlike Machiavelli, the founders were moralists. But they also took a *realpolitik* view of humanity and the need to guard a Republic so that it would not fall as Rome's had done. America's founders had also to contend with the sheer size of the land they intended to govern, and the territorial expansion they had planned. It was in disputes over the division of land, they well knew, that the Roman Republic was eventually destroyed. Conventional wisdom at the time—articulated most memorably by the French theorist Charles Louis de Secondat, Baron de Montesquieu—was that "it is natural for a republic to have only a small territory. Otherwise it cannot last long."[24]

The Antifederalists, who opposed ratifying the proposed constitution of the United States, raised this very objection. If the republic were to endure, authority had to be invested primarily and overwhelmingly in the separate states. As debates raged in the late 1780s over whether to ratify the Constitution, its defenders set out their arguments in a series of newspaper essays that became known as the *Federalist Papers*.

In the 10th of these *Federalist Papers*, James Madison argued that a large population would in fact be an advantage, not a threat, for the new republic's health and longevity. A large people spread over a wide space would have more room to negotiate and compromise with one another, he argued: "Extend the sphere, and you take in a greater variety of parties and interests; you make it less probable that a majority of the whole will have a common motive to invade the rights of other citizens; or if such a common motive exists, it will be more difficult for all who feel it to discover their own strength, and to act in unison with each other."

America's broad expanse, Madison hoped, would dissipate class or factional tensions rather than exacerbate them:

> The influence of factious leaders may kindle a flame within their particular States, but will be unable to spread a general conflagration through the other States. A religious sect may degenerate into a political faction in a part of the Confederacy; but the variety of sects dispersed over the entire face of it must secure the national councils against any danger from that source. A rage for paper money, for an abolition of debts, for an equal division of property, or for any other improper or wicked project, will be less apt to pervade the whole body of the Union than a particular member of it; in the same proportion as such a malady is more likely to taint a particular county or district, than an entire State.

More space would mean more tolerance in the true sense—not that every American community needed to approve of every other, but that all of them, if they obeyed the Constitution and laws handed down by Congress, could be free to compete and coexist within a federal union. Unless a truly egregious set of circumstances galvanized a real majority of the whole people to take up arms, radical movements would have little chance of upsetting the general peace.

Once you understand the intentions behind this arrangement, you can begin to see why the politics of the early twenty-first century have been so profoundly alarming to Americans of almost every political party. Instinctively if not explicitly, Americans can sense that they are facing not just the prospect of political change but the gradual erosion of civic peace. In this sense, comparisons between the present and the 1860s, when civil war really did break out, are understandable (if somewhat overblown). Riots in the street and at the Capitol building alike suggest that growing numbers of people feel shut out of American political and economic arrangements.

People take to the streets when they feel, as the Roman veterans did, that their fortunes are being managed with little reference to their own actual needs or desires. More and more Americans sense that their daily lives are governed, not by local governments that they can control, but by a small, closed set of people—a virtual oligarchy of the heads of Big Tech, Big Media, and Big Government—who wield extraordinary power over the entire nation. Considering the diverse and expansive republican America that Madison envisioned, this is a catastrophe.

We are toying with the kinds of forces that can easily undo a republic, as Polybius and Machiavelli observed and documented. It is not simply a passing set of run-of-the-mill political issues (arguments over taxation or regulation), or a rocky period in our history: it is a full-on regime crisis, an instability in the basic foundations of how our politics now operates. And it is not going away in the span of one election cycle. The problems are "systemic" and "structural" (to use two words now much in vogue). That being the case, one wonders whether the American republic can survive.

CHAPTER 10

Political Love

The Empire That Never Was

America is starting to feel like an ailing republic at home and a failed empire overseas. America, and the liberal order it imposed and upheld after the Second World War, became the first worldwide hegemon—without ever acknowledging the fact. And despite the triumphant thrill of seeing the Berlin Wall come down in 1989, America's general trajectory of global dominance appears to be heading into swift decline, to be replaced by a strategically disciplined and increasingly ruthless Communist China.

"The failures of the war [in Afghanistan] reveal a need for deeper introspection into what has gone wrong with American democracy and its institutions—including the story of failed expertise," wrote former Columbia University research fellow Richard Hanania in the *New York Times* in 2021.[1] In other words, protracted ineptitude abroad should be the occasion for serious introspection at home—where, unfortunately, the picture is similarly bleak. "The three jobs with the most projected growth in [America] all earn less than $27,000 a year, and . . . all the secondary institutions that once gave structure and meaning to hundreds of millions of American lives—jobs and unions but also local newspapers, churches, Rotary Clubs, main streets—have been decimated," wrote Alana Newhouse, editor-in-chief of *Tablet* magazine, shortly after the 2020 election.[2] Newhouse cited Michael Lind from the University of Texas, who has argued extensively that a new ruling elite, led in large part by tech magnates, has used the "global economy" to depress American wages and offshore American jobs, creating a permanent and growing underclass.

Digital technology, which holds out such promise and potential to decentralize power, has in effect often worked to consolidate power among a very few. The upshot is that the republic has begun to look more like a corrupt oligarchy, run by those who may be good at getting wealthy or climbing bureaucratic ladders, but who have little respect for, or even knowledge of, republican ideals. The unprecedented COVID lockdowns imposed in 2020 made it hard to think of ourselves anymore as Madison's locally governed nation of free men and women with irrevocable, God-given rights. The national lockdown, imposed on the advice of an unelected medical expert (and the highest paid member of a federal administrative perma-state), gave leeway for state and local leaders to invoke "emergency" powers of their own that treated "unalienable rights" as very alien indeed. The lockdowns, mask mandates, and the tolerance in many locales for 2020's Antifa and Black Lives Matter protests—which resulted in $2 billion dollars' worth of property damage, 700 injured law enforcement officers, and as many as 19 deaths[3]—led some to wonder whether their fundamental right to property or even life was simply forfeit when the ruling class deemed it so. It came to seem as if major decisions about Americans' personal and civic lives were no longer in the hands of Americans themselves.

The New Marxism

Barring secession—which would likely be catastrophic and bloody—there are limited options when a republic starts decaying into oligarchy. One is the option proposed by the German philosophers Karl Marx and Friedrich Engels back in the 1800s: a revolution that totally restructures society and fundamentally rearranges its economy.

In *The German Ideology*, Marx and Engels articulated what they called "the materialist conception of history." Frustrated with the high abstraction of earlier German philosophers, most notably certain followers of Friedrich Hegel, Marx began from the premise that man is not fundamentally a political or a rational animal but an economic one: "Men can be distinguished from animals by consciousness, by religion, or by whatever else you prefer. They themselves begin to distinguish themselves from animals as soon as they begin to produce their means of subsistence, a step which is conditioned by their physical organization."[4] To Marx, man's gods, his myths, his dreams, and his high ideals are not, as I have been arguing throughout this book, intimations of supernatural truth. Instead, they are pretexts, misapprehensions, and justifications that emerge reliably out of what Wordsworth called "getting and spending."[5] Material wealth and survival is what drives mankind and guides his actions.

Thus Marx deemed republican political theory, like most other high ideals, as mere window-dressing that allowed the powerful to disguise—from their subjects and from themselves—a mere struggle for power. "In an age and in a country where royal power, aristocracy, and bourgeoisie contend for mastery, and where mastery is therefore shared, the doctrine of the separation of powers proves dominant and is expressed as an 'eternal law.'"[6] In reality, though, it is only another means to subjugate the working class.

In America, decades of leftist political activism has shifted Marxism from its primary economic focus to an "intersectional" one, in which aggrieved minorities, especially racial minorities, play the part of the working class.[7] Marx's shadow looms behind liberalism's ever more intense skepticism about Western civilization and American ideals, and as such Neo-Marxism goes far beyond socialism. Marx's own theory was largely about class and class warfare. But in the mid-twentieth century, America's robust middle class made it difficult to animate a revolution based on purely economic resentments. So "class" became a matter not simply of money, but of other identity markers as well. In Europe, Marxists like Antonio Gramsci and Rudi Dutschke helped move cultural issues to the fore. In America, theorists like Ted Allen and Noel Ignatiev fixated on race and "white-skin privilege" as predominant fault lines in American society. "The first question is not 'can the white workers be radicalized?' but 'can the white radicals be radicalized?'" Allen wrote.[8] Could American Leftists be taught to see slavery as an ineradicable evil whose legacy underwrote and intensified all other forms of inequality? In this sense, Marx is the intellectual forefather of the identity-based grievances that currently dominate our political culture. "We actually do have an ideological frame," said Black Lives Matter co-founder, Patrisse Cullors. "We are trained Marxists."[9]

Marxism explains why "anti-racists" and other "woke" groups tend to believe that all intellectual arguments are reducible to material interests, making their opponents guilty of "false consciousness" or bad faith. Anti-racist theorists like Ibram X. Kendi and Robin DiAngelo insist that though you may *think* you aspire to colorblindness and meritocracy, those are just pretexts for consolidating the power and privilege you derive from ancient economic arrangements built on slavery and the exploitation of black labor. Your "white fragility" is in effect one expression of your class allegiance. "The very heartbeat of racism is denial," said Kendi in an address at the University of Rochester.[10]

Neo-Marxist convictions also explain why political groups like the Democratic Socialists of America constantly yoke other alleged inequalities to calls for economic redistribution of wealth. "Our fight to end capitalist exploitation is inextricably tied to our fight to end oppression," their platform declares: "A democratic socialist society must end all systemic domination, whether it's based on race, religion, ethnic origin, sexual orientation, disability, or gender."[11]

If indeed our problems in America are at heart the result of a class struggle between an oligarchic elite and an oppressed underclass, then a

Marxist would argue the only way out is to overturn the system altogether—not only the republic but the whole method of trade and incentives known as "capitalism," because, for Marx, capitalism underlies monarchies, republics, and oligarchies. The only way to escape their problems is through a Communist revolution, "revolutionizing the existing world," and "attacking and changing existing things."[12] The people must rise up, seize control of the means of production, and form a government where all goods are held in common and distributed according to need.

This is why America's far Left turns to rioting more readily than its far Right—and with much more encouragement from mainstream figures and politicians. For conservatives or reactionaries, revolution remains a last resort. For Marxists, it is always and everywhere the only solution—one to be hastened and encouraged at every turn. "There needs to be unrest in the streets for as long as there's unrest in our lives," said Congresswoman Ayanna Pressley during the summer of 2020.[13] Marxism's guiding idea is that the whole cultural, economic, and political system, root and branch, must be revolutionized until private property is abolished and inequality eradicated for good.

Fine Wine

Leaving aside for a moment the many failures and atrocities that have attended previous socialist and communist uprisings, it is worth noting that abolishing private property is not a suggestion that originated with Marx. Already in the *Republic*, Plato could see what Rome would learn and what Machiavelli would describe: economic resentment is a deadly danger to the health of a regime. That is why he suggested that rulers, at least, should live in a state of total *koinōnia*—a Greek word meaning "having things in common."

Plato's version of *koinōnia* looks remarkably like a communist utopia. Not only property, but families, are shared: "the possession of women, marriage, and procreation of children must as far as possible be arranged according to the proverb that friends have all things in common."[14] In the *Communist Manifesto*, Marx and Engels also called for the "abolition of the family," a demand which was recently renewed by the feminist theorist Sophie Lewis. In her book *Full Surrogacy Now: Feminism Against Family*, Lewis argues that a truly just society would be one in which "we break down our assumptions that children 'belong' to those whose genetics they share."[15]

"Want true equity? California should force parents to give away their children," wrote Joe Matthews in *The San Francisco Chronicle*. Matthews cited Plato as support for the idea that "the rich should give their children to the poor, and the poor should give their children to the rich."[16] The principle behind free love is the same as that behind communism: If competition and resentment is destroying the peace, why not share everything and abolish envy altogether?

The answer to this question is nearly as old as the communist impulse itself. Responding to Plato's suggestion, Aristotle made what remains a succinct and effective attack on communism, which ought to disqualify it as the solution to America's or anyone's political problems. In the end it is *philia*—friendship, or love—that binds political communities together. And "just as mixing a little wine with a lot of water makes the wine impossible to taste," so too does holding all property and family in common dilute the character and quality of personal affection. So "a law like that will necessarily have the opposite of the desired result . . . for in cities, we think that the highest good is love."[17]

This explains why calls for communal childcare slide seamlessly into the promotion of child*lessness*: "I've been opening up about how I do not enjoy being a mom," tweeted the writer Arianna Rebolini to the tune of 12,000 "likes." "I think a large part is my belief that normalizing (/celebrating!) the decision to be childfree can lead to more communal childcare."[18] The profusion of articles by parents who regret having children, or people who think the world isn't worth bringing children into, suggests that our newfound desire to share child-rearing comes along with a diminished desire to have children at all.[19] Communism dilutes love.

Love, responsibility, and ownership go together. Tacitly but reliably, holding property in common means valuing it less.

The love we feel for our own home, for our own children, for *this* woman or *this* friend and no other—for what is *ours* and no one else's—forms the basis of all real and lasting political union. To be someone's friend is to "desire for him the things that you believe to be good, not for your own sake, but for his—and to be inclined, so far as you can, to bring those good things about."[20] People become friends for various reasons: because they enjoy each other's company, because they have some advantage to offer each other, or simply and purely because they recognize one another's excellence of character. But there is a certain kind of friendship—a certain kind of love—which comes into being between neighbors.

People who share space and time, who develop rituals of "intermarriage, family allegiances, festivals, and all the other pastimes of living together" are, maybe without knowing it, engaged in what Aristotle calls "a labor of love." They are about the business of creating another, more natural kind of *koinōnia* than the one that Plato theorized, or that Marx hoped would come through revolution. The basic routines of life together are, for Aristotle, the building blocks of politics. They are the stuff of the small-c constitution, the framework of family devotion and economic partnership that turns a group of people from a random ethnic or geographical mass into a real political community. And the affection that suffuses this kind of life is called *politikē philia*—civic friendship, or civic love.[21]

In the modern era, it sounds naïve to suggest that mere love can fix our problems. We tend to assume that citizens of fractious, pluralistic, multiethnic republics cannot hope to share a common vision of higher truth. Instead, we imagine, they must get by on the minimal grounds of working together in mutual (largely economic) self-interest. Leo Strauss called this the "low but solid ground" of modern political philosophy: rather than joining together in shared faith, work, and love, citizens in the modern state seem to be little more than self-centered consumers who share nothing other than space.[22] Philosophers like Thomas Hobbes, John Locke, and John Stuart Mill have helped shape a vision of society organized on the lowest possible common denominator of safety, comfort, and non-intervention in each other's lives. It seems to have worked up to a point—but only up to a point, and its limitations as a political system have become more apparent as our own republic appears to degenerate. That is why "classical liberalism" has come under fire from critics, like political philosopher Patrick Deneen, who see within it seeds of our present spiritual emptiness, isolation, cultural uniformity, and loss of freedom.

We live next to one another in identical apartments stacked across a bland urban landscape; we rely on our leaders to arrange it so that everyone can order cheap goods from China on Amazon; government is a matter for bureaucrats. So long as we refrain from seriously inconveniencing or hurting one another, so long as we follow the bureaucratic *diktats*, nobody gets much into anybody else's business. Friendship in this society is irrelevant, including even the low kind of friendship that arises from shared ambition. Society is a mere non-aggression pact, a kind of indifference masquerading as love—which is to say, not love at all. Perhaps that is all we can expect from the modern state. Perhaps friendship of the kind Aristotle envisioned is impossible beyond the confines of a single city—maybe we are doomed to dilute our love after all.

But that is not how America's founders saw it. Taking leave of his presidency and bidding adieu to public service in his famous farewell address, George Washington told his citizens, "With slight shades of difference, you have the same religion, manners, habits, and political principles. You have in a common cause fought and triumphed together." He looked on his country with "that fervent love towards it which is so natural to a man who views in it the native soil of himself and his progenitors for several generations."[23]

In this same vein, John Adams wrote to the Massachusetts militia that "our Constitution was made only for a moral and religious People. It is wholly inadequate to the government of any other."[24] The letter of the law will be useless unless it guides a people who already share some common spirit—some mutual devotion to God and country that goes beyond simple self-preservation. The founders understood this, as did Lincoln: "We are not enemies, but friends," he said, pleading with a nation whose bonds of affection were fraying. "We must not be enemies. Though passion may have strained, it must not break our bonds of affection."[25] America cannot survive on its large-C Constitution alone. It needs a small-c constitution, too, a shared spirit of common purpose and ritual. And for that, we must become friends again.

What Comes Next

Much has been made of the argument over whether America is a "creedal" nation—that is, whether its existence depends wholly on maintaining certain beliefs, such as a dedication to individual liberty, or whether there is also some important ethnic and cultural component to our small-c constitution. And it is true that American identity, like Roman citizenship, has proven adaptable and extendible up to a point: it has been the nation's pride and joy to welcome and assimilate members of practically every nation and faith. Often immigrants—especially refugees from oppressive regimes like Cuba—demonstrate the deepest devotion possible to American values like freedom and impartial justice.

But just as no human soul floats abstracted in the air without a human body, just as no form becomes visible except when encapsulated in matter, so no creed is carried forward except in the common life and memory of a people. That is why conservatives object so strenuously to crises like the one that is unfolding at our southern border, where illegal immigration is at flood tide. It is not that "brown people" can't be good Americans. It is that a massive influx of people from outside would be a shock to *any* national system, let alone one as culturally anemic as America's in the 2020s. "The one absolutely certain way of bringing this nation to ruin . . . would be to permit it to become a tangle of squabbling nationalities," said Theodore Roosevelt in 1915.[26]

Roosevelt was discussing the now-ubiquitous phenomenon of "hyphen-ated Americans"—those who qualify their allegiance to this country by reserving some attachment to another national or cultural identity. Italian-Americans, Chinese-Americans, Muslim-Americans, and so on may all in practice be devoted patriots. But in principle it is a manner of speaking which dilutes the character of citizenship. Not for nothing were new arrivals required by the Naturalization Act of 1795 to "renounce forever all allegiance and fidelity to any foreign prince, potentate, state or sovereignty whatever."[27]

The antidote to social crackup is not more openness but more cohe-sion, more careful attention to the ancestral memory and shared history of the people already struggling to live together in this country. Rhet-oric that is truly "divisive" and "partisan" is not that which invokes America's national identity but that which encourages Americans to think of one another in terms of race, sex, or even vaccination status. In this context consider what it means that President Biden and his administration regularly talked in terms of a "pandemic of the unvac-cinated"—as if some portion of the American citizenry was tantamount to a disease. Consider also what it means that Brittney Cooper, a pro-fessor at Rutgers University, said publicly that "I think that white people are committed to being villains in the aggregate."[28] Examples of this sort of talk abound, and they are truly corrosive. The most damning indictment of our political and cultural elites is that they seem dedicated, with almost every word and action, to eroding the civic friendship that remains our only real hope of survival and restoration. Too many of our leaders seek to be demagogues, exploiting the already tense divisions between us for their own venal ends.

The net effect of our bitter national politics is to alienate us from ourselves and each other, to get us thinking in grand terms of epochal crisis and tribal warfare. And to make matters worse we may well *be* living through an epochal crisis of the kind Polybius would have recog-nized. Faced with foreign policy incompetence and retreat, and a heavy-handed, self-dealing, and disingenuous federal bureaucracy— the global and federal nature of our apparently imminent collapse—it's common for average citizens, people with no formal political power except the vote, to feel either helpless or reckless. Whether we riot or simply surrender, we suspect the cycle of regimes is crushing us under foot, no matter how we might fight back.

But the way out of this mess, paradoxically, is to think smaller and not bigger. The truth is that you and I are *not*, in fact, powerful enough to Save America or Save the World. Nor indeed will we get anywhere by continuing to think only in grand abstractions, even lofty and noble ones like "America," "the republic," or indeed "the West." We need those ideals to guide us, it is true—if I did not think so, I would not have written this book. But one article of wisdom that comes down to us through the history of Western thought is that all such high ideals are embodied in the small concerns and daily activities of the here and now. We fight for them by living them out in our own lives, and we preserve them by taking some part of them into ourselves. If it is true that our regime crisis is a failure of civic friendship, then the antidote is not grand schemes to redistribute wealth or overturn the 2020 election but re-investment in our neighbors *as* our neighbors.

"If anyone says, 'I love God,' but hates his brother, he is a liar. For the man who hates his brother, whom he has seen, cannot love God, whom he has not seen" (1 John 4:20). All politics is local, and the bonds of civic friendship are formed locally: face to face, shoulder to shoulder, at the volunteer fire department, in church, on Little League baseball fields. Social media has obscured this to a large degree, because it creates the illusion that everyone is equally close to us and all concerns are equally, crushingly, ours to bear. But it is not so: we are still and will always be embodied souls, human beings in time and place with other people near to us who share our concerns.

Here's an exercise to try: conduct a searching inventory of your emotional state. Are you anxious? Dejected? Fearful? Dismayed? Now ask yourself how much of that feeling is related to things that are actually going on around you in physical space, and how much of it is about catastrophic disasters that you fear happening "out there." If the atmosphere of your emotional world is more directly tied to your Twitter feed than to how your kids are doing at school or your relationship with your wife, something is deeply wrong.

This is not at all to say that when you turn your attention to the people and things immediately surrounding you, there will be no problems to contend with. There might be terrible problems like drug addiction, child abuse, contentious school board meetings over racial and sexual extremism, or the threat or reality of poverty. But the strangely comforting thing about even these problems is that they are *you*-sized: unlike the global disasters which you perceive or imagine, your personal and local problems represent the potential for you and those around you to get on with the actual work of civic engagement and republican friendship. In this context you actually can make things better—as parents around the country are starting to do with their local schools, and as ordinary people do every day, over the breakfast table and on the street, in acts of charity and kindness. The burden of building a family and cherishing it, the burden of fighting through the rubble of this broken world toward the good, the true, and the beautiful: *these* burdens, no more and no less, are yours to bear.

When you do get about that work, you may find that the tribal designations you have attached to yourself hold less and less weight. It may surprise you to learn that a "Republican" is not actually a type of person, and neither is a "Democrat." In our transformative age of realignment, the divide is really, more than anything, between people who want to live in the real world—the world where there are two sexes, kids are important, and the weak need protecting—and people who want to deny or upend that world.

Seek the people who want to live in reality, and you may find yourself side by side with hunters *and* environmentalists, Trump voters *and* old-school feminists. You may also find that some aspects of high tech can help you, rather than hurt you, in restoring peace to some small patch of your community. What if cryptocurrency, for example, could help you shore up your financial assets and start your own online business? The irony is that digital technology, if we use it well, has the potential to make us *more* independent from urban centers. The internet can free some of us to work remotely while we live in small towns and devote ourselves to local communities, rather than flocking into densely populated hubs where "all the action is happening." San Francisco and New York do not have to be the center of the world anymore. That is in our power too—if we choose to use new technology wisely.

None of these things is going to transform the course of history on its own. But all of them will get you back in the saddle of your own life and give you real agency. They will get you thinking like a citizen of a republic, with friends and fellow citizens at your side. There are still times, thank God, when we are called upon to vote and campaign and demonstrate—for presidents and senators and congressmen—who have power to shape national politics. When we do, we should demand that they show seriousness about representing our real interests—including and especially breaking up the tech monopolies which commodify us and our tribal allegiances while accruing unaccountable power over our communications technology. But in order even to know what our major concerns really are, we will need to know what life is really like in our neighborhoods, our cities, and our states.

That means going to the farmers' market, to city council meetings, and, yes, even to church. There is no getting around this. Classical liberalism, republican liberty, and even the American Constitution: none of it was meant to survive on its own. They are jewels set in a crown, upheld and supported only by the grand traditions of the West, including worship. Our inalienable rights are granted to us by a *Creator*—for that sentence to make any sense at all, the word "Creator" has to mean something.

I have stressed throughout this book that all the good and noble things we want to fight for cannot exist unless God does. And there will be no "saving the republic," no "escaping the cycle of regimes," without God. The reason we all feel so anxious to save the world is because we don't trust that He is there to do that job. And so we take upon ourselves world-saving responsibilities for which we are quite laughably unequipped. But it will be He who determines whether our republic stands or falls, and whether this nation tomorrow goes the way that all nations must one day go. And if it does, then only He will endure and only our investment in Him will have turned out not to have been in vain.

Because the West, which is God's, does not depend on the survival of America. The truth, which is His, has endured the rising and falling of many nations, the coming and going of the cities that were great in Herodotus's youth and the empire that once belonged to Rome. When the princes of the world are deposed, when powers that seemed eternal vanish like the Persian dust, there are things that remain.

Even for all the manuscripts that are lost heedlessly or burned in war, for all the towers that come crashing down, some things—the memory of lost republics, the nagging conviction that justice is eternal—endure. They endure because they too are God's.

After defecting from the Soviet underground, Whittaker Chambers, even in his darkest mood, wrote of "snatching a fingernail of a saint from the rack or a handful of ashes from the faggots" to preserve for a better day "when a few men begin again to dare to believe that there was once something else."

No one knows the hour or the day when Rome will fall. No one knows the role he will play in history's retrospect. But you and I wake up every day in a world that is real, surrounded by people who are also real, and that is enough. It is everything. And if you and I wake up determined that we will live as if the eternal truths handed down to us by our ancestors are as real as ourselves and the world around us—if we do that in faith, then that's better than good. That is how to save the West.

A Few Last Words

Max Planck, forefather of quantum theory, had a saying: "that is real which can be measured." Perhaps he simply meant that if you can measure something, it exists. But if he meant that *only* measurable things exist, then in some sense this book can be read as an extended argument against Planck—an argument that the things which *cannot* be measured are the realest things of all. If there is one thing I hope you will take away from all these reflections on the current state of the West, it is this: hold on to what is truly real.

From Plato's cave on down to the days of virtual reality we are in a constant fight to see our way beyond the borders of our own solipsism, to recognize that certain truths are immutable whether we choose them or not. Beauty, love, virtue: these things are what they are wherever and whenever we find them, even if living them out looks different in every age.

Yet even though these ultimate realities are not figments of our imagination, they are also not matter that we can simply see and touch. The excellence of courage and the majesty of nature make themselves known to us in the immeasurable spaces of our minds: the yearning quality of our memories when we look back on meeting our first love, or the rush of triumph we feel scaling a mountain, even if our bodies are straining to the point of agony. The thing in us which knows truth and beauty is called a soul.

And though the soul is not a physical thing, it is the organizing principle of our bodies—which means our flesh has a purpose. This explains why so many basic facts are currently out of fashion or under assault—that there are two sexes, that it is good to be healthy, that beauty exists. These basic realities point us toward the deeper truth that what we are is more than mere atoms to be reconfigured or edited or manipulated at will by machinists. We are embodied souls, rational animals, whose purpose is to seek excellence at being ourselves—at being human.

Everything, from your exercise routine to your sex life, has this purpose. Your life is not some toy for you to bat listlessly at in search of a new thrill. It is a holy thing, made holy by the fact that everything you do and say has meaning. Ultimately, like it or not, you are going to want more than to languish in a tiny apartment smoking weed and uploading your consciousness to the cloud. You may find some numbness or pleasure in that kind of life for a while, and it may be advertised to you as an exciting freedom of limitless possibility. But in reality it will turn out to be a paralyzing kind of freedom, a flat plane of infinite choice where it looks as if nothing is more valuable than anything else.

We know this is not so: all our experience with art, with culture, and with the very structure of our DNA suggests that this earthly life we live points us to something higher and better, toward those old eternal truths and beauties that Plato longed for and Saint Paul saw through a glass darkly. The whole world is encoded with *meaning*, and meaning suggests a basic truth.

That basic truth is the existence of God, the realest thing there is. He has not been disproven by science or rendered obsolete by technology. In fact, the limitless possibility of technology makes Him even more necessary as a guiding force, and science increasingly requires Him to make sense of what it is discovering. You do not have to accept the Nicene Creed overnight. But if you do not, you should ask yourself why you *do not want* to believe. Given what belief in God entails, a healthy human person *should want* to believe. In a way, you likely already do. You believe your life and your actions have meaning. The cloud of anxiety and impending doom that hovers over social media comes from the frenzy of people searching for meaning, because they have lost the meaning that is right in front of them. You do not need to be a part of that madness: sanity lies on the side of your better instincts, the instincts that tell you that what you do in life matters, and that reality is in fact real.

We are at a crucial juncture in history, when the forces at work are exactly the kind that can pull a republic apart and dissolve an empire. But if that is so, then the one thing most needful is civic friendship, the bond of mutual respect that comes from working together with real people, in real time, to solve immediate problems. Salvation is not going to come from one grand election. It will come gradually, among people doing the daily things that have always built the West: starting families, going to church, working, saving, investing, feeding the hungry, clothing the naked, and comforting the afflicted.

In all this, the question "how's that working out for you?" is a perfect diagnostic test. If some practice is making you sick, depressed, fat, and ashamed in the here and now, there is no reason to listen to anyone who tells you that same practice will soon change your life for the better if you just do more of it. Our obsession with studies and statistics has made us distrustful of our own immediate experience. But happiness and human flourishing are to be sought and found precisely through the trial and error of our own lives, guided by the wisdom of those who lived good lives before us.

Excellence is not something to be dreamed of "out there" or to be hoped for from a utopia that will materialize if we make ourselves a little bit more miserable in the short term, or if we embark on yet another communist revolution of the kind that, in practice, has always ended in nothing but immiseration, tyranny, and executions. Joy is not something to be manufactured with more drugs, nor virtue something to be play-acted on an imaginary landscape called the "world stage." The best and realest things you will do, will be done at home while playing with your kids, or at church, or at work, or at the town hall. You are not going to save the world. You are going, God willing, to seek virtue and love justice in the city where you find yourself.

If digital technology has distracted us from all this, it has also given us tools that we do not need anyone's permission to use: vast online libraries, new forms of currency, and innovative sources of income. There is only one thing powerful enough to make the difference between a drugged and docile future controlled by oligarchs, and a future shaped by the agency of individual humans who are strengthened, and not dominated, by technology. That one thing is the human soul. Ancient and invisible though it is, it still exists—it is the realest thing about you, and you must hold on to what is truly real.

"Finally, brothers," wrote Saint Paul in his letter to Europe's first Christian church, in the Macedonian city of Philippi, "whatever is true, whatever is honorable, whatever is just, whatever is sacred, whatever merits love or admiration—if anything is excellent or laudable—devote your attention to these things. Whatever you have learned or received or heard or seen in me, put it into practice" (4:8). Goodness, truth, and beauty are, in the last analysis, things which you can know and grasp in your immediate surroundings.

Let no one talk you out of your instincts: in your heart of hearts, with time and prayer, you can learn to see what is honorable, right, pure, and lovely. To defend the West itself, we must *be* the West: we have to live it in our everyday lives. You are a thing fearfully and wonderfully made for the glory of God, and you can live like it. I cannot promise you that your life will be happy. But I can promise that wherever you are, however well or badly things are going right now, your life has meaning. I can promise that truth, beauty, and goodness are not figments of your imagination or accidents of your biology—that they exist, and that you are a creature designed to seek them. Nothing is more real than that.

Bibliography

Abramovitch, Seth. "Sam Hyde Speaks." *The Hollywood Reporter.* December 8, 2018. https://www.hollywoodreporter.com/news/ general-news/sam-hyde-speaks-meet-man-behind-adul- swims-canceled-alt-right-comedy-show-954487/

"About." Black Lives Matter. https://blacklivesmatter.com/about/.

Acharya, Sourya, and Samarth Shukla. "Mirror Neurons." *Journal of Natural Science Biology and Medicine* 3.2 (2012): 118–24.

Dalberg-Acton, John. "The History of Freedom in Antiquity." February 26, 1877. https://www.acton.org/research/ history-freedom-antiquity.

Adams, John. "Letter to the Massachusetts Militia." Founders Online. October 11, 1789. https://founders.archives.gov/documents/Adams /99-02-02-3102.

———. "Letter to John Rogers." Founders Online. February 6, 1801. https://founders.archives.gov/documents/Adams/99-02-02-4799.

Alighieri, Dante. *The Divine Comedy.* Translated by Allen Mandelbaum. New York: Knopf, 1980.

Allen, Joe. "Transhumanists Gather in Spain to Plan Global
    Transformation." *The Federalist.* October 15, 2021. https://
    thefederalist.com/2021/10/15/transhumanists-gather-in-spain
    -to-plan-global-transformation/.
Allen, Theodore. "Can White Workers Radicals Be Radicalized?" In
    Revolutionary Youth and the New Working Class, edited by Carl
    Davidson, 167–81. Pittsburgh, PA: Changemaker, 2011.
Allison, David, ed. *The New Nietzsche.* New York: Delta, 1977.
American Psychiatric Association. *Diagnostic and Statistical Manual
    of Mental Disorders, Fifth Edition.* Washington, D.C.: American
    Psychiatric Publishing, 2013.
Anderson, Mike B., dir. *The Simpsons.* Season 16, episode 15, "Future
    Drama." Aired April 17, 2005, on Fox.
Anthony, Andrew. "You Ask the Questions." *The Guardian,* 19
    March 2017. https://www.theguardian.com/culture/2017/mar/19
    /yuval-harari-sapiens-readers-questions-lucy-prebble-arianna
    -huffington-future-of-humanity.
Appiah, Kwame Anthony. "There is No Such Thing as Western
    Civilization." *The Guardian,* November 9, 2016. https://www
    .theguardian.com/world/2016/nov/09/western-civilisation
    -appiah-reith-lecture.
Appian. *The Civil Wars.* Translated by John Carter. London: Penguin,
    1996.
Aquinas, Thomas. *The Summa Theologica of Saint Thomas Aquinas.*
    Translated by Fathers of the English Dominican Province. 2nd ed.
    Notre Dame, IN: Christian Classics, 1981.
Aristophanes, Four Plays: Clouds, Birds, Lysistrata, Women of the
    Assembly. Trans. Aaron Poochigian. New York: Liveright, 2021.
Aristophanes and Plato. *Four Texts on Socrates: Plato's* Euthyphro,
    Apology, *and* Crito *and Aristophanes'* Clouds. Translated by
    Thomas G. West. Ithaca, NY: Cornell University Press, 1984.
Aristotle. *De Anima.* Translated by Christopher Shields. Oxford:
    Oxford University Press, 2016.

———. *Metaphysics.* Translated by Hugh Lawson-Tancred. London: Penguin Classics, 1998.

———. *Physics.* Translated by C. D. C. Reeve. Indianapolis, IN: Hackett, 2018.

———. *Poetics.* Translated by Stephen Halliwell. London: Bristol Classical Press, 1998.

———. *Politics.* Translated by Carnes Lord. Chicago: University of Chicago Press, 1984.

———. *Art of Rhetoric.* Translated by Robert C. Bartlett. Chicago: University of Chicago Press, 2019.

Asa-El, Amotz. "The American Empire is Ready to End." *Jerusalem Post*, August 27, 2021. https://www.jpost.com/international /the-american-empire-is-ready-to-end-677831.

Augustine. *The Confessions.* Translated by Henry Chadwick. Oxford: Oxford University Press, 2008.

Bacardi, Francesca. "Kardashian Team Working Hard to Remove Unwanted Khloé Photo." *Page Six*, April 5, 2021. https://pagesix .com/2021/04/05/kardashian-team-working-hard-to-remove -unwanted-khloe-photo/.

Bacon, Francis. *Novum Organum.* Edited by Lisa Jardine and Michael Silvertorne. Cambridge: Cambridge University Press, 2000.

Baldas, Tresa. "Feds: FBI Informant Tried to Help the Whitmer Kidnap Plot Suspects." *Detroit Free Press*, January 6, 2022. https://www.freep.com/story/news/local/michigan/2022/01/06 /fbi-informant-tried-help-whitmer-kidnap-plot-suspects /9120090002/.

Ball, Matthew. "Evolving User + Business Behaviors and the Metaverse." The Metaverse Primer, MatthewBall.vc, June 28, 2021. https://www.matthewball.vc/all/userbehaviorsmetaverse.

Balleza, Maureen, and Kate Zernike, "Memos on Bush are Fake But Accurate, Typist Says." *New York Times*, September 15, 2004. https://www.nytimes.com/2004/09/15/us/the-2004

-campaign-national-guard-memos-on-bush-are-fake-but-accurate
.html.

Barbaro, Michael. "Microsoft and the Metaverse." Produced by
Daniel Guillemette, Rachelle Bonja, Eric Krupke and Luke Vander
Ploeg. *New York Times*, January 20, 2022. https://www.nytimes
.com/2022/01/20/podcasts/the-daily/metaverse-microsoft
-activision-blizzard.html.

de Beauvoir, Simone. *The Second Sex*. Translated by Constance Borde
and Sheila Malovany-Chevallier. New York: Vintage Books, 2009.

Beckett, Louis. "At Least 25 Americans Were Killed During Protests
and Political Unrest in 2020." *The Guardian*, October 31, 2020.
https://www.theguardian.com/world/2020/oct/31
/americans-killed-protests-political-unrest-acled.

Benner, Katie, Kenneth P. Vogel, and Michael S. Schmidt. "Hunter
Biden Paid Tax Bill, but Broad Federal Investigation Continues."
New York Times, March 16, 2022. https://www.nytimes.com
/2022/03/16/us/politics/hunter-biden-tax-bill-investigation.html.

Bernstein, Richard. "In Dispute on Bias, Stanford is Likely to Alter
Western Culture Program." *New York Times*, January 19, 1988.
https://www.nytimes.com/1988/01/19/us/in-dispute-on-bias
-stanford-is-likely-to-alter-western-culture-program.html.

Brian Bethune, "Was Jan. 6 the Beginning of the End for America?"
Maclean's, January 4, 2022. https://www.macleans.ca/politics
/washington/was-jan-6-the-beginning-of-the-end-for-america/.

Bettelheim, Bruno. *The Uses of Enchantment: The Meaning and
Importance of Fairy Tales*. London: Thames & Hudson, 1976.

Blackmore, Susan. *The Meme Machine*. Oxford: Oxford University
Press, 1999.

Bostrom, Nick. "Why I Want to Be Posthuman When I Grow Up." In
Medical Enhancement and Posthumanity (107-137), edited by
Bert Gordijn and Ruth Chadwick. Berlin: Springer. 2008.

Bovard, Rachel. "What the New Right Must Do Next Time It Earns
Power." *The Federalist*, November 4, 2021. https://thefederalist
.com/2021/11/04/national-conservatism-must-prioritize

-fights-over-american-values-not-just-legislation/#.YZKJPifzRh8
.sms.

Boynton, Emily. "It's OK if You Gained Weight During the Stay-at-Home Order." Right as Rain, June 24, 2020. https://rightasrain
.uwmedicine.org/mind/well-being/body-image.

Bradbury, Ray. *Fahrenheit 451*. New York: Simon & Schuster, 1953.

Brennan, Margaret, and Anthony Fauci. "Transcript: Dr. Anthony Fauci on 'Face the Nation.'" *CBS News*, November 28, 2021. https://www.cbsnews.com/news/transcript-dr-anthony-fauci
-on-face-the-nation-november-28-2021/.

Burke, Edmund. *Reflections on the Revolution in France*, edited by Conor O'Brien. London: Penguin, 1982.

Butler, Judith. *Gender Trouble*. New York: Routledge, 1990.

Calvin, John. *Institutes of the Christian Religion*. Edited by John T. McNeill. Translated by Ford Lewis Battles. Philadelphia, PA: The Westminster Press, 1960.

Carrington, Damian. "Want to Fight Climate Change? Have Fewer Children." *The Guardian*, July 12, 2017. https://www.theguardian
.com/environment/2017/jul/12/want-to-fight-climate-change-have
-fewer-children.

CBS. "Baby Plays with iPad, is Frustrated by Paper Mag." YouTube. October 14, 2011. https://www.youtube.com/watch?v=
UoOJqeAbDaQ&feature=emb_title.

Chambers, Whittaker. *Odyssey of a Friend*, edited by William F. Buckley Jr. New York: National Review, 1970.

Chesterton, G. K. *Spiritual Classics Collection*. Independently published, 1908–1925.

———. *What I Saw in America*. London: Hodder and Stoughton, 1922.

Chu, Andrea Long. "My New Vagina Won't Make Me Happy." *New York Times*, November 24, 2018. https://www.nytimes.com/2018
/11/24/opinion/sunday/vaginoplasty-transgender-medicine.html.

"Citizen's Guide to Federal Law on Obscenity." Child Exploitation and Obscenity Section, United States Department of Justice,

November 9, 2021. https://www.justice.gov/criminal-ceos
/citizens-guide-us-federal-law-obscenity.

"Civic Integrity." Twitter. https://about.twitter.com/en/our-priorities
/civic-integrity.

Clinton, Bill. "Clinton's Grand Jury Testimony, Part 4." *Washington Post*, August 17, 1998. https://www.washingtonpost.com/wp-srv
/politics/special/clinton/stories/bctest092198_4.htm.

CNET Highlights. "Meta! Watch Zuckerberg Reveal Facebook's New Name." October 28, 2021. https://www.youtube.com/watch?v=
KIxPRwgXFQg.

Cohen, David. "What Does it Mean to be Posthuman?" *NewScientist*, May 8, 2013. https://www.newscientist.com/article/
mg21829162-400-what-does-it-mean-to-be-posthuman/.

Comte, Auguste. *The Positive Philosophy*. Translated by Harriet Martineau. Cambridge: Cambridge University Press, 1853.

"Connect." Meta. Accessed May 24, 2022. https://facebookconnect
.com/en-us/.

Conwall, Gail. "The Two Reasons Parents Regret Having Kids." *The Atlantic*, August 31, 2021, https://www.theatlantic.com/family
/archive/2021/08/why-parents-regret-children/619931/.

"Conway: Press Secretary Gave 'Alternative Facts,.'" *NBC News*, January 22, 2017. https://www.nbcnews.com/meet-the-press/video
/conway-press-secretary-gave-alternative-facts-860142147643.

Cooke, Mervyn, ed. *The Hollywood Film Music Reader*. Oxford: Oxford University Press, 2010.

Cooper, Darryl. "The Disillusionment of the Deplorables." *American Mind*, July 10, 2021. https://americanmind.org/salvo/
the-disillusionment-of-the-deplorables/.

Cragg, Michael. "Terrible Name, Terrific Sitcom: How Schitt's Creek Became a Surprise Hit." *The Guardian*, May 9, 2020. https://
www.theguardian.com/tv-and-radio/2020/may/09/terrible-name
-terrific-sitcom-how-schitts-creek-became-a-surprise-hit.

Daily Wire. "Daily Wire Backstage: Live at the Ryman." YouTube. Streamed October 12, 2021. https://www.youtube.com/watch?v= D3S9hSy0AKk.

D'Angour, Armand. *Socrates in Love: The Making of a Philosopher.* London: Bloomsbury, 2019.

Dawid, Richard. "Undetermination and Theory Succession from the Perspective of String Theory." *Philosophy of Science* 73.3 (July 2006): 298–322.

Dawkins, Richard. *The Extended Phenotype.* Oxford: Oxford University Press, 1982.

———. *The Selfish Gene.* 1st ed. 1976. 40th Anniversary ed., 2016. Oxford: Oxford University Press.

Daymare, EG. "No Joke: Untangling the DNA Code of Alt-Right Comedy." *Mute*, April 10, 2017. https://www.metamute.org /editorial/articles/no-joke-untangling-dna-code-alt-right-comedy.

Dee, Katherine. "Tumblr U." *American Mind*, July 16, 2021. https:// americanmind.org/salvo/tumblr-u/.

———. "Tumblr Transformed Online Politics." *American Conservative*, August 11, 2021. https://www .theamericanconservative.com/articles/tumblr-transformed -american-politics/.

Deutsch, David. *The Beginning of Infinity: Explanations that Transform the World.* London: Penguin, 2011.

Deneen, Patrick. *Why Liberalism Failed.* New Haven, CT: Yale University Press, 2018.

Dennett, Daniel. *Consciousness Explained.* Boston: Little, Brown, and Company, 1991.

Deoni, Sean C. L., Jennifer Beauchemin, Alexandra Volpe, Viren D'Sa, and the RESONANCE Consortium. "Impact of the COVID-19 Pandemic on Early Child Cognitive Development: Initial Findings in a Longitudinal Observational Study of Child Health," August 11, 2021. https://www.medrxiv.org/content/10.11 01/2021.08.10.21261846v1.full.pdf.

Descartes, René. *Discourse on Method and Meditations on First Philosophy.* Translated by Donald A. Cress. 4th ed. Indianapolis, IN: Hackett, 1998.

———. *Meditations on First Philosophy.* 2nd edition. Translated by John Cottingham. Cambridge: Cambridge University Press, 2017.

Deutsch, David. *The Beginning of Infinity: Explanations that Transform the World.* London: Penguin, 2011.

Douthat, Ross. *The Decadent Society: How We Became the Victims of Our Own Success.* New York: Avid Reader Press, 2020.

"DSA Political Platform." Democratic Socialists of America. https://www.dsausa.org/dsa-political-platform-from-2021-convention/.

DuBois, W. E. B. *Writings.* 1896-1940. Edited by Nathan Huggins. New York: Library of America, 1986.

Dunham, Hayden. "Pippa Gardner and Hayden Dunham on the Struggle of Being Inside Bodies." *Interview,* May 19, 2021. https://www.interviewmagazine.com/art/pippa-garner-and-hayden -dunham-on-the-struggle-of-being-inside-bodies?utm_source= twitter&utm_medium=social&utm_campaign=may21.

Eliot, T. S. *Collected Poems, 1906-1962.* San Diego: Harcourt Brace Jovanovich, 1991.

Ellis, George. "Does the Multiverse Really Exist?" *Scientific American,* August 1, 2011. https://www.scientificamerican.com /article/does-the-multiverse-really-exist/.

———, and Joe Silk. "Scientific Method: Defend the Integrity of Physics." *Nature* 516 (December 16, 2014): 321–23. https://www .nature.com/articles/516321a.

EMBER (@emberpearl) "'he's challenging gender norms,' and he's losing. the gender norms are beating his ass." *iFunny,* 2021. https://ifunny.co/picture/ember-he-s-challenging-gender-norms -and-he-s-losing-oLk0S9K69.

Engels, Friedrich, and Karl Marx. *The Marx-Engels Reader.* Edited by Robert C. Tucker. New York: W. W. Norton, 1978.

Erickson, Erick. "Watching 'Game of Thrones' as a Christian." *Medium*, July 19, 2017. https://medium.com/@ewerickson /watching-game-of-thrones-as-a-christian-5e7a3031cebf.

Fan, Wenxin, and Keith Zai. "China's Curbs on Videogames, Celebrity Fandom Seek to Make Kids Tougher." *Wall Street Journal*, September 1, 2021. https://www.wsj.com/articles /chinas-videogame-limits-signal-move-to-regulate-private -lives-shape-next-generation-11630437404.

Ferguson, Niall. *Colossus: The Rise and Fall of the American Empire*. New York: Hudson, 2004.

———. "Niall Ferguson on Why the End of the American Empire Won't Be Peaceful." *The Economist*, August 20, 2021. https:// www.economist.com/by-invitation/2021/08/20/niall-ferguson -on-why-the-end-of-americas-empire-wont-be-peaceful.

———. "Putin Misunderstands History. So, Unfortunately, Does the U.S.," *Bloomberg*, March 22, 2022. https://www.bloomberg.com /opinion/articles/2022-03-22/niall-ferguson-putin-and -biden-misunderstand-history-in-ukraine-war.

Feuerherd, Ben, and Laura Italiano. "Rapper Raz Simone Accused of being 'Warlord' in Seattle's Police-Free CHAZ." *New York Post*, June 12, 2020. https://nypost.com/2020/06/12/raz-simone -accused-of-acting-like-warlord-in-seattles-chaz/.

Frates, Elizabeth Pegg. "Did We Really Gain Weight During the Pandemic?" *Harvard Health Publishing*, October 5, 2021. https:// www.health.harvard.edu/blog/did-we-really-gain-weight-during -the-pandemic-202110052606.

Freud, Sigmund. *Totem and Taboo*. Translated by A. A. Brill. London: Routledge, 1919.

Gabriele, Matthew, and David Perry. "Steve King Says he was Just Defending 'Western Civilization.' That's Racist, Too." *Washington Post*, January 15, 2019. https://www.washingtonpost.com/outlook /2019/01/15/steve-king-says-he-was-just-defending-western -civilization-thats-racist-too/.

Gallese, Vittorio, Luciano Fadiga, Leonardo Fogassi, and Giacomo Rizzolatti. "Action Recognition in the Premotor Cortex." *Brain* 119 (1996): 593–609, https://doi.org/10.1093/brain/119.2.593.

Girard, René. *I See Satan Fall Like Lightning*. Translated by James G. Williams. New York: Orbis, 1999.

Gustini, Ray. "No One Knows Why Teens Aren't Having Sex." *The Wire*, March 4, 2011. https://www.theatlantic.com/national/archive/2011/03/teen-sex-decline/348607/.

Givens, Dana. "Rep. Ayanna Presley Calls for 'Unrest in the Streets' Over the Failures of the Trump Administration." *Black Enterprise*, August 17, 2020. https://www.blackenterprise.com/rep-ayanna-pressley-calls-for-unrest-in-the-streets-over-the-failures-of-the-trump-administration/.

Hamburger, Philip. "The Constitution Can Crack Section 230." *Wall Street Journal*, January 29, 2021. https://www.wsj.com/articles/the-constitution-can-crack-section-230-11611946851.

Hampton, Rachelle, and Madison Malone Kircher. "'Body Positivity' is Meaningless." *ICYMI*, produced by Slate, April 24, 2021. https://podcasts.apple.com/us/podcast/body-positivity-is-meaningless/id1554115325?i=1000518429299.

Hanania, Richard. "'Just Trust the Experts,' We're Told. We Shouldn't." *New York Times*, September 20, 2021. https://www.nytimes.com/2021/09/20/opinion/afghanistan-experts-expertise.html.

Hankins, James. "St. Basil's Guide to Cultural Appropriation." *First Things*, December 7, 2021. https://www.firstthings.com/web-exclusives/2021/12/st-basils-guide-to-cultural-appropriation.

Hannah-Jones, Nikole. "Our Democracy's Founding Ideals Were False When They Were Written. Black Americans Have Fought to Make Them True." *New York Times*, August 14, 2019. https://www.nytimes.com/interactive/2019/08/14/magazine/black-history-american-democracy.html.

Harari, Yuval Noah. *Homo Deus: A Brief History of Tomorrow*. New York: Harper, 2015.

Harrington, Mary. "The Fight Against Erasing Women." *American Mind*, October 19, 2021. https://americanmind.org/features/the-fight-against-erasing-women/.

Hatchett, Keisha. "*Foundation* EP on Centering Black Women in Apple TV+'s Sci-Fi Epic." *TV Line*. September 23, 2021. https://tvline.com/2021/09/23/foundation-apple-tv-plus-david-goyer-preview/.

Hawking, Stephen. *A Brief History of Time*. New York: Bantam, 1988.

———, and Leonard Mlodlinow. "Why God Did Not Create the Universe." *Wall Street Journal*, September 3, 2010. https://www.wsj.com/articles/SB100014240527487042068045755467921609024244.

Hayek, Friedrich. *The Road to Serfdom*. Chicago: University of Chicago Press, 1944.

Heidegger, Martin. *The Question Concerning Technology and Other Essays*. Translated by William Lovitt. New York: Harper Perennial, 1977.

Helprin, Mark. "Once More, With Feeling." *The Claremont Review of Books*, Fall 2021. https://claremontreviewofbooks.com/once-more-with-feeling/.

Herodotus of Halicarnassus. *The Histories*. Translated by Aubrey de Sélincourt. New York: Penguin, 1954, rev. 2003.

Hitchens, Christopher. *God is Not Great: How Religion Poisons Everything*. New South Wales: Allen & Unwin, 2007.

Ho, Rosemarie. "Want to Dismantle Capitalism? Abolish the Family." *The Nation*, May 16, 2019. https://www.thenation.com/article/archive/want-to-dismantle-capitalism-abolish-the-family/.

Hobbs, Tawnell D., and Lee Hawkins. "The Results are In for Remote Learning: It Didn't Work." *Wall Street Journal*, June 5, 2020. https://www.wsj.com/articles/schools-coronavirus-remote-learning-lockdown-tech-11591375078.

Hofstadter, Douglas. *I Am a Strange Loop*. New York: Basic Books, 2007.

Honigman, Brian. "How Tumblr is Changing Online Activism."
    Forbes, February 18, 2014. https://www.forbes.com/sites/citi/2014
    /02/18/how-tumblr-is-changing-online-activism/?sh=
    562799fa3200.

Hopf, G. Michael. *Those Who Remain*. Self-published, Createspace,
    2016.

Human Rights Campaign Foundation, "Gender Snowperson:
    Understanding Identity." *Welcoming Schools*. Accessed May 23,
    2022. https://assets2.hrc.org/welcoming-schools/documents/WS
    _Lesson_Gender_Snowperson.pdf.

Hume, David. *An Enquiry Concerning Human Understanding*.
    Edited by Tom L. Beauchamp. Oxford: Oxford University Press,
    1999.

Ifill, Gwen. "Hillary Clinton Defends Her Conduct in Law Firm."
    New York Times, March 17, 1992. https://www.nytimes.com
    /1992/03/17/us/the-1992-campaign-hillary-clinton-defends
    -her-conduct-in-law-firm.html.

IT Dashboard. "Welcome to IT Dashboard." Accessed April 5, 2022.
    https://viz.ogp-mgmt.fcs.gsa.gov/#learn-basic-stats.

Jankowicz, Mark. "Fauci Said US Government Held Off Promoting
    Face Masks Because It Knew Shortages Were So Bad that Even
    Doctors Couldn't Get Enough." Business Insider, June 15, 2020.
    https://www.businessinsider.com/fauci-mask-advice-was
    -because-doctors-shortages-from-the-start-2020-6.

Saint Jerome, *Commentary on Ezekiel*. Translated by Thomas P.
    Scheck. New York: The Newman Press, 2017.

Jones, Dan. *Powers and Thrones: A New History of the Middle Ages*.
    New York: Penguin Random House, 2021.

Jones, Jeffrey M. "LGBT Identification Rises to 5.6% in Latest U.S.
    Estimate." Gallup, February 4, 2021. https://news.gallup.com/poll
    /329708/lgbt-identification-rises-latest-estimate.aspx.

———. "LGBT Identification in US Ticks Up to 7.1%." Gallup.
    February 17, 2022. https://news.gallup.com/poll/389792
    /lgbt-identification-ticks-up.aspx.

Khan, Zalan. "Does Afghanistan Mark the End of American Empire?" *Al-Jazeera*, August 28, 2021. https://www.aljazeera.com /opinions/2021/8/28/does-afghanistan-mark-the-end-of -american-empire.

Kant, Immanuel. *Critique of Pure Reason*. Translated by Paul Geyer and Allen W. Wood. Cambridge: Cambridge University Press, 1989.

Karlin, Sarah. "We Asked People to Illustrate Their Gender Dysphoria." BuzzFeed, May 10, 2016. https://www.buzzfeed.com /skarlan/we-asked-people-to-illustrate-what-their-gender -dysphoria-fe.

Kelly, Jack. "When the Narrative is Right but the Facts are Wrong." *Courier Times*, April 13, 2012.

Kendi, Ibram X. "The Very Heartbeat of Racism is Denial." *Rutgers University*, February 25, 2021. https://www.rochester.edu /newscenter/ibram-x-kendi-the-very-heartbeat-of-racism-is-denial -470332/.

Kilner, J. M., and R. N. Lemon. "What We Currently Know about Mirror Neurons." *Current Biology* 23 (December 2, 2013): R1057-R1062.

Kingston, Anne. "'I Regret Having Children.'" *Maclean's*. Accessed May 23, 2022. https://www.macleans.ca/regretful-mothers/.

Kirkup, James. "What Explains the Rising Number of Children with Transgender Issues?" *The Spectator*, August 14, 2020. https:// www.spectator.co.uk/article/do-tv-characters-of-old-transwomen -really-influence-the-gender-of-young-girls-.

Klavan, Andrew. *The Truth and Beauty: How the Lives and Works of England's Greatest Poets Point the Way to a Deeper Understanding of the Words of Jesus*. Grand Rapids, MI: Zondervan Books, 2022.

Koenig, Melissa. "'People are Aroused by Electrocution.'" *Daily Mail*, June 4, 2021. https://www.dailymail.co.uk/news/article-9650967 /Leaked-porn-lecture-given-Manhattan-school-reveals-pupils -taught-electro-porn.html.

Van der Kolk, Bessel. *The Body Keeps the Score: Brain, Mind, and Body in the Healing of Trauma.* New York: Penguin, 2015.

Kurtz, Stanley. *The Lost History of Western Civilization.* New York: Association of National Scholars, 2020. https://www.nas.org /reports/the-lost-history-of-western-civilization.

Lacqua, Francine, Stéphane Bancel, Richard Hatchett, Anthony S. Fauci, and Annelies Wilder-Smith. "COVID-19: What's Next?" *Bloomberg* and The World Economic Forum, January 17, 2022. https://www .weforum.org/events/the-davos-agenda-2022/sessions/covid-19 -what-s-next.

Laertius, Diogenes. *Lives of the Eminent Philosophers.* Translated by Pamela Mensch. Edited by James Miller. Oxford: Oxford University Press, 2018.

Leo X. "Session 4 – 10 May 1515." Fifth Lateran Council, Intratext, May 4, 1515. http://www.intratext.com/IXT/ENG0067/_PG .HTM.

Lewis, C. S. *The C. S. Lewis Signature Classics.* New York: HarperOne, 2017.

———. *The Space Trilogy.* Croydon: HarperCollins, 1938–45.

Lewis, Sophie. *Full Surrogacy Now: Feminism Against Family.* New York: Verso, 2019.

Lincoln, Abraham. "First Inaugural Address of Abraham Lincoln." The Avalon Project, Yale Law School, March 4, 1861. https:// avalon.law.yale.edu/19th_century/lincoln1.asp.

Lind, Michael. *The New Class War.* New York: Penguin Random House, 2020.

Littman, Lisa. "Parent Reports of Adolescents and Young Adults Perceived to Show Signs of a Rapid Onset Gender Dysphoria." *Plos One*, August 16, 2018. https://journals.plos.org/plosone /article?id=10.1371/journal.pone.0202330.

Livy. *The Rise of Rome: Books 1–5.* Translated by T. J. Luce. Oxford: Oxford University Press, 1998.

Lizzo. "Please use the body positive movement to empower yourself. But we need to protect and uplift the bodies it was created for and by." TikTok, April 8, 2021. https://www.tiktok.com/@lizzo/video /6948850681293917446?sender_device=pc&sender_web_id= 7031925730834810374&is_from_webapp=v1&is_copy_url=0.

Lord, Garret, and Lindsey Pollak. "Gen Z and the Death of the Networking Mixer." *Quartz*, November 15, 2021. https://qz.com /work/2089039/gen-z-is-finding-meaningful-professional -connections-online/.

Lucretius. *On the Nature of Things*. Translated by Martin Ferguson Smith. Indianapolis, IN: Hackett, 1969.

Lumsden, Lottie, and Annabelle Lee. "11 Women Who Prove Wellness isn't 'One Size Fits All'." *Cosmopolitan*. January 1, 2021. https://www.cosmopolitan.com/uk/body/a34915032/ women-bodies-wellness-healthy-different-shape-size/.

Machiavelli, Niccolò. *Discourses on Livy*. Translated by Julia Conaway Bondanella and Peter Bondanella. Oxford: Oxford University Press, 1997.

———. *The Essential Writings of Machiavelli*. Edited by Peter Constantine. New York: Random House, 2007.

Manent, Pierre. *Natural Law and Human Rights*. Translated by Ralph C. Hancock. Notre Dame, IN: Notre Dame University Press, 2021.

Manskar, Noah. "Riots Following George Floyd's Death May Cost Insurance Companies up to $2B." *New York Post*, September 16, 2020. https://nypost.com/2020/09/16/riots-following -george-floyds-death-could-cost-up-to-2b/.

Matthews, Joe. "Want True Equity? California Should Force Parents to Give Away Their Children." *San Francisco Chronicle*, January 16, 2022. https://www.msn.com/en-us/news/us/want-true -equity-california-should-force-parents-to-give-away -their-children/ar-AASShA8.

McNeil, Donald G., Jr., "How Much Herd Immunity is Enough?"
New York Times, December 24, 2020. https://www.nytimes.com
/2020/12/24/health/herd-immunity-covid-coronavirus.html.

Menand, Louis. "Why We Are No Longer Shocked by 'Ulysses'." *New
Yorker*, June 16, 2016. https://www.newyorker.com/culture
/cultural-comment/why-we-are-no-longer-shocked-by-ulysses.

Meta, "The Metaverse and How We'll Build It Together." YouTube,
October 28, 2021. https://youtu.be/Uvufun6xer8.

Marche, Stephen. *The Next Civil War*. New York: Simon & Schuster,
2022.

Meyer, Stephen C. *Return of the God Hypothesis*. New York:
HarperOne, 2021.

Meyerowitz, Anya. "This Adidas Campaign Shows Bare Boobs in All
Shapes and Sizes, and It's So Empowering to See." *Glamour*,
February 10, 2022. https://www.glamourmagazine.co.uk/article
/adidas-bare-boobs-sports-bra-ad.

Miller, Joshua Rhett. "Bail Fund Backed by Kamala Harris Freed
Minneapolis Man Charged with Murder." *New York Post*,
September 8, 2021. https://nypost.com/2021/09/08/bail-fund
-backed-by-kamala-harris-freed-man-charged-with-murder/.

Milton, John. *The Complete Poems and Essential Prose of John
Milton*. Edited by William Kerrigan, John Rumrich, and Stephen
M. Fallon. New York: Knopf, 2007.

———. *Paradise Lost*. Edited by Gordon Teskey. New York: W. W.
Norton & Company, 2020.

Mitchell, Joshua. *American Awakening*. New York: Encounter, 2020.

Murdoch, Iris. "The Sublime and the Good," *Chicago Review* 13.3
(1959): 42–55, 51.

———. *The Sovereignty of Good Over Other Concepts*. London:
Routledge, 1970.

Murray, Douglas. *The Madness of Crowds*. London: Routledge, 2019.

Nabokov, Vladimir. *Lolita*. New York: Vintage International, 1956.

"National Tracking Poll, October 8–11, 2021." *Morning Consult* and
Politico. Accessed May 23, 2022. https://www.politico.com/f/?id=

0000017c-7a96-db91-affd-fb9e5d350000&nname=playbook-pm
&nid=0000015a-dd3e-d536-a37b-dd7fd8af0000&nrid=
0000014e-f115-dd93-ad7f-f91513e50001&nlid=964328.

Netz, Reviel. *Scale, Space, and Canon in Ancient Literary Culture.*
Cambridge: Cambridge University Press, 2020.

Newhouse, Alana. "Everything is Broken." *Tablet*, January 14, 2021.
https://www.tabletmag.com/sections/news/articles/everything-is
-broken.

Newsdesk. "Netflix Transgender Employees Condemn Dave
Chappelle Special." *Tittle Press*, October 8, 2021. https://
tittlepress.com/entertainment/1208798/.

Nietzsche, Friedrich. *Basic Writings.* Translated by Walter Kaufmann.
New York: Modern Library, 1967.

———. *Daybreak: Thoughts on the Prejudices of Morality.* Translated
by Maudemarie Clark and Brian Leiter. Cambridge: Cambridge
University Press, 1997.

———. *The Gay Science.* Translated by Josephine Nauckhoff.
Cambridge: Cambridge University Press, 2001.

O'Neill, Jesse. "Rep. Marjorie Taylor Greene Suggests a 'National
Divorce' between Red and Blue States." *New York Post*, December
29, 2021. https://nypost.com/2021/12/29/rep-greene
-suggests-a-national-divorce-between-red-and-blue-states/.

Obama, Barack. "Remarks by the President at National Prayer
Breakfast." Office of the Press Secretary, Obama White House,
February 5, 2015. https://obamawhitehouse.archives.gov/the-press
-office/2015/02/05/remarks-president-national-prayer-breakfast.

Orwell, George. "Politics and the English Language." *Horizon*, April
1946. https://www.orwellfoundation.com/the-orwell-foundation
/orwell/essays-and-other-works/politics-and-the-english-language/.

Ospina, Juan Manuel. "Welcome to the End of Western Dominance."
El Espectador, March 8, 2022. https://worldcrunch.com
/world-affairs/decline-of-the-west.

Paley, William. *Natural Theology.* Edited by Matthew W. Eddy and
David Knight. Oxford: Oxford University Press, 2006.

Pang, Ken C., et al. "Association of Media Coverage of Transgender and Gender Diverse Issues with Rates of Referral of Transgender Children and Adolescents to Specialist Gender Clinics in the UK and Australia." *Jama* 3.7 (July 28, 2020). https://jamanetwork.com/journals/jamanetworkopen/fullarticle/2768726.

Paglia, Camille. *Glittering Images*. New York: Vintage Books, 2012.

Pandey, Manish. "Schitt's Creek 'Normalises LGBTQ Relationships.'" *BBC*, September 21, 2020. https://www.bbc.com/news/newsbeat-54240141.

Parmenides of Elea. *Fragments*. Translated by David Gallop. Toronto: University of Toronto Press, 1991.

"Paving the Way to the Modern Internet." DARPA. https://www.darpa.mil/about-us/timeline/modern-internet.

Pells, Rachael. "Number of British People Seeking to Change Their Gender Soars." *Independent*, July 10, 2016. https://www.independent.co.uk/life-style/health-and-families/health-news/number-of-british-people-seeking-to-change-their-gender-soars-a7130006.html.

Peterson, Andrea. "Former NSA and CIA Director Says Terrorists Love Using Gmail." *Washington Post*, September 15, 2013. https://www.washingtonpost.com/news/the-switch/wp/2013/09/15/former-nsa-and-cia-director-says-terrorists-love-using-gmail.

Plato. *Complete Works*. Edited by John M. Cooper. Indianapolis, IN: Hackett, 1997.

———. *Five Dialogues*. Translated by G. M. A. Grube. Revised by John M. Cooper. Indianapolis, IN: Hackett, 2002.

———. *Republic*. Translated by Allan Bloom. New York: Basic Books, 1986.

———. *Symposium*. Translated by Robin Waterfield. Oxford: World's Classics, 1994.

———. *Theaetetus* (vol. 1), *Sophist* (vol. 2) and *Statesman* (vol. 3), in *The Being of the Beautiful*, translated by Seth Benardete. Chicago: University of Chicago Press, 1986.

———. *Timaeus and Critias*. Translated by Robin Waterfield. Oxford: Oxford University Press, 2008.

Plotinus, *Enneads* (7 vols). Translated by A. H. Armstrong. Cambridge: Harvard University Press, 1969–88.

———. *The Enneads: Abridged Edition*. Translated by Stephan MacKenna. London: Penguin, 1991.

Plutarch. *Roman Lives*. Translated by Robin Waterfield. Oxford: Oxford University Press, 1999.

Podhoretz, Norman. "'Lolita,' My Mother-in-Law, the Marquis de Sade, and Larry Flynt." *Commentary*. April 1997. https://www.commentary.org/articles/norman-podhoretz/lolita-my-mother-in-law-the-marquis-de-sade-and-larry-flynt/.

Polybius. *The Histories*. Translated by Robin Waterfield. Oxford: Oxford University Press, 2010.

Popper, Karl. *The Logic of Scientific Discovery*. London: Routledge, 1959.

Poulos, James. *Human, Forever*. Self-published, humanforever.us, 2021.

"*DAMN.*, by Kendrick Lamar." The Pulitzer Prize Board. 2018. https://www.pulitzer.org/winners/kendrick-lamar.

Reuters. "Mark Zuckerberg Speaks at Facebook's Annual AR/VR Conference." YouTube, Oct 28, 2021, https://www.youtube.com/watch?v=XOn2CZWnxxY.

Rieff, David. "Multiculturalism's Silent Partner." *Harper's Magazine*, August 1993.

"Roosevelt Bars the Hyphenated." *New York Times*, October 13, 1915.

Roston, Aram. "Proud Boys Leader Enrique Tarrio was an FBI Informant." *The Guardian*, January 27, 2021. https://www.theguardian.com/us-news/2021/jan/27/proud-boys-leader-enrique-tarrio-fbi-informant.

Ross, Katherine. "Why Weren't We Wearing Masks from the Beginning? Dr. Fauci Explains." *TheStreet*, June 12, 2020. https://

www.thestreet.com/video/dr-fauci-masks-changing
-directive-coronavirus.

Rothblatt, Martine. *From Transgender to Transhuman.*
Self-published, Amazon Digital Services, 2011.

Rufo, Christopher. "Disney's Ideological Capture." *City Journal,*
March 30, 2022. https://www.city-journal.org/disneys-ideological
-capture.

Safronova, Valeriya. "A Private-School Sex Educator Defends Her
Methods." *New York Times,* July 7, 2021. https://www.nytimes
.com/2021/07/07/style/sex-educator-methods-defense.html.

Saïd, Edward. *Orientalism.* New York: Pantheon, 1976.

Saikia, Anku M., Jahnabi Das, Pavel Barman, and Mintu D. Bharali.
"Internet Addiction and its Relationships with Depression,
Anxiety, and Stress in Urban Adolescents of Kamrup District,
Assam." *Journal of Family and Community Medicine* 26.2
(May-August 2019): 108–12.

Salimbene. *Chronicles.* In *The Internet Medieval Sourcebook.*
Fordham University. Accessed May 23, 2022. https://sourcebooks
.fordham.edu/source/salimbene1.asp.

Salo, Jackie. "'We've Got to Take These Motherf—kers Out': Rutgers
Professor Calls White People 'Villains'." *New York Post,* October
29, 2021. https://nypost.com/2021/10/29/rutgers-professor
-calls-white-people-villains/.

Sax, Leonard. "The Ambiguity of the Evidence," Fall 2021.
Claremont Review of Books 21.4. https://claremontreviewofbooks
.com/the-ambiguity-of-the-evidence/.

Saxe, Rebecca. "The Forbidden Experiment." *Boston Review,* June 27,
2012. https://bostonreview.net/articles/saxe-the
-forbidden-experiment/.

Schrödinger, Erwin. *Interpretation of Quantum Mechanics: Dublin
Seminars (1949–1955) and Other Unpublished Essays.* Edited by
Michel Bitbol. Woodbridge, Connecticut: Ox Bow Press, 1995.

Schaffer, Simon. "Scientific Discoveries and the End of Natural
Philosophy." *Social Studies of Science* 16.3 (1986): 387–420.

Schwartz, Ian. "Ocasio-Cortez: People More Concerned About Me Being 'Factually Correct' than 'Morally Right'." Real Clear Politics, January 6, 2019. https://www.realclearpolitics.com/video/2019/01/06/ocasio-cortez_people_being_more_concerned_about_me_being_factually_correct_than_morally_right.html.

Scruton, Roger. "Memo to Hawking: There's Still Room for God." *Wall Street Journal*, September 24, 2010. https://www.wsj.com/articles/SB10001424052748703989304575503952480317596.

"Section 230: The 'Most Important Law in Tech.'" Computer & Communications Industry Association, Last accessed May 20, 2022. https://www.ccianet.org/section230/.

"See Meme-ified Richard Dawkins Saatchi's New Directors Showcase Opener." Adage. June 23, 2013. https://adage.com/creativity/work/just-hits-opener/31942.

Seth, Anil. *Being You: A New Science of Consciousness*. New York: Dutton, 2021.

Shakespeare, William. *Hamlet*. Edited by Barbara A. Mowat and Paul Werstine. New York: Simon & Schuster, 1992.

———. *Macbeth*. Edited by Barbara A. Mowat and Paul Werstine. New York: Simon & Schuster, 1992.

———. *The Merchant of Venice*. Edited by Barbara A. Mowat and Paul Werstine. New York: Simon & Schuster, 1992.

Shattuck, Roger. *The Forbidden Experiment: The Story of the Wild Boy of Averon*. Tokyo: Kodansha International, 1980.

Shaw, Amatullah. "15 Parents Are Sharing Why They Regret having Kids." BuzzFeed, August 21, 2021. https://www.buzzfeed.com/amatullahshaw/parents-are-sharing-regret.

Shideler, Kyle. "Shideler Testifies before Senate Subcommittee on the Constitution." *Center for Security Policy*, August 4, 2020. https://centerforsecuritypolicy.org/shideler-testifies-before-senate-subcommittee-on-the-constitution/.

———. "Taking it to the Streets." *Claremont Review of Books* 21, no. 3 (Summer 2021), https://claremontreviewofbooks.com/taking-it-to-the-streets/.

Shrier, Abigail. "How 'Peer Contagion' May Play into the Rise of Teen Girls Transitioning." *New York Post*, June 27, 2020. https://nypost.com/2020/06/27/how-peer-contagion-plays-into-the-rise-of-teens-transitioning/.

———. *Irreversible Damage: The Transgender Craze Seducing Our Daughters*. Washington, D.C.: Regnery, 2020.

Silverman, Sarah. "Maybe we should break up." *The Sarah Silverman Podcast*, September 12, 2021. https://twitter.com/SarahKSilverman/status/143723689088575488 0?s=20.

Smith, Noah. "Coronavirus Makes America Seem Like a Civilization in Decline." *Bloomberg*, March 29, 2020. https://www.bloomberg.com/opinion/articles/2020-03-29/coronavirus-makes-america-seem-like-a-civilization-in-decline.

Smolkin, Rachel. "Justice Delayed." *American Journalism Review* 29, no. 4 (August-September 2007). https://go.gale.com/ps/i.do?id=GALE%7CA167843986&sid=googleScholar&v=2.1&it=r&link access=abs&issn=10678654&p=AONE&sw=w&userGroupName=anon%7E8417028a.

Solzhenitsyn, Aleksandr. *The Gulag Archipelago*. Translated by Thomas P. Whitney. New York: HarperCollins, 1973.

Sosa, Adriana, et al. "An Open Letter to Spotify." WordPress, January 14, 2022. https://spotifyopenletter.wordpress.com/2022/01/10/an-open-letter-to-spotify/.

Steinbuch, Yaron. "Black Lives Matter Co-Founder Describes Herself as 'Trained Marxist.'" *New York Post*, June 25, 2020. https://nypost.com/2020/06/25/blm-co-founder-describes-herself-as-trained-marxist/

Stephenson, Neal. *Snow Crash*. New York: Bantam Books, 1992.

Strauss, Leo. *Natural Right and History*. 1953. Chicago: University of Chicago Press.

———. "Jerusalem and Athens: Some Introductory Reflections." *Commentary*, June 1967. https://www.commentary.org/articles/leo-strauss/jerusalem-and-athens-some-introductory-reflections/.

Schwarzenbach, Sibyl A. "On Civic Friendship." *Ethics* 107, no. 1 (October 1996): 97–128.

"The State of the World's Children." UNICEF and Gallup, 2021. Last accessed January 18, 2022. https://www.unicef.org/reports/state-worlds-children-2021.

Tacitus. *Agricola, Germania, Dialogus.* Translated by M. Hutton and W. Peterson. Cambridge: Harvard University Press, 1914, revised 1970.

Thucydides. *History of the Peloponnesian War.* Edited by Robert B. Strassler. Translated by Richard Crawley. New York: Free Press, 1996.

Toomey, Russell B., Amy K. Syvertsen, Maura Shramko, "Transgender Adolescent Suicide Behavior." *Pediatrics* 142, no. 2 (October 1, 2018), https://doi.org/10.1542/peds.2017-4218.

Uldricks, Nathan. "The Importance of Management Policy in American Governance." *American Mind*, March 1, 2022. https://americanmind.org/features/the-importance-of-management-policy-in-american-governance/.

United States Surgeon General's Advisory. "Protecting Youth Mental Health." December 7, 2021. https://www.hhs.gov/sites/default/files/surgeon-general-youth-mental-health-advisory.pdf.

United States v. One Book Entitled Ulysses by James Joyce. 72 F. Supp. 2d 705. (2d Cir. 1934).

U.S. Congress. *Naturalization Act of 1795.* Public Law 3-20. 3rd Cong., 2nd sess. (January 29, 1975). https://govtrackus.s3.amazonaws.com/legislink/pdf/stat/1/STATUTE-1-Pg414a.pdf.

Vulture Editors, "Wait, What's Going On with Netflix and *Cuties?*" *Vulture*, October 7, 2020. https://www.vulture.com/2020/10/netflix-cuties-twerking-poster-drama-explained.html.

Warren, Michael. "Golden Trump Statue Turns Heads at CPAC." CNN, February 26, 2021. https://www.cnn.com/2021/02/26/politics/trump-gold-statue-cpac-2021/index.html.

Warren, Tom. "Microsoft Teams Enters the Metaverse Race with 3D
    Avatars and Immersive Meetings." *The Verge*, November 2, 2021.
    https://www.theverge.com/2021/11/2/22758974/
    microsoft-teams-metaverse-mesh-3d-avatars-meetings-features.

Washington, George. "Farewell Address." *Daily American Advertiser*,
    1796. https://www.senate.gov/artandhistory/history/resources/pdf/
    Washingtons_Farewell_Address.pdf.

———. "Farewell Address." September 19, 1796. Founders Online.
    https://founders.archives.gov/documents/Washington/05-20-02-
    0440-0002.

Whorecress. "why i'm not body positive." TikTok. March 14, 2021.
    https://www.tiktok.com/@whoreceress/video/6939549924782624
    006?is_copy_url=1&is_from_webapp=v1.

Wittgenstein, Ludwig. *Philosophical Investigations*. Translated by
    G. E. M. Anscome, P. M. S. Hacker, and Joachim Schulte.
    Hoboken, New Jersey: Wiley-Blackwell, 2009.

Weiss, Bari. "The Miseducation of America's Elites." *City Journal*,
    March 9, 2021. https://www.city-journal.org/
    the-miseducation-of-americas-elites.

"Who Wins with Virtual Recruiting?" Handshake. Summer 2021.
    https://joinhandshake.com/network-trends/virtual-recruiting/.

Wolchover, Natalie, and Quanta Magazine. "Life as We Know It
    Hinges on One Very Small Decimal." *The Atlantic*, December 5,
    2020. https://www.theatlantic.com/science/archive/2020/12/
    the-magic-number-that-shapes-the-universe/617288/.

Wood, Peter. "Diversity's Descent." In *A Dubious Expediency: How
    Race Preferences Damage Higher Education*, edited by Gail
    Heriot and Maimon Schwarzchild, 87–110, 94. New York:
    Encounter, 2021.

Woolsey, John M. *United States v. One Book Called "Ulysses,"*
    December 6, 1933. U.S. District Court for the Southern District of
    New York.

Wright, Robin. "Does the Great Retreat from Afghanistan Mark the
    End of the American Era?" *New Yorker*, August 15, 2021. https://

www.newyorker.com/news/our-columnists/does-the-great-retreat-from-afghanistan-mark-the-end-of-the-american-era.

Zuboff, Shoshana. *The Age of Surveillance Capitalism*. New York: PublicAffairs, 2019.

Zuckerberg, Mark. "The hardest technology challenge of our time may be fitting a supercomputer into the frame of normal-looking glasses. But it's the key to bringing our physical and digital worlds together." Facebook. April 29, 2021. https://www.facebook.com/zuck/posts/10112933648910701.

Zuckerberg, Mark. "Mark Zuckerberg Speaks at Facebook's Annual AR/VR Conference." Reuters, October 28, 2021. https://www.youtube.com/watch?v=XOn2CZWnxxY.

Notes

Introduction

1. Brian Bethune, "Was Jan. 6 the Beginning of the End for America?" *Maclean's,* January 4, 2022, https://www.macleans.ca/politics/washington/was-jan-6-the-beginning-of-the-end-for-america/; Stephen Marche, *The Next Civil War* (New York: Simon & Schuster, 2022), 177–224; Noah Smith, "Coronavirus Makes America Seem Like a Civilization in Decline," *Bloomberg,* March 29, 2020, https://www.bloomberg.com/opinion/articles/2020-03-29/coronavirus-makes-america-seem-like-a-civilization-in-decline; Michael MacKay (@mhmck), "Russia's invasion of Ukraine is life or death for Western civilization. But so far, only Central and Eastern European countries—led by Ukraine—recognize it," Twitter, April 5, 2022, https://twitter.com/mhmck/status/1511451981084340228?s=20&t=VELLEajJ6C nXX_yV3mdNAQ; Juan Manuel Ospina, "Welcome to the End of Western Dominance," *El Espectador,* March 8, 2022, https://worldcrunch.com/world-affairs/decline-of-the-west; Robin Wright, "Does the Great Retreat from Afghanistan Mark the End of the American Era?" *New Yorker,* August 15, 2021, https://www.newyorker.com/news/our-columnists/does-the-great-retreat-from-afghanistan-mark-the-end-of-the-american-era.
2. Tacitus, *Dialogus,* 18.3.
3. John Dalberg-Acton, "The History of Freedom in Antiquity," Acton Institute, February 26, 1877, https://www.acton.org/research/history-freedom-antiquity.
4. Jerome, *Commentary on Ezekiel,* trans. Tomas P. Scheck (New York: The Newman Press, 2017), III (preface).
5. Edward Saïd, *Orientalism* (New York: Pantheon, 1978), 273.
6. See Peter Wood, "Diversity's Descent" in *A Dubious Expediency: How Race Preferences Damage Higher Education,* ed. Gail Heriot and Maimon Schwarzchild (New York: Encounter, 2021), 87–110, 94; Stanley Kurtz, *The Lost History of*

Western Civilization, ebook edition (New York: Association of National Scholars, 2020), 73–93, https://www.nas.org/reports/the-lost-history-of-western-civilization; Richard Bernstein, "In Dispute on Bias, Stanford Is Likely to Alter Western Culture Program," *New York Times*, January 19, 1988, https://www.nytimes.com/1988/01/19/us/in-dispute-on-bias-stanford-is-likely-to-alter-western-culture-program.html.

7. David Rieff, "Multiculturalism's Silent Partner," *Harper's Magazine*, August 1993.

8. Barack Obama, "Remarks by the President at National Prayer Breakfast," Speeches and Remarks, White House Office of the Press Secretary, February 5, 2015, https://obamawhitehouse.archives.gov/the-press-office/2015/02/05/remarks-president-national-prayer-breakfast.

9. David Perry and Matthew Gabriele, "Steve King Says He Was Just Defending 'Western Civilization.' That's Racist, Too," *Washington Post*, January 15, 2019, https://www.washingtonpost.com/outlook/2019/01/15/steve-king-says-he-was-just-defending-western-civilization-that's-racist-too/.

10. Kwame Anthony Appiah, "There Is No Such Thing as Western Civilization," *The Guardian*, November 9, 2016, https://www.theguardian.com/world/2016/nov/09/western-civilisation-appiah-reith-lecture.

11. Bari Weiss, "The Miseducation of America's Elites," *City Journal*, March 9, 2021, https://www.city-journal.org/the-miseducation-of-americas-elites.

12. See Meghan Cox Gurdon, "Even Homer Gets Mobbed," *Wall Street Journal*, December 27, 2020, https://www.wsj.com/articles/even-homer-gets-mobbed-11609095872?page=1; Heather Silva (Levine) (@heathered_love), "Hahaha—very proud to say we got the Odyssey removed from the curriculum this year!" Twitter, June 4, 202, 11:25 a.m., https://twitter.com/heathered_love/status/1268564623231528960.

13. Disrupt Texts (@DisruptTexts), "#DisruptTexts," Twitter, as of January 26, 2022, https://twitter.com/DisruptTexts; see further Disrupt Texts, "Homepage," https://disrupttexts.org.

14. Seneca, *Epistles,* trans. Robin Campbell (London: Penguin Classics, 1969), 47.

15. W. E. B. DuBois, "The Souls of Black Folk," in *Writings*, ed. Nathan Huggins (New York: Library of America, 1903), 438.

16. Niccolò Machiavelli, *The Essential Writings of Machiavelli*, ed. Peter Constantine (New York: Random House, 2007), 505–6.

17. Leo Strauss, "Jerusalem and Athens: Some Introductory Reflections," *Commentary*, June 1967, https://www.commentary.org/articles/leo-strauss/jerusalem-and-athens-some-introductory-reflections/.

18. Philip Hamburger, "The Constitution Can Crack Section 230," *Wall Street Journal*, January 29, 2021, https://www.wsj.com/articles/the-constitution-can-crack-section-230-11611946851. Hamburger argues that the federal government has granted these censorship powers to big tech in hopes of using them for its own ends.

19. See Andrea Peterson, "Former NSA and CIA Director Says Terrorists Love Using Gmail," *Washington Post*, September 15, 2013, https://www.washingtonpost.com/news/the-switch/wp/2013/09/15/former-nsa-and-cia-director-says-terrorists-love-using-gmail.

20. Shoshana Zuboff, *The Age of Surveillance Capitalism* (New York: PublicAffairs, 2019), 566. Kindle edition.

21. "Overview IT Dashboard," https://viz.ogp-mgmt.fcs.gsa.gov/#learn-basic-stats; DARPA, "Paving the Way to the Modern Internet," https://www.darpa.mil/about-us/timeline/modern-internet; Nathan Uldricks, "The Importance of Management Policy in American Governance," *American Mind,* March 1, 2022, https://americanmind.org/features/the-importance-of-management-policy-in-american-governance/.

22. James Poulos, *Human, Forever: The Digital Politics of Spiritual War* (Blockchain, 2021), 228.

23. Rachel Bovard, "What the New Right Must Do Next Time It Earns Power," The Federalist, November 4, 2021, https://thefederalist.com/2021/11/04/national-conservatism-must-prioritize-fights-over-american-values-not-just-legislation/#.YZKJPifzRh8.sms.

24. DailyWire+, "Daily Wire Backstage: Live at the Ryman," YouTube, October 12, 2021, https://www.youtube.com/watch?v=D3S9hSy0AKk.

25. Ray Bradbury, *Fahrenheit 451* (New York: Simon & Schuster, 1953), 150.

Chapter 1: The Reality Crisis

1. "Connect," Meta, https://facebookconnect.com/en-us/; Meta, "The Metaverse and How We'll Build It Together—Connect 2021," Youtube, October 28, 2021, https://youtu.be/Uvufun6xer8, 1:01–1:18.

2. Meta, "The Metaverse and How We'll Build It Together—Connect 2021," YouTube, October 28, 2021, https://youtu.be/Uvufun6xer8, 3:47–6:04.

3. Michael Barbaro, "Microsoft and the Metaverse," *The Daily,* produced by Daniel Guillemette, Rachelle Bonja, Eric Krupke, and Luke Vander Ploeg, *New York Times,* January 20, 2022, https://www.nytimes.com/2022/01/20/podcasts/the-daily/metaverse-microsoft-activision-blizzard.html.

4. William Shakespeare, *Hamlet,* ed. Barbara A. Mowat and Paul Werstine (New York: Simon & Schuster, 1992), III.i.70–71.

5. Ibid., II.ii.273–75.

6. Niccolo Soldo, "The Dubrovnik Interviews: Marc Andreessen—Interviewed by a Retard," Fisted by Foucault, May 31, 2021, https://niccolo.substack.com/p/the-dubrovnik-interviews-marc-andreessen.

7. "A Peek into the Metaverse," *Horizon,* January 24, 2022, https://fb.watch/aM0UYnh8TV/.

8. "Conway: Press Secretary Gave 'Alternative Facts,'" NBC News, January 22, 2017, https://www.nbcnews.com/meet-the-press/video/conway-press-secretary-gave-alternative-facts-860142147643.

9. Maureen Balleza and Kate Zernike, "Memos on Bush are Fake but Accurate, Typist Says," *New York Times,* September 15, 2004, https://www.nytimes.com/2004/09/15/us/the-2004-campaign-national-guard-memos-on-bush-are-fake-but-accurate.html. In 2015, Rather was the subject of a movie, *Truth,* which made a remarkable effort to rehabilitate him by blurring the lines between "truth" and "falsehood" altogether.

10. Rachel Smolkin, "Justice Delayed," *American Journalism Review* 29, no. 4 (August–September 2007), https://ajrarchive.org/article.asp?id=4379; Jack Kelly, "When the Narrative Is Right but the Facts Are Wrong," *Courier Times,* April 13,

2012, https://www.buckscountycouriertimes.com/story/opinion/columns/your-voice/2012/04/13/when-narrative-is-right-but/17949396007/.

11. Ian Schwartz, "Ocasio-Cortez: People More Concerned about Me Being 'Factually Correct' than 'Morally Right,'" RealClearPolitics, January 6, 2019, https://www.realclearpolitics.com/video/2019/01/06/ocasio-cortez_people_being_more_concerned_about_me_being_factually_correct_than_morally_right.html.

12. "Clinton's Grand Jury Testimony, Part 4," *Washington Post*, August 17, 1998, https://www.washingtonpost.com/wp-srv/politics/special/clinton/stories/bctest092198_4.htm.

13. George Orwell, "Politics and the English Language," Orwell Foundation, https://www.orwellfoundation.com/the-orwell-foundation/orwell/essays-and-other-works/politics-and-the-english-language/.

14. Friedrich Hayek, *The Road to Serfdom* (Chicago: University of Chicago Press, 1944), 178–79.

15. Friedrich Nietzsche, *The Gay Science,* book 3, section 125.

16. Martin Heidegger, "The Word of Nietzsche" in *The Question Concerning Technology and Other Essays,* trans. William Lovitt (New York: Harper Perennial, 1977), 61.

17. Friedrich Nietzsche, *Genealogy of Morals*, essay 2, section 11.

18. Nietzsche, *The Gay Science,* book 4, section 335.

19. Heidegger, "The Word of Nietzsche," 68.

20. Andy Stone (@andymstone), "While I will intentionally not link to the New York Post, I want be [*sic*] clear that this story is eligible to be fact checked by Facebook's third-party fact checking partners. In the meantime, we are reducing its distribution on our platform," Twitter, October 14, 2020, 11:10 a.m., https://twitter.com/andymstone/status/1316395902479872000?s=20.

21. Katie Benner, Kenneth P. Vogel, and Michael S. Schmidt, "Hunter Biden Paid Tax Bill, but Broad Federal Investigation Continues," *New York Times*, March 16, 2022, https://www.nytimes.com/2022/03/16/us/politics/hunter-biden-tax-bill-investigation.html.

22. "Civic Integrity," Twitter, https://about.twitter.com/en/our-priorities/civic-integrity.

23. Aristophanes, *Clouds*, ll.98–99.

24. Aristotle, *Art of Rhetoric*, 1402a. Aristotle associates this kind of teaching especially with the sophist par excellence, Protagoras of Abdera (ca. 490–420 BC).

25. Ibid.

26. Thucydides, *History of the Peloponnesian War*, book 2, chapter 65, l.10.

27. See Guardian News, "Yanny or Laurel Video: Which Name Do You Hear?–Audio," YouTube, May 16, 2018, https://www.youtube.com/watch?v=7X_WvGAhMlQ.

28. Plato, *Theaetetus*, 160d–e.

29. Plato, *Republic*, I, 338b–c, 340b.

30. Shakespeare, *Hamlet*, II.2.268–70.

31. Thucydides, *History,* 5.89.

32. Ibid., 3.82.

33. Plato, *Apology*, 21d–23a.

Chapter 2: Outside the Cave

1. This was the posture of Heraclitus's disciple, Cratylus, who gave up speech altogether and simply moved his finger around. Aristotle, *Metaphysics*, trans. Hugh Lawson-Tancred (London: Penguin Classics, 1998), 1010a7–15.

2. Plato, *Phaedo*, 77c6–9b8.

3. Plato, *Symposium*, 175b.

4. Ibid., 211d–e.

5. Plato, *Republic*, VII, 514a.

6. Mark Zuckerberg, "The hardest technology challenge of our time may be fitting a supercomputer into the frame of normal-looking glasses. But it's the key to bringing our physical and digital worlds together," Facebook post, April 29, 2021, https://www.facebook.com/zuck/posts/10112933648910701.

7. Matthew Ball, "Evolving User + Business Behaviors and the Metaverse," MatthewBall.vc, June 28, 2021, https://www.matthewball.vc/all/userbehaviors metaverse.

8. Zuckerberg, "The hardest technology. . . ." (See note 5).

9. UNICEF and Gallup, "The State of the World's Children," 2021, https://www.unicef.org/reports/state-worlds-children-2021.

10. *Protecting Youth Mental Health: The United States Surgeon General's Advisory* (Department of Health and Human Services, December 7, 2021), https://www.hhs.gov/sites/default/files/surgeon-general-youth-mental-health-advisory.pdf, 9.

11. Sean C. L. Deoni, Jennifer Beauchemin, Alexandra Volpe, Viren D'Sa, and the Resonance Consortium, "Impact of the COVID-19 Pandemic on Early Child Cognitive Development: Initial Findings in a Longitudinal Observational Study of Child Health," medRxiv, August 11, 2021, https://www.medrxiv.org/content/10.11 01/2021.08.10.21261846v1.full.pdf, abstract.

12. Herodotus, *The Histories*, II.2.

13. Salimbene, "Chronicles" in G. Coulton, *St. Francis to Dante* (London: David Nutt, 1906), 242–43. See further Dan Jones, *Powers and Thrones* (London: Viking, 2021); Roger Shattuck, *The Forbidden Experiment: The Story of the Wild Boy of Aveyron* (Tokyo: Kodansha International, 1980); Rebecca Saxe, "The Forbidden Experiment," *Boston Review*, June 27, 2012, https://bostonreview.net/articles/saxe-the-forbidden-experiment/.

14. CBS, "Baby Plays with iPad, Is Frustrated by Paper Mag," YouTube, October 14, 2011, https://www.youtube.com/watch?v=UoOJqeAbDaQ&feature=emb_title.

15. "Who Wins with Virtual Recruiting?" Handshake, summer 2021, https://joinhandshake.com/network-trends/virtual-recruiting/. Quote from Garrett Lord, CEO of Handshake, and Lindsey Pollak in "Gen Z and the Death of the Networking Mixer," Quartz, November 15, 2021, https://qz.com/work/2089039/gen-z-is-finding-meaningful-professional-connections-online/.

16. Iris Murdoch, *The Sovereignty of Good over Other Concepts* (London: Routledge, 1970), 8.

17. Iris Murdoch, "The Sublime and the Good," *Chicago Review* 13, no. 3 (1959): 42–55, 51.

18. Aleksandr Solzhenitsyn, *The Gulag Archipelago*, trans. Thomas P. Whitney (New York: HarperCollins, 1973), vol. 1, 100–101.

19. René Girard, *I See Satan Fall Like Lightning*, trans. James G. Williams (New York: Orbis, 1999), 175.

20. Tom Warren, "Microsoft Teams Enters the Metaverse Race with 3D Avatars and Immersive Meetings," The Verge, November 2, 2021, https://www.theverge .com/2021/11/2/22758974/microsoft-teams-metaverse-mesh-3d-avatars -meetings-features.

21. Shoshana Zuboff, *The Age of Surveillance Capitalism* (New York: Public Affairs, 2019), 15.

22. Plato, *Republic*, 10.600c.

23. Ibid., 7.517a.

24. T. S. Eliot, "Burnt Norton" in *Collected Poems, 1906-1962* (San Diego: Harcourt Brace Jovanovich, 1991), 44–45.

25. Plato, *Apology*, 39c.

Chapter 3: The Body Crisis

1. Lottie Lumsden and Annabelle Lee, "11 Women Who Prove Wellness Isn't 'One Size Fits All,'" *Cosmopolitan,* January 1, 2021, https://www.cosmopolitan.com /uk/body/a34915032/women-bodies-wellness-healthy-different-shape-size/; Anya Meyerowitz, "This Adidas Campaign Shows Bare Boobs in All Shapes and Sizes, and It's So Empowering to See," *Glamour,* February 10, 2022, https:// www.glamourmagazine.co.uk/article/adidas-bare-boobs-sports-bra-ad.

2. Michael Anton, "Unprecedented," *New Criterion* 41, no. 3 (December 2021): https://newcriterion.com/issues/2021/12/unprecedented, 9.

3. Yuval Harari, *Homo Deus: A Brief History of Tomorrow* (New York: Harper, 2015), 109. See further Daniel Dennett, *Consciousness Explained* (Boston: Little, Brown, and Company, 1991) for the argument that qualitative subjectivity, or the "I" of the mind, is an illusion. Similar though distinct is Douglas Hofstadter, *I Am a Strange Loop* (New York: Basic Books, 2007). Hofstadter argues in chapter 3 that the mind, being immaterial, cannot "push the body around," i.e., is just an experience we have while our bodies perform their mechanical functions according to the laws of physics. Incidentally, Hofstadter's view was already parodied in C. S. Lewis's character Dr. Frost from *That Hideous Strength* (1945).

4. See, for example Stephen Hawking, *A Brief History of Time* (New York: Bantam, 1988), chapter 12; David Deutsch, *The Beginning of Infinity: Explanations That Transform the World* (London: Penguin, 2011), 154.

5. A popular proponent of this view is Anil Seth, whose work at the Sackler Centre for Consciousness Science has produced fascinating information about brain activity but has not, contra Seth himself, gotten us any closer to understanding the mysterious connection between that chemistry and what he calls the "hallucination" of consciousness. See *Being You: A New Science of Consciousness* (New York: Dutton, 2021).

6. Harari, *Homo Deus,* 106. Harari is not the only person to adopt this fractured view of the human subject: cf. Michael Haar on Nietzsche: "All psychological categories (the ego, the individual, the person) derive from the illusion of substantial identity." Michael Haar, "Nietzsche and Metaphysical Language," in *The New Nietzsche,* ed. David Allison (New York: Delta, 1977), 17–18.

7. C. S. Lewis, *The Problem of Pain* (New York: HarperOne, 2001), 135.

8. Aristotle, *De Anima*, III.2, 425b.
9. St. Jerome, *Commentary on Ezekiel*, 1.7.
10. Immanuel Kant, *Critique of Pure Reason*, I.II.ii.3.
11. Porphyry, *On the Life of Plotinus and the Order of His Books*, 2. Another version of the text reads, "I am striving to return the Divine in myself to the Divine in the All."
12. Porphyry, *On the Life of Plotinus*, 23.
13. Plato, *Timaeus*, 42e–43a.
14. Plato, *Phaedrus*, 246a.
15. Plotinus, *Enneads*, 4.3.9.
16. Plato, *Timaeus*, 49b–c.
17. René Descartes, *Discourse on Method and Meditations on First Philosophy*, 6.9.
18. Hayden Dunham, "Pippa Gardner and Hayden Dunham on the Struggle of Being inside Bodies," *Interview*, May 19, 2021, https://www.interviewmagazine .com/art/pippa-garner-and-hayden-dunham-on-the-struggle-of-being-inside -bodies?utm_source=twitter&utm_medium=social&utm_campaign=may21.
19. Francesca Bacardi, "Kardashian Team Working Hard to Remove Unwanted Khloé Photo," *Page Six*, April 5, 2021, https://pagesix.com/2021/04/05/ kardashian-team-working-hard-to-remove-unwanted-khloe-photo/.
20. Lizzo, "Please use the body positive movement to empower yourself. But we need to protect and uplift the bodies it was created for and by," TikTok, April 8, 2021, https://www.tiktok.com/@lizzo/video/6948850681293917446?sender _device=pc&sender_web_id=7031925730834810374&is_from_webapp=v1&is _copy_url=0.
21. American Psychiatric Association, *Diagnostic and Statistical Manual of Mental Disorders,* 5th ed. (Washington, D.C.: American Psychiatric Publishing, 2013), 451–60.
22. Simone de Beauvoir, *The Second Sex*, trans. Constance Borde and Sheila Malovany-Chevallier (New York: Vintage Books, 2009), 330.
23. Judith Butler, *Gender Trouble* (New York: Routledge, 1990), 10–12. See further 151–57.
24. Sarah Karlin, "We Asked People to Illustrate Their Gender Dysphoria," *BuzzFeed,* May 10, 2016, https://www.buzzfeed.com/skarlan/we -asked-people-to-illustrate-what-their-gender-dysphoria-fe.
25. Rachael Pells, "Number of British People Seeking to Change Their Gender Soars," *The Independent,* July 10, 2016, https://www.independent.co.uk/life-style/health-and-families/health-news/number-of-british-people-seeking-to-change-their-gender-soars-a7130006.html.
26. Jeffrey M. Jones, "LGBT Identification Rises to 5.6% in Latest U.S. Estimate," Gallup, February 4, 2021, https://news.gallup.com/poll/329708/lgbt-identification-rises-latest-estimate.aspx.
27. Jeffrey M. Jones, "LGBT Identification in US Ticks Up to 7.1%," Gallup, February 17, 2022, https://news.gallup.com/poll/389792/lgbt-identification-ticks-up.aspx.
28. Lisa Littman, "Parent Reports of Adolescents and Young Adults Perceived to Show Signs of a Rapid Onset Gender Dysphoria," *Plos One*, August 16, 2018, https:// journals.plos.org/plosone/article?id=10.1371/journal.pone.0202330.
29. See further Abigail Shrier, "How 'Peer Contagion' May Play into the Rise of Teen Girls Transitioning," *New York Post,* June 27, 2020, https://nypost.com/2020/06/27/ how-peer-contagion-plays-into-the-rise-of-teens-transitioning/.

30. Human Rights Campaign Foundation, "Gender Snowperson: Understanding Identity," Welcoming Schools, https://assets2.hrc.org/welcoming-schools /documents/WS_Lesson_Gender_Snowperson.pdf.

31. Ken C. Pang et al., "Association of Media Coverage of Transgender and Gender Diverse Issues with Rates of Referral of Transgender Children and Adolescents to Specialist Gender Clinics in the UK and Australia," *JAMA Network Open* 3, no. 7 (July 28, 2020), https://jamanetwork.com/journals/jamanetworkopen/ fullarticle/2768726.

32. Brian Honigman, "How Tumblr Is Changing Online Activism," *Forbes,* February 18, 2014, https://www.forbes.com/sites/citi/2014/02/18/how-tumblr-is-changing-online-activism/?sh=562799fa3200. See further Katherine Dee, "Tumblr U.," The American Mind, July 16, 2021, https://americanmind.org/salvo/tumblr-u/; Katherine Dee, "Tumblr Transformed Online Politics," *American Conservative*, August 11, 2021, https://www.theamericanconservative.com/articles/ tumblr-transformed-american-politics/.

33. Abigail Shrier, *Irreversible Damage: The Transgender Craze Seducing Our Daughters* (Washington, D.C.: Regnery, 2020), 197–208. See further Ray Gustini, "No One Knows Why Teens Aren't Having Sex," *The Atlantic,* March 4, 2011, https://www.theatlantic.com/national/archive/2011/03/teen-sex-decline/348607/.

34. Gwen Ifill, "Hillary Clinton Defends Her Conduct in Law Firm," *New York Times*, March 17, 1992, https://www.nytimes.com/1992/03/17/us/the-1992-campaign-hillary-clinton-defends-her-conduct-in-law-firm.html.

35. For "menstruaters," see Pooja Makhijani, "Menstruation Gets a Gen-Z Makeover," *New York Times*, January 24, 2022, https://www.nytimes.com /2022/01/20/well/sustainable-period-products.html. For "chest feeders" see Lexi Lonas, "UK Hospital Replaces Term 'Breast Milk' with 'Human Milk' to be More Inclusive," *The Hill*, February 10, 2021, https://thehill.com/policy/ international/538319-uk-hospital-replaces-term-breast-milk-with-human-milk-to-be-more/. For "birthing people," see Cori Bush (@RepCori), "Every day, Black birthing people and our babies die because our doctors don't believe our pain. My children almost became a statistic. I almost became a statistic. I testified about my experience @OversightDems today. Hear us. Believe us. Because for so long, nobody has," Twitter, May 6, 2021, 1:05 p.m., https://twitter.com/repcori/status/13903521275795 94753?lang=en.

36. Douglas Murray, *The Madness of Crowds* (London: Routledge, 2019), 225. Video at https://archive.org/details/olson-kennedy-breasts-go-and-get-them.

37. Mary Harrington, "The Fight against Erasing Women," The American Mind, October 19, 2021, https://americanmind.org/features/the-fight-against -erasing-women/.

38. Martine Rothblatt, *From Transgender to Transhuman* (self-published, 2011), 115. Technically, Rothblatt should have written "persona creata." It is suggestive, too, that "persona" in Latin does not in fact mean "person" in the sense Rothblatt seems to think it does: it means "false mask" or "outward show" rather than personality or essence. See further Yuval Noah Harari: "I think that *Homo sapiens* as we know them will probably disappear within a century or so, not destroyed by killer robots or things like that, but changed and upgraded with biotechnology and artificial intelligence into something else, into something different," in Andrew Anthony, "You Ask the Questions," *The Guardian*, March 19 2017, https://

www.theguardian.com/culture/2017/mar/19/yuval-harari-sapiens-readers-questions-lucy-prebble-arianna-huffington-future-of-humanity.

39. See further Pierre Manent, *Natural Law and Human Rights*, trans. Ralph C. Hancock (South Bend, Indiana: Notre Dame University Press, 2021), 6.

40. Andrea Long Chu, "My New Vagina Won't Make Me Happy," *New York Times*, November 24, 2018, https://www.nytimes.com/2018/11/24/opinion /sunday/vaginoplasty-transgender-medicine.html.

41. EMBER (@emberpearl) "'he's challenging gender norms' and he's losing. the gender norms are beating his ass," iFunny, November 20, 2021, https://ifunny.co/picture/ ember-he-s-challenging-gender-norms-and-he-s-losing-oLk0S9K69.

Chapter 4: Spirit and Flesh

1. See, e.g., Diogenes Laertius, *Lives of the Eminent Philosophers*, V.4.
2. Aristotle, *Metaphysics*, I.6, 987b.
3. Aristotle, *De Anima*, III.8, 432a.
4. See Aristotle, *De Anima*, I.1, 403a; Aristotle, *Metaphysics*, VII.1–5, 1028a–30a.
5. Aristotle, *Physics*, V.2, 194b-5a; *Metaphysics* II.3, 994a–b.
6. Aristotle, *De Anima*, II.1, 412b.
7. Ibid., III.1, 412a.
8. See especially Plato, *Republic*, IV, 427d–444b.
9. Nick Bostrom, "Why I Want to Be Posthuman When I Grow Up," *Medical Enhancement and Posthumanity*, eds. Bert Gordijn and Ruth Chadwick (Berlin: Springer, 2008), 107–8.
10. Ibid., 124 n.38.
11. Ibid., 127.
12. Aristotle, *Nicomachean Ethics*, X, 6–7, 1176a–8a.
13. Tertullian, *Prescriptions against Heretics*, 7.
14. Aquinas, *Summa Theologica*, I.Q76.A1.
15. Ibid., supplement to part III.Q69.A1; cf. Q97.A5.

Chapter 5: The Crisis of Meaning

1. Richard Dawkins, *The Selfish Gene*, 1st ed. (Oxford: Oxford University Press, 1976), xxxv.
2. Christopher Hitchens, *God Is Not Great: How Religion Poisons Everything* (Australia: Allen & Unwin, 2007), 5, 165.
3. Aristotle, *Physics*, 2.1, 192b20–23.
4. On the gradual transformation of natural philosophy into what we now call "science," see Simon Schaffer, "Scientific Discoveries and the End of Natural Philosophy," *Social Studies of Science* 16 no. 3 (1986): 387–420; Reviel Netz, *Scale, Space, and Canon in Ancient Literary Culture* (Cambridge: Cambridge University Press, 2020), 421.
5. Dawkins, *The Selfish Gene*, 1.
6. Ibid., 249. See further Susan Blackmore, *The Meme Machine* (Oxford: Oxford University Press, 1999).
7. See James Vincent, "Video: Richard Dawkins Attempts Memedom via Saatchi & Saatchi," *The Independent*, June 26, 2013, https://www.independent.co.uk/

life-style/gadgets-and-tech/video-richard-dawkins-attempts-memedom-via-saatchi-saatchi-8674875.html.

8. Aristotle, *Poetics*, 1, 1448b.
9. See Sourya Acharya and Samarth Shukla, "Mirror Neurons," *Journal of Natural Science Biology and Medicine* 3, no. 2 (2012): 118–24; J. M. Kilner and R. N. Lemon, "What We Currently Know about Mirror Neurons," *Current Biology* 23 (December 2, 2013): R1057–R1062; Bessel Van der Kolk, *The Body Keeps the Score: Brain, Mind, and Body in the Healing of Trauma* (New York: Penguin, 2015), 37.
10. William Wordsworth, *The Prelude: The Four Texts (1798, 1799, 1805, 1850)* (London: Penguin, 2004), II.239–245.
11. Andrew Klavan, *The Truth and Beauty: How the Lives and Works of England's Greatest Poets Point the Way to a Deeper Understanding of the Words of Jesus* (Grand Rapids, Michigan: Zondervan Books, 2022), 76–77.
12. Ludwig Wittgenstein, *Philosophical Investigations.* trans. G. E. M. Anscome, P. M. S. Hacker, and Joachim Schulte (Hoboken, New Jersey: Wiley-Blackwell, 2009), 84.
13. John Keats, "On First Looking into Chapman's Homer," ll.1–4.
14. See Diogenes Laertius, *Lives of the Eminent Philosophers*, 7.60.1–6
15. Aristotle, *Poetics*, 1, 1447b.
16. Thomas Wyatt, "Whoso List to Hunt, I Know Where Is an Hind," 11–14.
17. Dawkins, *The Selfish Gene*, 248.
18. Leonard Sax, "The Ambiguity of the Evidence," *Claremont Review of Books* 21 no. 4 (Fall 2021), https://claremontreviewofbooks.com/the-ambiguity-of-the-evidence/.
19. Plato, *Timaeus*, 38a.
20. Ibid., 39e.
21. Ibid., 29e.
22. Ibid., 41c.
23. Plato, *Republic*, X, 600c.
24. David Deutsch, *The Beginning of Infinity: Explanations That Transform the World* (London: Penguin, 2011), 409. Incidentally, this can provide a response to Deutsch's rather Platonic attack on the idea of imitation: Deutsch points out that when we replicate memes, we are trying to understand "the meaning of the behavior" we are observing, not the behavior itself. But the meaning is *contained* in the behavior, and imitating the latter is part of how we access the former.
25. Dawkins, *The Selfish Gene*, 260.
26. René Girard, *I See Satan Fall Like Lightning*, trans. James G. Williams (New York: Orbis, 1999).
27. G. K. Chesterton, "The Eternal Revolution," *Orthodoxy* in *Spiritual Classics Collection. 1908-1925* (Independently published), 183–34.
28. Deutsch, *The Beginning of Infinity*, 395.

Chapter 6: Life Imitates Art

1. The Pulitzer Prize Board, "*DAMN.*, by Kendrick Lamar," The Pulitzer Prizes, 2018, https://www.pulitzer.org/winners/kendrick-lamar.
2. Plato, *Timaeus*, 47d.
3. Aristotle, *Politics*, VIII.5, 1340a.
4. Boethius, *De Institutione Musica*, I.1.
5. Plato, *Republic*, III, 411a–b.

6. Bruno Bettelheim, *The Uses of Enchantment: The Meaning and Importance of Fairy Tales* (London: Thames & Hudson, 1976), 74–75.

7. Plato, *Republic*, III, 389c.

8. *United States v. One Book Called "Ulysses,"* 5 F. Supp. 182 (S.D.N.Y 1933).

9. *United States v. One Book Entitled Ulysses by James Joyce*, 72 F. Supp. 2d 705 (2nd Cir. 1934).

10. Norman Podhoretz, "'Lolita,' My Mother-in-Law, the Marquis de Sade, and Larry Flynt," *Commentary,* April 1997, https://www.commentary.org/articles/norman-podhoretz/lolita-my-mother-in-law-the-marquis-de-sade-and-larry-flynt/.

11. Vladimir Nabokov, "On a Book Entitled *Lolita*" in *Lolita* (New York: Vintage International, 1956).

12. Louis Menand, "Why We Are No Longer Shocked by 'Ulysses,'" *New Yorker,* June 16, 2016, https://www.newyorker.com/culture/cultural-comment/why-we-are-no-longer-shocked-by-ulysses.

13. See Vulture Editors, "Wait, What's Going On with Netflix and *Cuties?*" Vulture, October 7, 2020, https://www.vulture.com/2020/10/netflix-cuties-twerking-poster-drama-explained.html.

14. Anita Anabel, "Netflix Indicted by US Grand Jury over Controversial 'Cuties' Film," The Latch, October 8, 2020, https://thelatch.com.au/cuties-netflix/.

15. See Michael Cragg, "Terrible Name, Terrific Sitcom: How Schitt's Creek Became a Surprise Hit," *The Guardian,* May 9, 2020, https://www.theguardian.com/tv-and-radio/2020/may/09/terrible-name-terrific-sitcom-how-schitts-creek-became-a-surprise-hit; Manish Pandey, "Schitt's Creek 'Normalises LGBTQ Relationships,'" BBC, September 21, 2020, https://www.bbc.com/news/newsbeat-54240141.

16. Keisha Hatchett, "*Foundation* EP on Centering Black Women in Apple TV+'s Sci-Fi Epic," TVLine, September 23, 2021, https://tvline.com/2021/09/23/foundation-apple-tv-plus-david-goyer-preview/.

17. Christopher Rufo, "Disney's Ideological Capture," *City Journal,* March 30, 2022, https://www.city-journal.org/disneys-ideological-capture.

18. Newsdesk, "Netflix Transgender Employees Condemn Dave Chappelle Special," Tittle Press, October 8, 2021, https://tittlepress.com/entertainment/1208798/.

19. Camille Paglia, *Glittering Images.* (New York: Vintage Books, 2012), xii.

20. Erick Erickson, "Watching 'Game of Thrones' as a Christian," Medium, July 19, 2017, https://medium.com/@ewerickson/watching-game-of-thrones-as-a-christian-5e7a3031cebf.

21. William Shakespeare, *Macbeth*, V.v.19–28.

22. Ibid., III.iv.136–38.

Chapter 7: The Crisis of Religion

1. John Calvin, *Institutes of the Christian Religion*, ed. John T. McNeill, trans. Ford Lewis Battles (Philadelphia: The Westminster Press, 1960), I.ii.8.

2. Francis Bacon, "Aphorisms" in *Novum Organum*, eds. Lisa Jardine and Michael Silvertorne (Cambridge: Cambridge University Press, 2000), I, 39–44.

3. Bacon, "Aphorisms," 45–46.

4. David Hume, *An Enquiry Concerning Human Understanding*, ed. Tom L. Beauchamp (Oxford: Oxford University Press, 1999), 2.5.

5. Ibid., 10.2.35.

6. Auguste Comte, *The Positive Philosophy*, trans. Harriet Martineau (Cambridge: Cambridge University Press, 1853) 1:27–29.

7. Sigmund Freud, *Totem and Taboo*, trans. A. A. Brill (London: Routledge, 1919), IV.6.

8. Kant, *Critique of Pure Reason*, trans. Tomas P. Scheck (New York: Newman Press, 2017), II.ii.3.

9. Francine Lacqua, Stéphane Bancel, Richard Hatchett, Anthony S. Fauci, and Annelies Wilder-Smith, "COVID-19: What's Next?" World Economic Forum, January 17, 2022, https://www.weforum.org/events/the-davos-agenda-2022 /sessions/covid-19-what-s-next.

10. Margaret Brennan and Anthony Fauci, "Transcript: Dr. Anthony Fauci on 'Face the Nation,'" CBS News, November 28, 2021, https://www.cbsnews.com/news/ transcript-dr-anthony-fauci-on-face-the-nation-november-28-2021/.

11. Katherine Ross, "Why Weren't We Wearing Masks from the Beginning? Dr. Fauci Explains," The Street, June 12, 2020, https://www.thestreet.com/video/ dr-fauci-masks-changing-directive-coronavirus.

12. Donald G. McNeil Jr. "How Much Herd Immunity Is Enough?" *New York Times*, September 22, 2021, https://www.nytimes.com/2020/12/24/health/herd-immunity-covid-coronavirus.html.

13. G. K. Chesterton, *What I Saw in America* (London: Hodder and Stoughton, 1922), 12.

14. Joshua Mitchell, *American Awakening* (New York: Encounter, 2020), §10, xxi.

15. Friedrich Nietzsche, *Daybreak: Thoughts on the Prejudices of Morality*, trans. Maudemarie Clark and Brian Leiter (Cambridge: Cambridge University Press, 1997), 49.

16. Plato, *Apology*, 22c–e.

17. *The Simpsons*, season 16, episode 15, "Future Drama," directed by Mike B. Anderson, aired April 17, 2005, on Fox.

Chapter 8: The Real Story

1. See David Deutsch, *The Beginning of Infinity: Explanations That Transform the World* (London: Penguin, 2011), 276; Erwin Schrödinger, *Interpretation of Quantum Mechanics: Dublin Seminars (1949–1955) and Other Unpublished Essays*, ed. Michel Bitbol (Oxford: Oxbow, 1955), 19–37.

2. See further Natalie Wolchover and Quanta Magazine, "Life as We Know It Hinges on One Very Small Decimal," *The Atlantic*, December 5, 2020, https:// www.theatlantic.com/science/archive/2020/12/the-magic-number-that-shapes-the-universe/617288/; Leonard Sax, "The Ambiguity of the Evidence," *Claremont Review of Books* 21, no. 4 (Fall 2021), https://claremontreviewofbooks.com/the-ambiguity-of-the-evidence/; Stephen C. Meyer, *Return of the God Hypothesis* (New York: HarperOne,2021), 200–226.

3. Some have answered Paley that if creation implies a designer, *he too* must have been designed for the purpose of designing, meaning he too must have been designed, creating an infinite regress. But of course God, if he is the ultimate designer, need not have been structured *for the purpose* of designing: being designed means being structured for a purpose, but performing an action does not mean that action is the purpose for which you were designed. God is capable of creating life and freely

chooses to do so—but he is not *designed* to do so for the simple reason that he is not designed to do anything at all. As the ultimate purpose of all things, he has no purpose of his own except himself.

4. George Ellis and Joe Silk, "Scientific Method: Defend the Integrity of Physics," *Nature* 516 (December 16, 2014): 321–23, https://www.nature.com/articles /516321a.

5. Meyer, *Return of the God Hypothesis*, 507.

6. George Ellis, "Does the Multiverse Really Exist?" *Scientific American*, August 2011, https://www.scientificamerican.com/article/does-the-multiverse-really-exist/.

7. Richard Dawid, "Undetermination and Theory Succession from the Perspective of String Theory," *Philosophy of Science* 73, no. 3 (July 2006): 298–322.

8. Karl Popper, *The Logic of Scientific Discovery* (London: Routledge, 1959), 23–24.

9. Ibid., 89–90.

10. Diogenes Laertius, *Lives of the Eminent Philosophers*, trans. Pamela Mensch, ed. James Miller (Oxford: Oxford University Press, 2018), 10.45. See further 10.88–90.

11. Lucretius, *De Rerum Natura*, book 2, ll. 1023–1174; see further Diogenes of Oinoanda, fragment 63.

12. David Hume, *An Enquiry Concerning Human Understanding*, ed. Tom L. Beauchamp (Oxford: Oxford University Press, 1999), 11.17.

13. John Adams, "From John Adams to John Rogers, 6 February 1801," Founders Online, https://founders.archives.gov/documents/Adams/99-02-02-4799.

14. Aristotle, *Poetics*, 2, 1448a.

15. Diogenes Laertius, *Lives of the Eminent Philsophers*, 10.127–28.

16. Valeriya Safronova, "A Private-School Sex Educator Defends Her Methods," *New York Times*, July 7, 2021, https://www.nytimes.com/2021/07/07/style/sex-educator-methods-defense.html.

17. See, for instance, Melissa Koenig, "'People Are Aroused by Electrocution,'" *Daily Mail*, June 4, 2021, https://www.dailymail.co.uk/news/ article-9650967/Leaked-porn-lecture-given-Manhattan-school-reveals-pupils-taught-electro-porn.html.

18. Roger Scruton, "Memo to Hawking: There's Still Room for God," *Wall Street Journal*, September 24, 2010, https://www.wsj.com/articles/SB10001424052748703 989304575503952480317596, in reply to Stephen Hawking and Leonard Mlodlinow, "Why God Did Not Create the Universe," *Wall Street Journal*, September 30, 2010, https://www.wsj.com/articles/SB100014240527487042068045 75467921609024244.

19. Saint Augustine, *Confessions*, 11.7.

20. Ibid., 11.4.

21. Saint Augustine in *Summa Theologica*, I.Q13.A2.

22. See "Igor Stravinsky on Film Music" (1946) in Mervyn Cooke, ed., *The Hollywood Film Music Reader* (Oxford: Oxford University Press, 2010), 273–80.

23. William Shakespeare, *Merchant of Venice*, ed. Barbara A. Mowat and Paul Werstine (New York: Simon & Schuster, 1992), V.1.71.

24. Dante, "Paradiso," *The Divine Comedy*, IV.37–48.

25. C. S. Lewis, *Out of the Silent Planet*, *The Space Trilogy* (Croydon: HarperCollins, 1938–1945), 28.

26. John Milton, "Comus" in *The Complete Poems and Essential Prose of John Milton*, ed. William Kerrigan, John Rumrich, and Stephen M. Fallon (New York: Knopf, 2007), 1019–21.

27. Perhaps no one understood this better than Jorge Luis Borges, whose famous short story "The Library of Babel" seems to me a good metaphor for quantum indeterminacy, among other things.

Chapter 9: Regime Crisis

1. Whittaker Chambers, *Odyssey of a Friend*, ed. William F. Buckley Jr. (New York: National Review, 1970), 201.
2. Zalan Khan, "Does Afghanistan Mark the End of American Empire?" *Al-Jazeera*, August 28, 2021, https://www.aljazeera.com/opinions/2021/8/28/ does-afghanistan-mark-the-end-of-american-empire.
3. Amotz Asa-El, "The American Empire Is Ready to End," *Jerusalem Post*, August 27, 2021, https://www.jpost.com/international/the-american-empire-is -ready-to-end-677831.
4. Niall Ferguson, "Niall Ferguson on Why the End of the American Empire Won't Be Peaceful," *The Economist*, August 20, 2021, https://www.economist.com/by -invitation/2021/08/20/niall-ferguson-on-why-the-end-of-americas-empire-wont -be-peaceful.
5. Niall Ferguson, "Putin Misunderstands History. So, Unfortunately, Does the U.S.," Bloomberg, March 22, 2022, https://www.bloomberg.com/opinion /articles/2022-03-22/niall-ferguson-putin-and-biden-misunderstand-history-in -ukraine-war.
6. Mark Helprin, "Once More, with Feeling," *Claremont Review of Books* (Fall 2021), https://claremontreviewofbooks.com/once-more-with-feeling/.
7. Herodotus, *The Histories*, trans. Aubrey de Sélincourt, rev. ed. (New York: Penguin, 2003), 1.6.
8. Ibid., 1.30–86.
9. Aeschylus, *The Persians and Other Plays*, 739–44.
10. Thucydides, *History of the Peloponnesian War*, 1.23.
11. See Plato, "Statesman," in *The Being of the Beautiful*, trans. Seth Benardete (Chicago: Chicago University Press, 1986), 302c–d; Herodotus, *The Histories*, 3.80–84.
12. Alfred Lord Tennyson, "Ulysses" in *The Major Works* (Oxford: Oxford University Press, 2009), 36–38.
13. Aristotle, *Politics*, III.7, 1279b.
14. Ibid., 1.2, 1253a.
15. Polybius, *The Histories*, VI.4.8–10.
16. G. Michael Hopf, *Those Who Remain* (Self-published, 2016), 20.
17. Livy, *Histories*, 2.1.
18. Machiavelli, "The Prince" in *The Essential Writings of Machiavelli*, ed. Peter Constantine (New York: Random House, 2007), I.
19. Machiavelli, *Discourses on Livy*, trans. Julia Conaway Bondanella and Peter Bondanella (Oxford: Oxford University Press, 1997), I.58.
20. Ibid., I.5.
21. Plato, *Republic*, IV, 422e–423a.
22. Plutarch, "Life of Tiberius Gracchus" in *Roman Lives*, trans. Robin Waterfield (Oxford: Oxford Univeristy Press, 1999), 9.4.
23. Appian, *The Civil Wars*, trans. John Carter (London: Penguin,1996), I.1.

24. Montesquieu, *Spirit of the Laws*, trans. John Carter (London: Penguin, 1996), I.viii.16.

Chapter 10: Political Love

1. Richard Hanania, "'Just Trust the Experts,' We're Told. We Shouldn't," *New York Times*, September 20, 2021, https://www.nytimes.com/2021/09/20 /opinion/afghanistan-experts-expertise.html.

2. Alana Newhouse, "Everything Is Broken," Tablet, January 14, 2021, https:// www.tabletmag.com/sections/news/articles/everything-is-brokenhttps://www .tabletmag.com/sections/news/articles/everything-is-broken.

3. Louis Beckett, "At Least 25 Americans Were Killed during Protests and Political Unrest in 2020," *The Guardian*, October 31, 2020, https://www.theguardian .com/world/2020/oct/31/americans-killed-protests-political-unrest-acled; Jemina McEvoy, "14 Days of Protests, 19 Dead," *Forbes*, June 8, 2020, https:// www.forbes.com/sites/jemimamcevoy/2020/06/08/14-days-of-protests-19-dead/ ?sh=49f635cf4de4; Ebony Bowden, "More than 700 Officers Injured in George Floyd Protests across the U.S.," *New York Post*, June 8, 2020, https://nypost .com/2020/06/08/more-than-700-officers-injured-in-george-floyd-protests -across-us/.

4. Karl Marx and Friedrich Engels, *The German Ideology* in *The Marx-Engels Reader*, ed. Robert C. Tucker (New York: W. W. Norton, 1978), I.A.2. The manuscripts of *The German Ideology* are highly contested, and efforts have been made to disambiguate the views of Engels from those of Marx. But Thomas Sowell makes a cogent argument that Engels understood Marx perfectly, and that we can look to *The German Ideology* for real insight into Marxism. See Thomas Sowell, *Marxism: Philosophy and Economics* (Rock Hill, South Carolina: Quill, 1985), esp. chapters 3 and 4.

5. Marx and Engels, *The German Ideology*, I.B.ii.2.

6. See Kyle Shideler, "Shideler Testifies before Senate Subcommittee on the Constitution," *Center for Security Policy*, August 4, 2020, https:// centerforsecuritypolicy.org/shideler-testifies-before-senate-subcommittee-on-the -constitution/; Kyle Shideler, "Taking It to the Streets," *Claremont Review of Books* (Summer 2021), https://claremontreviewofbooks.com/taking-it-to-the-streets/.

7. Theodore Allen, "Can White Workers Radicals Be Radicalized?" in *Revolutionary Youth and the New Working Class*, ed. Carl Davidson. (Pittsburgh: Changemaker, 2011), 167–81, 172.

8. Yaron Steinbuch, "Black Lives Matter Co-Founder Describes Herself as 'Trained Marxist,'" *New York Post*, June 25, 2020, https://nypost.com/2020/06/25/ blm-co-founder-describes-herself-as-trained-marxist/.

9. Ibram X. Kendi, "The Very Heartbeat of Racism Is Denial," Rutgers University, February 25, 2021, https://www.rochester.edu/newscenter/ibram-x-kendi-the -very-heartbeat-of-racism-is-denial-470332/.

10. Democratic Socialists of America, "DSA Political Platform," https://www.dsausa .org/dsa-political-platform-from-2021-convention/.

11. Marx and Engels, *The German Ideology*, II.B.ii.2.

12. Dana Givens, "Rep. Ayanna Presley Calls for 'Unrest in the Streets' over the Failures of the Trump Administration," *Black Enterprise*, August 17, 2020, https://

www.blackenterprise.com/rep-ayanna-pressley-calls-for-unrest-in-the-streets-over-the-failures-of-the-trump-administration/. See further Joshua Rhett Miller, "Bail Fund Backed by Kamala Harris Freed Minneapolis Man Charged with Murder," *New York Post*, September 8, 2021, https://nypost.com/2021/09/08/bail-fund-backed-by-kamala-harris-freed-man-charged-with-murder/.

13. Plato, *Republic,* IV, 423e. Aristophanes brilliantly parodies this view in *Assemblywomen*.

14. Marx and Engels, "The Communist Manifesto," chapter II; Sophie Lewis, *Full Surrogacy Now: Feminism against Family* (New York: Verso, 2019), 125–34; Rosemarie Ho, "Want to Dismantle Capitalism? Abolish the Family," *The Nation*, May 16, 201, https://www.thenation.com/article/archive/want-to-dismantle-capitalism-abolish-the-family/.

15. Joe Matthews, "Want True Equity? California Should Force Parents to Give Away Their Children," *San Francisco Chronicle*, January 16, 2022, https://www.msn.com/en-us/news/us/want-true-equity-california-should-force-parents-to-give-away-their-children/ar-AASShA8.

16. Aristotle, *Politics*, II.4, 1262a–b.

17. Arianna Rebolini (@AriannaRebolini), "I've been opening up about how I do not enjoy being a mom, thinking about why I feel so passionately about talking about it, and I think a large part is my belief that normalizing (/celebrating!) the decision to be childfree can lead to more communal childcare," Twitter, January 26, 2022, 11:18 a.m., https://twitter.com/ariannarebolini/status/1486373073335037959.

18. See also Anne Kingston, "'I Regret Having Children,'" *Maclean's*, 2022, https://www.macleans.ca/regretful-mothers/; Gail Cornwall, "The Two Reasons Parents Regret Having Kids," *The Atlantic*, August 31, 2021, https://www.theatlantic.com/family/archive/2021/08/why-parents-regret-children/619931/; Amatullah Shaw, "15 Parents Are Sharing Why They Regret Having Kids," BuzzFeed, August 21, 2021, https://www.buzzfeed.com/amatullahshaw/parents-are-sharing-regret; Damian Carrington, "Want to Fight Climate Change? Have Fewer Children," *The Guardian*, July 12, 2017, https://www.theguardian.com/environment/2017/jul/12/want-to-fight-climate-change-have-fewer-children.

19. Aristotle, *Art of Rhetoric*, II.4, 1380b–1381a.

20. Aristotle, *Politics,* III.9, 1280b. See also *Nicomachean Ethics*, VIII.1, 1155a.

21. Leo Strauss, *Natural Right and History* (Chicago: University of Chicago Press, 1953), 247.

22. George Washington, "Farewell Address," Senate Document No. 106–21, https://www.senate.gov/artandhistory/history/resources/pdf/WashFarewell.pdf.

23. John Adams, "John Adams to Massachusetts Militia, 11 October 1798," Founders Online, https://founders.archives.gov/documents/Adams/99-02-02-3102.

24. Abraham Lincoln, "First Inaugural Address, Final Version," Library of Congress, Manuscript Division, March 4, 1861, https://goo.gl/aP8zAJ.

25. "Roosevelt Bars the Hyphenated," *New York Times*, October 13, 1915.

26. *Naturalization Act of 1795*, Public Law 3–20, 3rd Cong., 2nd sess. (January 29, 1795), 414–15, https://govtrackus.s3.amazonaws.com/legislink/pdf/stat/1/STATUTE-1-Pg414a.pdf.

27. Jackie Salo, "'We've Got to Take These Motherf—kers Out': Rutgers Professor Calls White People 'Villains,'" *New York Post*, October 29, 2021, https://nypost.com/2021/10/29/rutgers-professor-calls-white-people-villains/.

Index